Gender and the Secon

Gender and History Series

Series editors: Amanda Capern and Louella McCarthy

Published

Ann Taylor Allen   *Women in Twentieth-Century Europe*

Paul J. Bailey   *Women and Gender in Twentieth-Century China*

Catherine Baker   *Gender in Twentieth-Century Eastern Europe and the USSR*

Trev Lynn Broughton & Helen Rogers (eds)   *Gender and Fatherhood in the Nineteenth Century*

Ana Carden-Coyne (ed.)   *Gender and Conflict since 1914: Historical and Interdisciplinary Perspectives*

Krista Cowman   *Women in British Politics c.1689–1979*

Béatrice Craig   *Women and Business since 1500*

Shani D'Cruze & Louise A. Jackson   *Women, Crime and Justice in England since 1660*

Anne R. Epstein and Rachel G. Fuchs (eds)   *Gender and Citizenship in Historical and Transnational Perspective: Agency, Space, Borders*

William Henry Foster   *Gender, Mastery and Slavery: From European to Atlantic World Frontiers*

Rachel G. Fuchs & Victoria E. Thompson   *Women in Nineteenth-Century Europe*

Hannah Greig, Jane Hamlett & Leonie Hannan (eds)   *Gender and Material Culture in Britain since 1600*

Lesley A. Hall   *Sex, Gender and Social Change in Britain since 1880 (2nd edition)*

Laurence Lux-Sterritt & Carmen Mangion (eds)   *Gender, Catholicism and Spirituality: Women and the Roman Catholic Church in Britain and Europe, 1200–1900*

Corinna Peniston-Bird & Emma Vickers (eds)   *Gender and the Second World War: Lessons of War*

Perry Willson   *Women in Twentieth-Century Italy*

Angela Woollacott   *Gender and Empire*

Forthcoming

Jacqueline DeVries   *Women, Religion and Social Change in Britain since 1795*

Natasha Hodgson   *Gender and the Crusades*

Jane Martin   *Gender and Education in Britain since 1770*

Marianna Muravyeva   *Sexual Variations in Europe since 1600*

Gender and the Second World War

Lessons of War

Edited by

CORINNA PENISTON-BIRD

and

EMMA VICKERS

 macmillan education   palgrave

First published 2017 by
PALGRAVE

Palgrave in the UK is an imprint of Macmillan Publishers Limited,
registered in England, company number 785998, of 4 Crinan Street,
London, N1 9XW.

Palgrave® and Macmillan® are registered trademarks in the United States,
the United Kingdom, Europe and other countries.

ISBN: 978–1–137–52458–4 hardback
ISBN: 978–1–137–52457–7 paperback

This book is printed on paper suitable for recycling and made from fully
managed and sustained forest sources. Logging, pulping and manufacturing
processes are expected to conform to the environmental regulations of the
country of origin.

A catalogue record for this book is available from the British Library.

A catalog record for this book is available from the Library of Congress.

Printed and bound by CPI Group (UK) Ltd, Croydon, CR0 4YY

Other titles by the authors:

Peniston-Bird, Corinna M., with S. Barber (eds) (2009) *History Beyond the Text: A Student's Guide to Approaching Alternative Sources* (London and New York: Routledge) (Routledge guides to using historical sources.)

Peniston-Bird, Corinna M., with P. Summerfield (2007) *Contesting Home Defence: Men, Women and the Home Guard in the Second World War* (Manchester: Manchester University Press).

Peniston-Bird, Corinna M., with G. J. DeGroot (eds) (2000) *A Soldier and a Woman: Sexual Integration in the Military* (Harlow: Pearson Education).

Vickers, E. (2013) *Queen and Country: Same-sex Desire in the British Armed Forces, 1939–1945* (Manchester and New York: Manchester University Press).

To Amelie and Sarah,
and all our students of gender and war, past and present

Contents

List of Tables and Figures

Tables

Figures

List of Abbreviations

AAF	Army Air Force
ARP	Air Raid Precautions
BDM	*Bund Deutscher Mädel*
CIA	Central Intelligence Agency
CM	*Chongsindae* movement
CNR	Canadian National Railways
CPTP	Civilian Pilot Training Program
ENSA	Entertainments National Service Association
FFI	French Forces of the Interior
FHAR	*Front Homosexuel d'Action Révolutionnaire* (Homosexual Revolutionary Action Front)
FSA	Farm Security Administration
GI	Government/General Issue (US) used to refer to both equipment and soldiers
GPRF	*Gouvernement Provisoire de la République Française* (Provisional Government of the French Republic)
JPF	*Jeunesses Populaires Françaises*
KM	*kijich'on* movement
LCC	London County Council
MRP	*Mouvement Républicain Populaire*
NAAFI	Navy, Army and Air Force Institutes
OWI	Office of War Information
PNF	*Partito Nazionale Fascista* (National Fascist Party)
PPF	*Parti Populaire Français* (French Popular Party)
RSHA	Reich Security Main Office
RSI	Italian Social Republic (*Repubblica Sociale Italiana*)
SA	*Sturmabteilung*
SCAP	Supreme Command for the Allied Powers
SD	*Sicherheitsdienst des Reichsführers-SS* (Security Service)
SS	*Schutzstaffel*
WAC	Women's Army Corps
WASP	Women Airforce Service Pilots

Acknowledgements

Our thanks go first to our editors at Palgrave for all their constructive feedback, and in particular to Rachel Bridgewater who has dealt with our multiple queries with great patience.

Our authors have been a pleasure to work with, and we thank them for the numerous interchanges over the past months, and for their interest in the project from the outset. We would also like to thank all the contributors to the *Lessons of War* Conference held at Lancaster University, England in September 2013, who underlined the importance of continuing and expanding the discussions on gender and war.

The images in the chapters below are reproduced courtesy of the Imperial War Museum (Chapter 3); of Hilde Purwin (Chapter 5); of Akg-images/ Sputnik (Chapter 8); of Rachel Jenzen (Private Collection) (Chapter 9); of the Library of Congress (Chapter 11).

The quotations from Mass Observation in Chapter 4 are reproduced with permission of Curtis Brown Group Ltd, London on behalf of The Trustees of the Mass Observation Archive.

List of Contributors

Lorenzo Benadusi is an Assistant Professor of History at the University of Bergamo. His work analyses the history of militarism, masculinity, and homosexuality in the fascist period. He has multiple publications, including *The Enemy of the New Man: Homosexuality in Fascist Italy* (Wisconsin University Press, 2012) and George Mosse's *Italy* (Palgrave, 2014). He is also the author of *Ufficiale e gentiluomo. Virtù civili e valori militari in Italia* (Feltrinelli, 2015) and *Storia del Corriere della Sera* (Rizzoli, 2011).

Robert Dale is a Lecturer in Russian History at Newcastle University. He was awarded a PhD in January 2011 from Queen Mary, University of London, which was funded by the Arts and Humanities Research Council and the Harry Frank Guggenheim Foundation. He has previously held teaching fellowships at the University of York and Newcastle University, and a British Academy Postdoctoral Fellowship, based first at King's College London and then Nottingham Trent University. His first monograph *Demobilized Veterans in Late Stalinist Leningrad: Soldiers to Civilians* was published by Bloomsbury Academic in 2015. His current research builds upon his work on the demobilization and post-war readjustment of Red Army veterans and explores the post-war reconstruction of Soviet society. This work pays special attention to the Great Patriotic War's painful legacy, and the ways in which the war continued to destabilize and divide post-war society.

Kate Darian-Smith is Professor of Australian Studies and History in the Faculty of Arts and Professor of Cultural Heritage, in the Faculty of Architecture, Building and Planning at the University of Melbourne. She is also Co-Director of the Australian Collaboratory for Architectural History, Urban and Cultural Heritage at the University. She has published widely on Australian and imperial histories, memory and history, the history of childhood, Australia at war and cultural heritage, and led many cross-disciplinary research projects funded by the Australian Research Council. Her most recent book is *Conciliation on Colonial Frontiers: Conflict, Performance and Commemoration in Australia and the Pacific Rim* (Routledge, 2015; co-edited), and she is completing a co-authored book on the history of press photography in Australia. Kate has held government appointments and advisory roles in the education and cultural sectors, is a Fellow of the Academy of Social Sciences in Australia, and has been involved in the promotion of Australian Studies overseas, particularly in Asia, for over two decades.

Helen Glew is a Senior Lecturer in History at the University of Westminster. Her monograph *Gender, Rhetoric and Regulation: Women's Work in the Civil Service and the London County Council, 1900–55* is published by Manchester University Press (2016). She is now working on a social and cultural history of the marriage bar since the late nineteenth century, a project which examines policy and discourse surrounding married women's right to work as well as women's experiences of combining paid work and marriage. Recent publications also include 'The Married Woman Worker in *Chatelaine* Magazine, 1948–1964', in Sue Hawkins, Nicola Phillips, Rachel Ritchie, and S. Jay Kleinberg (eds), *Women in Magazines: Research, Representation, Production and Consumption* (Routledge, 2016) and chapters on women at the Regent Street Polytechnic and on Quintin Hogg and late nineteenth-century philanthropy in Elaine Penn (ed.), *Educating Mind, Body & Spirit: The Legacy of Quintin Hogg and the Polytechnic, 1864–1992.*

Emma Jackson currently works at the Office of the Independent Adjudicator for Higher Education, adjudicating on complaints and appeals between students and universities. She is also a governor for a local secondary school. Emma received a first-class honours degree in History from the University of Reading in 2013. Her interest in cross-dressing during the Second World War emerged from research that she undertook as part of her undergraduate dissertation.

Katherine Jellison is a Professor of History at Ohio University. Katherine's research focuses on gender issues in American consumer culture, and her publications include *Entitled to Power: Farm Women and Technology, 1913–1963* (University of North Carolina Press, 1993) and *It's Our Day: America's Love Affair with the White Wedding, 1945–2005* (University Press of Kansas, 2008). She is also the author or co-author of numerous journal articles and book chapters dealing with Anabaptist consumer practices in the 1930s and 1940s. She is currently working on a book manuscript about Amish women during the Great Depression.

Danke Li holds a PhD in history from the University of Michigan and is a Professor of History and Director of Asian Studies Program at Fairfield University in the United States. She serves as a national board member for Chinese Historians in the United States and the Society of Oral History on Modern China. Her research interests include women's history in China, women and the Second Sino-Japanese War, and the history of women's education in China. She is the author of many scholarly articles as well *Echoes of Chongqing: Women in Wartime in China* (University of Illinois Press, 2010) and *War, Women and Memory: 35 Chongqing Women's Wartime Experiences* (Chinese University of Hong Kong Press, July 2013). Her book *War, Women and Memory: 35 Chongqing Women's Wartime Experiences* won the 2014 Hong Kong Book Award.

Ariane Mak is a doctoral candidate at the École des Hautes Études en Sciences Sociales (School for Advanced Studies in the Social Sciences), Paris. Her doctoral research focuses on industrial militancy in British coalmines during the Second World War. Through a historical ethnography based on Mass Observation surveys and oral history interviews, her thesis explores the conflict between patriotism and social justice. Particular emphasis is placed on the disruption of occupational hierarchies and its consequences in terms of respectable masculinities and femininities. She is also researching the history of social sciences and is involved in several collaborative research projects in this field. Ariane Mak has been a History Research Associate at Queen Mary, University of London. She is also in charge of the EHESS oral history research programme 'Pour une histoire sonore de l'histoire orale'.

Sarah Myers is an Assistant Professor of History and Director of the Joseph E. & Shirley J. Keirn World War II Collection at Saint Francis University in Pennsylvania where she teaches public and military history. Her research fields include war and society in the United States, gender in the military, gender history, and oral history. She has presented at conferences including the Society for Military History and the Organization of American Historians. She attended the 2015 West Point Summer Seminar in Military History and the ROHO Advanced Oral History Summer Institute at the University of California, Berkeley.

Katrin Paehler is Associate Professor at Illinois State University. In her research and teaching she specializes in Nazi Germany, the Holocaust, foreign intelligence, genocide, and mass violence, as well as history, memory, and their representations. She is the author of chapters and articles on the Nazi Security and Intelligence Service, on Foreign Intelligence and the Holocaust, and on memories of World War II. She was a member of the Independent Historians Commission on the German Foreign Office and Nazism and Its Aftermath. She co-edited *A Nazi Past. Recasting German Identity in Postwar Europe* (2015) and her monograph on Office VI of the RSHA is forthcoming from Cambridge University Press.

Corinna Peniston-Bird is a Senior Lecturer in Gender History in the Department of History at Lancaster University with particular interests in the cultural circuit, and pedagogy in the discipline. Since 1998, her research and teaching has centred on gender dynamics in Britain in the Second World War, with an emphasis on the relationship between memories and cultural representations. Previous publications include 'Of Hockey Sticks and Sten Guns: British Auxiliaries and their Weapons in the Second World War', *Women's History Magazine*, Autumn 2014, no. 76; '"All in It Together and Backs to the wall": Relating Patriotism and the People's War in the 21st Century', *Oral History* Autumn, 2012; with Penny Summerfield, *Contesting Home Defence: Men, Women and the Home Guard in the Second World War* (Manchester University Press, 2007) as well as the co-edited special issue with Wendy Ugolini, *Journal of War and Culture Studies,* 'Silenced Mourning' (2014).

Helen Steele, currently at Leiden University, wrote her PhD on the experiences of Viennese women during the Second World War and Allied occupation. Her thesis was supervised by Jill Lewis at Swansea University and funded by the Arts and Humanities Research Council. During her candidature Helen held a two-month research scholarship awarded by the research platform 'Repositioning of Women's and Gender History' to work in the Collection of Women's Estates held at the University of Vienna. The research carried out during the scholarship is published as 'Daily Lives and Informal Networks in the Diaries of Two Viennese Women, 1943–1945', in Christa Hämmerle and Li Gerhalter (eds), *Krieg – Politik – Schreiben. Tagebucher von Frauen (1918 bis 1950)*, L'Homme Schriften (Böhlau, 2015). Helen works at Leiden University as a Tutor on the BA International Studies programme.

Florence Tamagne is Associate Professor at the University of Lille 3. A specialist in the history of homosexuality, she has published in English *A History of Homosexuality in Europe: Berlin, London, Paris, 1919–1939* (Algora Publishing, 2004), and has also contributed to Robert Aldrich (ed.), *Gay Life and Culture: A World History* (Universe, 2006), Louis-Georges Tin (ed.), *The Dictionary of Homophobia: A Global History of Gay and Lesbian Experience* (Arsenal Pulp Press, 2008), and Alain Corbin, Jean-Jacques Courtine, Georges Vigarello (ed.), *A History of Virility* (Columbia University Press, 2016).

Sachiyo Tsukamoto received a MA degree in politics and began her PhD in History at the University of Nottingham. In October 2014, she transferred her PhD studies to Politics at the University of Newcastle in Australia. Her research explores the politics of gendered memory of Japanese 'comfort women'. She is a member of VAWWRAC (Violence Against Women in War Research Center), which is the successor of VAWW-NET Japan. Her publication, 'From the Shadows of Silence and Shame to the Light of Voice and Dignity: Transnational Activism and the Contested Nature of the Historical Memory of the "Comfort Women" in Japan' appears in M. Paxton, E. Kolpinskaya, and J. Jonasova (eds), *Politics in Crisis?* (Cambridge Scholars Publishing, 2015).

Emma Vickers is a Senior Lecturer in History at Liverpool John Moores University. Her first monograph, *Queen and Country: Same Sex Desire in the British Armed Forces, 1939–1945* (Manchester University Press, 2013) explores the relationship between same-sex desire and service in the British armed forces during the Second World War. Emma has published articles in the *Lesbian Studies Journal* (2009) and *Feminist Review* (2010) and is currently working on *Dry Your Eyes Princess*, a project which uses oral testimony to uncover the experiences of trans* personnel in the British armed forces before 2000. Emma has worked with the BBC and collaborated with various museums and organizations, including the Ministry of Defence and the Historical Association. She is also an academic advisor for the National Festival of LGBT History.

Introduction

Corinna Peniston-Bird
and Emma Vickers

In 1942, the British cartoonist Joseph Lee described how the war had created a 'topsy turvy world'.[1] It was his perception of change in the nature of wartime gender relations and the gendered role reversals which provoked Lee's observation. The contemporary awareness that the Second World War was having a profound impact on gender identities and relationships took some time, however, to enter the subsequent historiography on the war. We have come a long way since Joan Wallach Scott pointed out that, 'Because, on the face of it, war, diplomacy, and high politics have not been explicitly about those relationships [between the sexes], gender seems not to apply, and so continues to be irrelevant to the thinking of historians concerned with issues of politics and power.'[2] Today, academic research is much more likely to acknowledge that the existence, definition, causes, practices, and consequences of war cannot be understood without using gender as a category of analysis.[3] The thirteen chapters offered here by established and emerging historians from across the globe are positioned firmly at this juncture of the historiography, and they also explore the idea that, as Joanne Bailey argued, 'War is a crucible for ideas about gender and a catalyst in reconstructing gender identities.'[4] Nonetheless, some authors here also successfully challenge the extent of that reconstruction, or indeed, the significance of the war for long-term change.

Collectively, this volume speaks to wartime femininities and masculinities, individuals and collectives, conformity and disruption, in isolation or in relation, in both the short and the longer term. The goal is to provide students and researchers with a collection of contemporary historical research on gender and the Second World War that positions that research in the broader historiography of the war. Recommended reading is included at the close of each chapter; the historiography covered in this introduction cannot address the breadth of geographical and temporal range covered in the chapters, but concentrates on coverage of the key themes of the collection. Unsurprisingly, most books which address the multiple geographical regions embroiled in the war are edited collections, introduced below. Each chapter here thus demonstrates the significance of specific spatial, political, cultural, and social contexts, but it is in the identification of the junctures and disjunctures between the different chapters that the reader may find the greatest insights into the lessons of war. The founding principle of this volume is that war is a 'clarifying moment' which throws gender into stark relief.[5] War reveals what in constructions of gender is negotiable and flexible, and what is not. The collection as a whole interrogates not only ideologies and public discourse, but also lived experience and memory. It is striking how wide a variety of source materials are drawn upon in this collection, from personal testimony to legislation, from court cases to literature, from a range of visual sources to patriotic songs. Neither practice nor representation, nor individual or collective, is subordinated to the other.

We make no claim to offer global coverage and there is still much work to be done if we are to understand the impact of the war on all the countries involved – over one hundred ranging from Afghanistan to Yugoslavia – but thirteen countries in four continents are represented here, both the victorious and the defeated.[6] This range is reflected in the different terminology used to describe the war which the editors deliberately chose not to reconcile: the Asia-Pacific War, the Second Sino-Japanese War, or the Great Patriotic War obviously describe a specific location, reading, and periodization of the war, while the distinction between the Second World War and World War II is more subtle, reflecting not only the historiographical conventions of different nations but a slight shift in emphasis on the global nature of the war. In the British coverage of the centenary of the First World War, for example, this subtle distinction is suggested by the contrast between the terminology adopted by the BBC (who have opted for World War I in various forms, with an eye to international audiences) and the Imperial War Museum (who refer consistently to the First World War). Together, the chapters allow the reader to explore some of the correlations and contradictions across differing cultural and geographical contexts, from both Allied and Axis perspectives: Robert Dale, Lorenzo Benadusi, and Florence Tamagne, for example, explore military masculinities in three contexts which suggest both the nationally specific – for example, the Stalinist construction of individual heroism rooted in the collective effort – and the universal, such as the intertwining of military masculinity with heterosexuality, or the paradoxical combination of aggressive military masculinity with temperate and tender homosociability on the front lines.

The serendipity of juxtaposition coexists with the systematic grouping of the thirteen chapters into four themes. Male and female experiences are represented in each section, and there is varied emphasis within and between the chapters on masculinities, femininities, and gender relations. Parts I and II explore gender identities in the military and the domestic contexts respectively.[7] In Part III, four chapters explore the meeting places between military and civilian identities. The idea of the latter being distinct, and the identification of two fronts – a battle front and a home front – may constitute a conventional convenience, but it serves to obscure the commonalities and disparities of experience between and within the categories. The interplay in wartime masculinities between military and civilian values is a rich and varied one; Benadusi, for example, suggests there is a dialectic to be explored between middle-class respectability and respectability in uniform in Italian Fascism, a finding which offers interesting parallels with Sonya Rose's work on temperate masculinities in Britain.[8] Part IV addresses contemporary and retrospective representations of the Second World War. As Kate Darian-Smith points out in her investigation into US marines in Melbourne, 'The rising wave of popular interest around the world in the experiences and reverberations of civilians and soldiers during World War II suggests – paradoxically – that as the war is no longer present within lived memory, the forms of its commemorative representations are becoming increasingly prominent in national understandings of its cultural and political impact.' All the chapters weave between the implicit and the explicit so fundamental in studies of gender identities, but that interweaving is most evident in the case studies of Part IV. Katherine Jellison, for example, explores the inherent but unheeded contradictions of representing the values for which the United States was at war through images of a group of women opposed to war, while Sachiyo Tsukamoto explores the gendered assumptions that explain the contested histories of 'comfort women' in Japan and South Korea. The editors hope that this will provide a spur to further comparative investigation of commemorative activity of the war across the globe.

The investigation of the impact of war on gender began with a focus on women in the 1950s, which continues to the present day. Research by Richard Titmuss, Arthur Marwick, and Penny Summerfield amongst others contributed to a multifaceted debate on the relationship between war and social change. The question was whether increased labour requirements offered increased opportunities and self-awareness for women – whether war allowed women to make political gains and spurred feminist politics. The emphasis on new opportunities was countered by analysis of the counteractive role of legislation and societal policing of change.[9] Ariane Mak's investigation of consumption in Welsh mining communities in this volume provides a perfect illustration of the policing of gender boundaries and the different evidence and strategies employed within, in this case, working-class communities significantly impacted by the war and the employment opportunities it introduced to previously depressed areas. Her research reminds us to locate such strategies at the three levels of the state, the community, and the individual.

Femininities are poised – sometimes torn – between the paradoxes created by the symbolic and the pragmatic mobilization of women for the war effort. As Katrin Paehler shows through her case study of Hildegard Beetz below, for example, Beetz simultaneously played and defied constructions of her gender. Even retrospective accounts of her role reveal deep-seated gender-based prejudices and preconceptions as to the individuals, professions, and behaviours worthy of historical investigation. Paehler's conclusions would suggest that scholarship on women continues to have the power 'fundamentally [to] transform disciplinary paradigms'. Feminist scholars had already pointed out in the 1970s that the study of women would not only add new subject matter but would also force a critical re-examination of the premises and standards of existing scholarly work:

> We are learning that the writing of women into history necessarily involves redefining and enlarging traditional notions of historical significance, to encompass personal, subjective experience as well as public and political activities. It is not too much to suggest that however hesitant the actual beginnings, such a methodology implies not only a new history of women, but also a new history.[10]

Oral and personal testimony were fundamental to that shift, and the subjective experience is a focus of analysis in many of the chapters below, constantly warning against sweeping assumptions.[11]

The 'new history' has led also to challenges to the invisibility of masculinities and to explorations of how men, too, experienced the demands and consequences of war.[12] In their edited collection, Stefan Dudink, Karen Hagemann, and John Tosh convincingly argued for the interrelatedness between gender, political, and military history, 'how politics and war have become the seemingly "natural" homelands of masculinity'.[13] *Lessons of War* suggests that across the participants of the Second World War, hegemonic masculinity became inextricably intertwined with military masculinity. Hegemonic masculinity is understood here as in John Tosh's definition – 'to stand for those masculine attributes which are most widely subscribed to – and least questioned – in a given social formation: the "common sense" of gender as acknowledged by all men save those whose masculinity is oppositional or deviant.'[14] However, our authors explore the space of what Anna Brava termed the 'muddled mixture' of masculinities, whether military or civilian, heterosexual or queer.[15] As several chapters suggest, deviant masculinities and military masculinity were also inextricably intertwined. Emma Vickers and Emma Jackson explore the boundaries of such intertwining with their investigation into male cross-dressing in the British armed forces, suggesting that masculinities could perhaps be more playful and subversive of the norm even in the military context than hitherto assumed. The significance of diversity in sexual and gender identities is an important theme which runs through these chapters. As Laura Sjoberg has argued and Tamagne's article in this collection exemplifies, 'it is important to understand the roles and representations not only of men and women during war, but also of other "sexes" and "genders", including but not limited to queer and transgendered people and representations ... [this] is informative both about the ways that rigid adherence to gender roles is essential to war efforts, and about the ways in which gender tropes are used to alienate and other enemies [*sic*].'[16]

The focus of *Lessons of War* is thus not only on the impact of conflict on sexual identities and practices, but also on the meanings – and the telling silences – imposed on these, not only at the time but for generations afterwards.[17] Academic attention has recently explored in greater depth the interconnectedness of war and sexual activity, intimate or violent, a focus which has grown alongside that on the body as a site of meeting between institution and individual, of objective and subjective experience.[18] In this field, the edited collection by Dagmar Herzog, *Brutality and Desire, War and Sexuality in Europe's Twentieth Century* (2008), is of particular note, owing to the way in which the collection nuanced military history through an examination of the sexual behaviours of both soldiers and civilians, both during war and in its aftermath. As many authors show here, sexual violence – and its denial – was central to the waging and experience of war in ways that have ricocheted through time and memory, both private and public.

In 1986, Joan Wallach Scott argued that the theme of gender challenges the conventional periodization of war.[19] In the case of this volume, that is partly a consequence of the geographical range of inclusions whose wars started at different times, but also in response to the question as to the significance of the war as a watershed in gender relations. When placed into the wider historical chronology adopted by many of the authors here, the war revealed both the transitory and the doggedly stable components of gender constructions. The latter can be explained by the range of strategies used to reassert traditional gender roles – from legislation to spin to silence – to reaffirm the return to 'normal'. Indeed, it is in the range of strategies employed and the determination with which they are pursued both during and after the war, that the threat of war to conventional ideas of gender can most clearly be seen. Numerous chapters including Helen Steele's analysis of bigamy cases in Austria all underline how long the impact of war was experienced, and the obstacles to the reassertion of the gender order in the aftermath of war. Conversely, however, attention to continuities can also challenge an overemphasis on the significance of the Second World War, as the chapters of Helen Glew and Florence Tamagne warn us. Furthermore, many shifts perhaps prompted by the war have taken decades to play out; the longer they take, obviously the more difficult it becomes to identify precisely what role can be ascribed to the war. Nonetheless, oral histories, as explored by Kate Darian-Smith, testify to the enduring significance of the war in individual life-review and personal understandings of gender identities for decades after the conflict.

Finally, a word to gender theory. A central dimension of gender and war studies has been the attempt to find a model that explains or at least describes the phenomenon of gender dynamics in wartime. On outbreak of war, a common phenomenon is polarization. At one end of the spectrum the militarized male goes to war to defend the domestic femininity at the other end. Jean Bethke Elshtain describes this phenomenon as 'Just Warriors' fight for 'Beautiful Souls'.[20] This phenomenon hinges on the gendered qualities of separate spheres, identified by Joanna Bourke as encompassing the manly, athletic, stoic, and courageous for men, and the gentle, domesticated, and virginal for women.[21] As Danke Li observes in this volume, in the early phases of the war, many Chinese politicians and artists simply did not realize that the war would be a long one that would require the active participation of Chinese women. Therefore most of the wartime cartoons and wood-block prints in that period represented the theme of men going to the front line to fight against Japanese invaders in order to protect women and children at home. Penny Summerfield's identification of a 'gender contract' describes a similar relationship between the sexes: 'men were pledged to fight for women, who undertook to maintain home and family. These were the patriotic wartime roles of the two sexes.'[22]

However polarization and the gender contract cannot survive the exigencies of war, and in particular, the increased demand for labour. In *Behind the Lines: Gender and the Two World Wars* (1989), Margaret and Patrice Higonnet introduced the iconic metaphor of the double helix to describe why, despite the potential, neither World War led to significant change in the distance between the sexes, in male dominance and female subservience:

> The female strand on the helix is opposed to the male strand, and position on the female strand is subordinate to position on the male strand. The image of the double helix allows us to see that, although the roles of men and women vary greatly from culture to culture, their relationship is in some sense constant.[23]

As discussed below, the double helix does not operate in every context, but it is supported by such evidence as pay and status differentials. The marriage bar offers an interesting dimension to the Higonnets' theory as it suggests the significance of inflection by age and marital status; as Glew suggests, in both Britain and Canada the practice outlived the compelling evidence of its impropriety.

The crux of these models is the combat taboo; all hinge on the idea that however much flux wartime brings, the exclusion of women from directly confronting and killing the enemy definitively separates the genders and ensures male supremacy. Cynthia Enloe, a key analyst of the relationship between war and gender, argues that women *must* be denied access to 'the front', to 'combat', so that men can claim uniqueness and superiority that will justify their dominant position in the social order.[24] The significance of the combat taboo can be read in the lengths gone to in its defence. Where military masculinity can be explored in all belligerent countries, military femininity defies ready definition, despite the attention paid by academics to the auxiliary forces.[25] Sarah Myers' investigation here into the American Women Airforce Service Pilots (WASP) confirms the strict boundary policing of such potentially subversive roles, located at multiple levels: the government; the institution; the individual, a finding which echoes that of Mak (see above).

The WASP and auxiliary services in general, however, can be more disruptive of gender boundaries than the models outlined above allow – an observation equally true of the expansion of roles on the home front. Most recently, Corinna Peniston-Bird has suggested a model of the impact of war on gender based on the concept of fuzzy boundaries, exploring the centre of the gender spectrum where masculinities and femininities overlapped most: in compulsory military service, for example, and in the areas where civilian and military – and male and female – roles were less obviously distinct, owing to proximity to the war effort, harsh living conditions, and the risk to life or limb.[26] This model also allows for the possibility of gender-blind perceptions of roles and service. It opens up the possibility of an alternative to what Denise Riley refers to as the 'dreadful air of constancy which sexual polarities possess'.[27] As testified in the following pages, all models are seen in operation in different places and times in the Second World War. The roles and identities explored in this volume proved more unstable and mutable than Riley's air of constancy would suggest, and polarities coexist with clear areas of 'fuzzy' overlap. The men and women at war had to negotiate these paradoxes; as our contributors illustrate, it is the responsibility of historians to hold these tensions, not impose a resolution denied the historical actors.

Notes

1. J. Lee (1942) 'Smiling Through: Topsy-Turvy World', *Evening News*, 27 January. British Cartoon Archive, JL2021. The full caption continues with the frustrated husband's words: 'Just like a woman! Bring all your friends home from the factory to supper when all I've got in the house is two tins of Spam.' The image shows some physical reversals, too, with the group of women lounging over the furniture in their dungarees while the husband complains from the kitchen door in his pinny.

2. J. W. Scott (1986) 'Gender: A Useful Category of Historical Analysis', *The American Historical Review*, vol. 91, no. 5, pp. 1053–75, here p. 1057.

3. L. Sjoberg (2013) *Gendering Global Conflict: Towards a Feminist Theory of War* (New York: Columbia University Press).

4. J. Bailey (2014) 'Questions of Gender', *History Today*, vol. 64, no. 6, p. 54. See context at http://www.historytoday.com/joanne-bailey/questions-gender, date accessed 3 May 2016.

5. In *Behind the Lines*, the editors argued that 'war has acted as a clarifying moment, one that has revealed systems of gender in flux and thus highlighted their workings. Emergency conditions either alter or reinforce existing notions of gender, the nation, and the family.' M. Randolph Higonnet, J. Jenson, S. Michel, and M. Collins Weitz (eds) (1988) *Behind the Lines: Gender and the Two World Wars* (New Haven, CT: Yale University Press), p. 5.

6. See, for example, N. M. Wingfield and M. Bucur (eds) (2006) *Gender and War in Twentieth-Century Eastern Europe*, Indiana-Michigan Series in Russian & East European Studies (Bloomington: Indiana University Press); S. Dudink, K. Hagemann, and J. Tosh (eds) (2004) *Masculinities in Politics and War: Gendering Modern History*, Gender in History Series (Manchester and New York: Manchester University Press).

7. We note with regret – and as encouragement – that there is still much work to be done on the experiences of civilian men during wartime. A pending publication is J. Pattinson, A. McIvor, and L. Robb (2016) *Men in Reserve: British Civilian Masculinities in the Second World War*, Cultural History of Modern War (Manchester and New York: Manchester University Press).

8. S. O. Rose (2003) *Which People's War? National Identity and Citizenship in Wartime Britain 1939–1945* (Oxford: Oxford University Press).

9. A very brief indicative sample of the British debate includes R. M Titmuss (1958) 'War and Social Policy' and 'The Position of Women: Some Vital Statistics' in *Essays on the Welfare State* (London: Allen and Unwin); A. Marwick (1968) *Britain the Century of Total War: War, Peace and Social Change 1900–1967* (London: Bodley Head); H. Smith (1986) 'The Effect of the War on the Status of Women' in H. L. Smith (ed.) (1986) *War and Social Change: British Society in the Second World War* (Manchester: Manchester University Press); or more recently, P. Summerfield (1998) *Reconstructing Women's Wartime Lives* (Manchester and New York: Manchester University Press). See also, J. E. Trey (1972) 'Women in the War Economy: World War II', *Review of Radical Political Economics*, vol. 4, no. 3, pp. 40–57.

10. A. D. Gordon, M. J. Buhle, and N. Shrom Dye (1976) 'The Problem of Women's History' in B. Carroll (ed), *Liberating Women's History* (Urbana: University of Illinois Press), p. 89.

11. As exemplified by S. Alexievich (1988) *War's Unwomanly Face* (Moscow: Progress Publishers).

12. See, for example, M. Roper and J. Tosh (eds) (1991) *Manful Assertions: Masculinities in Britain since 1800* (London and New York: Routledge): the introduction is a particularly useful insight into the origins of this field of study. For a more recent example, see G. Hayes and K. W. Goodlet (2014) 'Exploring Masculinity in the Canadian Army Corps, 1939–45', *Journal of Canadian Studies*, vol. 48, no. 2, pp. 40–69.

13. 'Introduction', in S. Dudink, K. Hagemann, and J. Tosh (eds) (2004) *Masculinities in Politics and War*, p. xii.

14. J. Tosh, 'Hegemonic Masculinity and the History of Gender' in S. Dudink, K. Hagemann, and J. Tosh (eds) (2004) *Masculinities in Politics and War*, p. 47.

15. For 'muddled mixture' see A. Bravo (1991) 'Simboli del materno', in *Donne e uomini nelle guerre mondiali*, (Rome-Bari: Laterza), p. 121 (discussed in Lorenzo Benadusi's chapter, Chapter 2, in this volume).

16. L. Sjoberg (2014) *Gender, War and Conflict* (Wiley) e-book: ch. 4.

17. J. Costello (1986) *Love, Sex and War: Changing values 1939–45* (London: Pan Books); E. Vickers (2013) *Queen and Country: Same-sex Desire in the British Armed Forces, 1939–1945* (Manchester: Manchester University Press); D. Herzog (ed.) (2011) *Brutality and Desire: War and Sexuality in Europe's Twentieth Century* (London: Palgrave); L. Bernadusi (2012) *The Enemy of the New Man: Homosexuality in Fascist Italy* (Madison: University of Wisconsin Press); Y. Smaal (2015) *Sex, Soldiers and the South Pacific, 1939–1945: Queer identities in Australia in the Second World War* (London: Palgrave Macmillan); P. Jackson (2004) *One of the Boys: Homosexuality in the military during World War II* (Montreal: McGill-Queen's University Press).

18. See, for example, Joanna Bourke's publications, including (2014) *The Story of Pain: From Prayer to Painkillers* (Oxford: Oxford University Press); (2007) *Rape: A History from 1860s to the Present* (London: Virago; Emeryville; CA: Shoemaker and Hoard); (1999) *An Intimate History of Killing: Face-to-Face Killing in Twentieth Century Warfare* (London: Granta and New York: Basic Books); (1996) *Dismembering the Male: Men's Bodies, Britain, and the Great War* (Chicago: University of Chicago Press), or Emma Newlands (2014) *Civilians into Soldiers: War, the Body and British Army Recruits* (Manchester: Manchester University Press). Many studies are of course nation-specific, such as A. Grossmann (1995) 'A Question of Silence: The Rape of German Women by Occupation Soldiers', *October*, vol. 72 (Spring), Berlin 1945: 'War and Rape "Liberators Take Liberties"', pp. 42–63.

19. This remains a key text: J. W. Scott (1986) 'Gender'.

20. J. B. Elshtain (1987) *Women and War* (Brighton: Harvester).

21. Bourke, *Dismembering the Male*, pp. 12–13.

22. P. Summerfield (1997) *'My Dress for an Army Uniform': Gender Instabilities in the Two World Wars*, Inaugural Lecture (Lancaster: University of Lancaster, 1997).

23. M. R. and P. L. R. Higonnet outlined 'The double helix' in M. Randolph Higonnet et al., (1988) *Behind the Lines*, pp. 31–47, here p. 34.

24. For a full list of Cynthia Enloe's publications, please see her home page at Clark University on http://www2.clarku.edu/faculty/facultybio.cfm?id=343, date accessed 13 July 2016.

25. G. J. DeGroot and C. M. Peniston-Bird (eds) (2000) *A Soldier and a Woman; Sexual Integration in the Military* (Harlow: Pearson Education); J. Wheelwright (1989) *Amazons and Military Maids: Women Who Dressed as Men in Pursuit of Life, Liberty and Happiness* (London: Pandora); R. D. Markwick and E. Charon Cardona (2012) *Soviet Women on the Frontline in the Second World War* (Basingstoke: Palgrave Macmillan); B. Fieseler, M. M. Hampf, and J. Schwarzkopf (2014) 'Gendering Combat: Military Women's status in Britain, the United States, and the Soviet Union during the Second World War', *Women's Studies International Forum* 47, pp. 115–26.

26. C. Peniston-Bird (2014) 'Of Hockey Sticks and Sten Guns: British Auxiliaries and Their Weapons in the Second World War', *Women's History Magazine*, vol. Autumn, no. 76, pp. 13–22; and 'Representing Invisible Men: The Memorialization of Reserved Occupations' in Juliette Pattinson and Linsey Robb (eds), *Men, Masculinities and Male Culture in the Second World War* (Palgrave Macmillan, forthcoming).

27. D. Riley (1986) 'Summary of Preamble to Interwar Feminist History Work', unpublished paper, presented to the Pembroke Center Seminar, May 1985, cited by J. W. Scott (1986), 'Gender'; see also D. Riley (1987) 'Does Sex Have a History? "Women" and Feminism', *New Formations*, Spring, no. 1, pp. 35–45, here p. 43.

Part 1
Gender Identities in the Forces

1

Battling Contested Airspaces: The American Women Airforce Service Pilots of World War II

Sarah Myers

Although women pilots had been in aviation in the decades prior to World War II, men in the Army Air Force (AAF) considered the American Women Airforce Service Pilots (WASP) above all else 'novelties' when they arrived at AAF bases after training.[1] In calling them 'novelties', the Central Flying Training Command, a regional section of the AAF, referenced male attitudes towards women flyers and the introduction of women into the male-dominated AAF. Many WASP encountered numerous male pilots during the war who did not even know that there were women flying for the AAF. As the Central Flying Training Command stated: 'War and Army flying in particular had been looked upon as a man's game. It was no wonder that male pilots as well as others looked askance at the possibility of using women as pilots in numerous and sundry activities vital to the war effort.'[2] These men, and often the American public, believed that not only war but military flying was 'a man's game' and it is no surprise that the WASP encountered hostility during their service. Amidst private and public debates about the capabilities of their physical bodies and their sexuality the WASP intrusively threatened and upset definitions of military service and the emerging image of an elite male AAF. This caused their military service to be dismissed as women's work and it ultimately led to a denial of full citizenship under the US government and the rights accorded to other male veterans. Throughout their training and assignments the women pilots asserted their place as professionals within contested airspaces as they battled male resistance and gendered debates about their physical, psychological, and intellectual abilities.

Early histories of American women in World War II, such as those of William Chafe, D'Ann Campbell, and Leila Rupp, initiated debates on how the war influenced women's lives and whether or not it was a 'watershed' moment because of new work opportunities.[3] Others, such as Sherna Gluck and Susan Hartmann, argue that women's experiences led to the women's liberation movement of the 1960s and 1970s.[4] Later historians, notably Leisa Meyer, move away from the watershed versus continuity arguments while examining the lives of military women in terms of sexuality and power.[5] This chapter complicates this historiography by exploring the ways that women fought for a place as professionals in gendered military spaces.

An experimental programme

The WASP programme was considered an experiment to test women's competence in military aircraft flying. The women went through military training for between five and seven and a half months. They had the same training as AAF men, minus the combat training of aerial gunnery and advanced aerobatics because it was assumed women should not fight in combat unless no other options existed.[6] They had similar test scores, graduation rates, and even washout rates (expulsion) to male pilots. Approximately 25,000 women pilots applied to the programme, 1,830 women were accepted, and 1,074 graduated. The washout rate for these check rides was the same for both men and women trainees because it was the job of the instructors to eliminate pilots who were not of the highest calibre.[7] After training, the women pilots were stationed at over 120 AAF bases in the continental United States and they served in assignments including ferrying planes cross-country, towing targets for male cadets to practise anti-aircraft artillery, instructing male pilots, and test piloting. They were restricted from flying in combat, but not dangerous missions. However, their duties were almost entirely contained to the continental United States, for fear that a woman's death in combat or even over an ocean might cause a public backlash against women's participation in the military.[8] Although officially considered civilians, the trainees followed military rules and regulations during the war. They performed the same duties as AAF officers in that they flew military aircraft, lived on military bases, worked with other military personnel, and obeyed AAF rules and regulations. Some of these regulations were unique to the women pilots because the AAF wanted to avoid the slander campaign that accused the Women's Army Corps (WAC) of serving as prostitutes for male soldiers while also questioning the sexuality of women in the military.[9] The AAF was successful in this endeavour due to their intense censorship of the media during the war.[10] What started as an experiment to see if women had the physical, emotional, and intellectual capabilities to fly military aircraft became an incredible success.

A love of flying, a hope for a career in aviation, and a patriotic desire to help with the war effort motivated the women who became the WASP. Although American women pilots in the 1920s and 1930s were from relatively wealthy families, since paying for flying hours was expensive, the majority of the WASP had families who could not financially support their flying. Rather, they earned their licences and accumulated flying time through the Civilian Pilot Training Program (CPTP). The CPTP made flying accessible to men and women of all social classes and backgrounds. Although the CPTP only trained one woman for every ten men, approximately 2,500 women received CPTP training prior to the US entrance into World War II in December 1941.[11] Women pilots needed to have a certain number of flying hours before applying for the WASP programme so the creation of the CPTP made their WASP experiences possible.[12] Although there were a small number who came from wealthy families, the majority of the WASP received their licence via the CPTP programme or by working extra jobs to pay for flying hours.[13] After receiving their pilots' licences in the CPTP, many women pilots were eager to use their valuable aviation skills professionally and in a patriotic capacity, as large numbers of them applied for the WASP programme.

Gendered assumptions

There were private and public discussions about the women's bodies, in terms of their physical abilities and potential limitations.[14] Medical professionals and male pilots often felt that women could not handle military aircraft or even flying because of the stereotype that women were physically weaker. To a greater extent than contemporary aircraft, 1940s aircraft required physical strength, rather than automation, to fly. When the WASP flew aircraft successfully, male journalists in the media dismissed the abilities and successes of the WASP as luck or as a fluke rather than as evidence of the women's skills. In doing so, the journalists furthered stereotypes about the military as a masculine space. These reactions existed despite the fact that the WASP passed the same AAF physical examination for flying.[15] One officer accused the women pilots of being 'too weak' to fly heavy aircraft and he supported his argument by explaining that women could not do more than ten push-ups.[16] Yet as the WASP programme continued due to the women pilots' successes, they were assigned after graduation to ferry heavier and faster aircraft, proving their abilities throughout the war. Heavier aircraft were those that were multiengine, such as bombers like the B-17 or B-29, and they were utilized to deliver bombs overseas. The faster aircraft that the WASP flew were typically pursuit aircraft, for example P-38 or P-51, which were utilized overseas for fast combat fighting and as protection for larger, slower bombers. These types of aircraft were harder to fly in terms of strength and skillset than lighter aircraft like the ones the WASP flew during training. During training, instructors taught the WASP how to handle heavy aircraft by having them perform exercises to build up their arm, wrist, and hand strength.[17] The WASP heard about AAF officers questioning the women's physical strength when discussing the militarization of the programme, as one WASP mentioned in a letter home to her family. Yet, she explained, while flying was tiring and required a 'great deal of physical stamina' it was 'worth it'.[18]

In addition to concerns about women's strength, there were also questions about other aspects of women's bodies.[19] Until the mid-1940s, some doctors and medical experts believed the physical strain caused by aeroplane aerobatics would damage a woman's reproductive organs.[20] There was also the belief that female pilots would need to be 'off duty for a few days each month' for emotional and physical reasons, therefore rendering them 'undependable' compared to male pilots.[21] The WASP resisted by refusing to report their cycles or by claiming they were 'irregular'.[22] Overall, the WASP proved they could 'safely, efficiently, and regularly' fly all types of military aircraft despite supposed physical restraints.[23] Furthermore, at the end of the programme, WASP Director Jacqueline Cochran concluded that the women's health had 'not interfered with their service'.[24] Part of Cochran's conclusion was drawn from a medical study conducted on the WASP during the course of the programme. The purpose of this study was not just to make conclusions about WASP performance, but also to consider the future incorporation of women pilots in the US military. Various flight surgeons and medical officers collected data from 430 reported cases of women's menstrual cycles.[25] This was the number after some of the cases were 'thrown out' when it was discovered the WASP were 'giving replies that they thought ... would enhance the percentage in favor of women pilots'! So, in addition to not always reporting their cycles, apparently the WASP also altered their responses to questions about them as well. When asked about cramps none of the trainees said they would be 'unable to bring a ship in if she happened to have cramps while flying'. Also considering the women's performance, the medical officers noted that there were no changes in 'visual acuity and depth perception' during flights. Finally, there was no correlation between a woman's period and her elimination from training, and 'of the 11 fatal accidents, 112 major, non-fatal accidents, there were no demonstrable contributing menstrual factors'. The conclusion of the study was that: 'Menstruation is not a handicap in selected candidates to prevent a woman from fulfilling her job as a military aircraft pilot.'[26] Through these studies it is clear that women's bodies were a source of debate among physicians, as they not only doubted the capabilities of women versus men as military pilots but the physicians also ignored the fact that women had flown planes in the decades prior to the war. These physicians accepted that men could fly military planes, which were larger than civilian aircraft, but they automatically assumed that a woman's reproductive organs were more restrictive or problematic than a man's.

In the end, these and other medical reports showed that the women pilots 'had as much endurance and were no more subject to fatigue and flew as regularly and for as long hours as the male pilots in similar work'.[27] Furthermore, WASP test scores, as well as washout and graduation rates out of training, were comparable to the male pilots' rates.[28] When the WASP proved their capabilities via these comparative test scores during training and graduation, the programme was deemed successful and they were assigned to more experimental roles so that the AAF could 'ascertain their adaptability for duties as other than ferry pilots'.[29]

Interactions with instructors

During training the interactions that women in the WASP had with their instructors, who exercised a certain degree of control over whether the women pilots passed or failed check rides during training, illuminate ways that the WASP confronted male reactions to their abilities.[30] On occasion, male pilots treated the WASP according to gendered assumptions about them. In instances of intimidation and harassment the WASP ignored or resisted their instructors or sought to prove their flying abilities. Yet not all interactions with male instructors and check pilots were adverse. Many WASP noticed that male pilots' acceptance came after the male pilots flew with female pilots.[31]

Some male instructors fuelled by gendered assumptions tried to prevent the WASP from passing training, perhaps because women challenged their own military identity. WASP Establishment Officer Leoti Deaton said at the conclusion of the WASP programme: 'Previously, many of the officers, particularly the check pilots, were openly disparaging and openly resentful toward the training of women pilots.'[32] Deaton's analysis from her years of working with the WASP at Sweetwater illuminates a distinction that sometimes existed between AAF pilots and civilian pilots. The women pilots frequently found check rides with civilian pilots to be better than with AAF pilots, as the latter 'were very unhappy being associated with a women's field'.[33] Some AAF check pilots said they intended to fail as many women as possible. An AAF check pilot told WASP Joanne Wallace, 'I came here … to see how many of you women I could wash out.'[34] Such experiences with male pilots were frequent enough that WASP classes would warn upcoming classes about the current instructors.[35] Whether intended for intimidation or a teaching method, these threats often encouraged the WASP to work even harder. Furthermore, female pilots had the same wash-out and graduation rates as male pilots, so regardless of their interactions with instructors, there were still a comparable number of women graduating.[36]

Some WASP believed these AAF men were embarrassed that their work involved teaching women. Perhaps this embarrassment derived from the belief that teaching women was insignificant or unimportant compared with teaching male students who would fight in combat or perform other forms of work readily identified as military. The WASP who encountered these instructors hesitated to report these men for fear of being washed out of training, as they could also receive demerits for 'improper or disrespectful' behaviour towards officers or instructors.[37] WASP Jean Hascall Cole had an encounter with an instructor who 'flipped the plane into a maneuver that was so violent that [she] was knocked unconscious' and blood came out of her nose and eyes. She chose not to report the man, even though he did not apologize, because she was worried that she would not graduate.[38] Another WASP described the abuses of her instructor: he screamed, swore, hit the stick against her knees until they bruised, and held his earphones out of the cockpit so that the loud noise of the wind would come through her earphones.[39] Instructors also used these tactics with male pilot trainees.[40] Many WASP talked about their instructors hitting the stick against their knees mid-flight and they even compared bruises with each other. One WASP explained that when a trainee made a mistake during a flight, her instructor would 'slam the stick back and forth banging [her] knees'. She felt that it was an 'effective' tactic but one which the trainees felt expressed a 'lack of respect'.[41] WASP Marjorie Osborne Nichol told her parents during training that although she had instructors who swore repeatedly at her and pounded her with the stick during flights, she would 'rather have a rugged instructor who makes flying hell than one who barely or perhaps doesn't get you through the civilian and Army checks'.[42] To these WASP, graduation meant more than any hardships suffered during training.

Some trainees chose to resist their instructors through various methods. It was possible to request a change of instructor, and some WASP had their requests fulfilled.[43] When WASP Kay Herman's instructor kept taking over the controls, she forcefully asked him to remove his hands from 'her' controls.[44] Other WASP made light of the tense interactions between WASP and male instructors by writing articles, poems, and cartoons in their newsletters. These newsletters were published and distributed among WASP trainees.[45] During World War II, other military groups, including servicemen and women in other branches of the US military, performed this military tradition of publishing newsletters.[46] Presumably the WASP could publish their own opinions about their training experiences, since it was published by the WASP not the AAF.[47] In one article a trainee posed a fictional interaction between an instructor and student, in which the instructor yelled, 'can't you do anything right?'[48] Although fictional, this article must have resonated with WASP trainees who wrote and read this newsletter.

Not all interactions with male instructors and check pilots were combative or antagonistic. Some instructors tried to be effective teachers to the women pilots.[49] Often, however, they attributed their belief that women trainees needed different treatment to men to their being the more emotional sex. These flexible instructors realized 'bluster' did not work as well as it did with male students, but found encouragement more effective.[50] Some WASP noticed patterns of male behaviour and believed from their interactions that male pilots eventually accepted the women pilots. This acceptance came after an initial period of 'rudeness' followed by 'complete acceptance and admiration' after the male pilots actually interacted with the women pilots.[51] These reactions were also evident in WASP encounters with male pilots on AAF bases during their assignments after training.

The trainees also interacted with their instructors outside of training and some even dated men on the field, which was forbidden and resulted in expulsion if caught. These pilots often found creative ways to meet and their interactions were frequently platonic, according to WASP Joanne Wallace Orr.[52] Although references to sex among military personnel are scarce in archival sources, there was a WASP song that warned against relationships with male officers. It told a fictional story of a WASP who slept with a pilot: 'The moral of this story, as you can plainly see, Is never trust a pilot an inch above the knee, He'll kiss you and caress you, and promise to be true, and have a girl at every field as all the pilots do.'[53] Despite this suggestion of the dangers of the pilots' sexual allure, however, the statistics would appear to support Orr's emphasis on platonic relationships. Medical records and AAF documents show that the number of documented pregnancies was extremely low. These WASP were required to resign, although at least one base allowed a married WASP to continue flying after she reported her pregnancy. She, too, eventually resigned, most likely when she started to show.[54] So, although there were questions about WASP abilities and the impact of flying on their reproductive organs, at least one flight surgeon allowed a woman to fly while pregnant. These records illuminate the continued regulation of the women pilots' bodies and sexuality.

Justifications for WASP assignments

The roles assigned to the WASP illuminate these gendered assumptions and a sexual division of labour within the AAF. Much of the work the WASP accomplished was dangerous, and the roles contradicted traditional notions of femininity. WASP often assumed the jobs men preferred not to perform during the war, such as the work of towing targets. Male pilots viewed it as more masculine and worthwhile to die in combat than on the home front. In addition, male pilots labelled jobs that the WASP were now performing with gendered language that set them apart as women's work. Once jobs in the AAF had been redefined as women's duties, male pilots expressed hostility at having to take jobs to which the WASP were being assigned.

One primary job that male pilots did not want to hold was that of towing targets for male Air Force cadets to practise shooting live ammunition. The assignment consisted of flying the same pattern in the air so that male cadets could practise shooting ammunition by aiming at the sheet target that was attached by cables to the plane. The ammunition was coloured so that when it hit the target it would leave behind a coloured mark. There was a round circle in the middle of the sheet, and since each cadet or group of cadets had a different colour, AAF officials could measure who hit closest to the target. WASP Bev Beesemyer said of the experience: 'It was the only flying I did where I flew … by the seat of my pants.'[55] Furthermore, some of the WASP would convince mechanics at the base to put longer cables on the plane so that the sheet could be a little farther away from it.

Despite and perhaps because of the fact that the WASP freed up some men for combat through the work of towing targets, male pilots who remained and who continued to tow targets resented women serving alongside them. The first AAF base where the WASP performed target-towing was at Camp Davis in North Carolina and it was infamous among the WASP for its disdain for women pilots.[56] Many of the men stationed there blatantly objected to the women's presence.[57] These reactions stem from male responses to women disrupting masculine stereotypes about dangerous work, but also their desire to claim the field of military aviation as masculine.[58] Target-towing was risky, not only because of the possibility that the cadets would miss the targets and hit the planes, but because the planes flown were heavily damaged from combat or were old machines.[59] As a result of this plane damage, male and female pilots towing targets flew war-weary planes unfit for combat. The mechanics on base had trouble keeping up with the amount of work and often ran out of replacement parts. For example, WASP Mabel Rawlinson died in a crash because of an unfixed faulty hatch.

The media and male pilots utilized several strategies for justifying the female pilots' job assignments as within the boundaries of conventional femininity even while the women worked in dangerous jobs. They referred to WASP assignments in the AAF as 'chores' even though male pilots also performed the same assignments.[60] Making this distinction placed a linguistic distance between men and women performing this assignment. Furthermore, there were assumptions about women in repetitive tasks. Male pilots claimed the work of towing targets was 'sheer boredom' because the process involved flying the same pattern repeatedly. The WASP themselves viewed some of their assignments as the 'dirty little routine jobs that AAF pilots do not like to do'. These reactions reinforce stereotypes that women were better suited for tedious, repetitive work. In addition to associating women with domestic chores and recurrent work, journalists also emphasized the WASP as maintaining their femininity. One journalist who visited a target-towing AAF base explained: 'Their quarters demonstrate they have not forsaken their femininity even though they are doing men's work.' This article was entitled 'The Girls Make Good: Women Pilots Overcome Both Masculine Tradition and a Tough Flying Chore'.[61] Thus, this journalist situated the WASP within conventional femininity. Furthermore, US General Henry Arnold thanked the WASP for taking the tasks that 'are not much desired by our hot-shot young men headed toward combat or just back from an overseas tour'.[62] As male pilots showed their preferences to risk their lives more honourably overseas, rather than at home, they minimized the women's roles in these tasks. Men justified women's wartime roles as feminine to protect their elite image of the AAF.[63] This image was one of military men performing highly skilled, courageous service in dangerous assignments. When the WASP performed on the same level as men on the home front, it disrupted this trope. Despite their treacherous assignments, the WASP had the same fatality and accident rates as male pilots 'in similar work'. There were a total of thirty-eight WASP fatalities, which averages to one WASP fatality per 16,000 hours of flying.[64] The fact that the WASP performed at the same level as male pilots also undermined their masculine AAF image.

Flying demonstrations

In addition to taking jobs that male pilots preferred not to hold, the WASP also proved the safety of aircraft to male pilots. If the WASP could fly aircraft effectively, then male pilots assumed they were safe and easy to fly, even if they had previously deemed the aircraft dangerous or difficult to pilot. These assumptions were continued from the 1920s and 1930s, when, with the growth of the aviation industry, women pilots successfully proved the safety of aeroplanes to the American public. Yet these early demonstrations often undermined the women pilots' professional skills and role in aviation.[65] Similarly, despite WASP mastery of new technological advancements in the form of aircraft and their attempts to claim their place as skilled military pilots in the predominately male space of the air, they were not taken seriously as professionals.

During the war, as new types of aircraft were developed and utilized, certain planes were viewed as more treacherous than others. As a result, male AAF pilots often dubbed these planes with nicknames such as 'widow maker' or 'flying prostitutes'. The former terms referenced the fact that several good pilots died in accidents while flying these aircraft. When this happened it lowered morale among pilots who were supposed to be flying the B-29.[66] The latter term, 'flying prostitutes', was a sexualized reference to the plane's lack of support, since the B-26 had short wings for its size making it appear less stable.[67] Both terms have gendered implications for the WASP, as the utilization of the term widow and not widower implies that pilots are men, while the reference to prostitutes seems derogatory towards women. Yet once men saw women pilots flying these aircraft, they changed their minds. The WASP also flew P-47s and B-29s when male pilots refused to fly them. General Paul Tibbets taught two WASP, Dora Dougherty Strother and Dorothea Johnson Moorman, to fly the B-29 and they demonstrated its safety to male pilots at various AAF bases. After each demonstration the WASP would take crews up to teach them how to fly the B-29. Male pilots originally considered this bomber unsafe to fly because the initial planes developed engine fires, but again, male opinion changed after the women's demonstrations.[68] One AAF officer, Patrick Timberlake, described the effect of the WASP flying onto an AAF base: 'The first one came in, and the people were out there to watch the airplane come in, and the door opened, and this dainty little WASP gets out ... She's ... the command pilot. Then the copilot gets out, and another WASP, the whole crew was WASP. It's funny, this didn't go on for long, because there wasn't enough of them, but it was a hell of a morale feature.'[69] Not only did this work like propaganda to demonstrate the safety of the aircraft to these AAF men, it also perpetuated the 'frail, timid, unathletic, and unmechanical' image of women pilots assumed in previous decades.[70]

Conclusion

Since 'War and Army flying ... had been looked upon as a man's game', the WASP were perceived as disruptive to the developing image of the military, technological environment of the AAF that revolved around a high level of professional prowess.[71] While the WASP successfully struggled in the contested airspace, they were never granted status as equals to male pilots during the war and they were continually considered an unusual phenomenon in the AAF. Through their AAF roles, including flying demonstrations, they reinforced military masculinity. As they fulfilled the purpose of the programme of freeing up men for combat, they allowed men to handle the more challenging work of serving overseas and in this way they reinforced gender norms. The programme was disbanded in December 1944 after the WASP militarization bill that would have granted them military status and benefits failed in Congress. When their dangerous duties were dismissed as women's work rather than military service for their country, it led to a denial of their important work in the AAF and ultimately of a permanent place in the AAF after the war. The AAF was the only branch of the US military that did not incorporate women on a permanent basis after the war. After the conclusion of the programme, the WASP waited over thirty years before receiving militarization in 1977.[72] Furthermore, women were excluded from military flying until the early 1970s. Shortly after World War II, the Air Force began including jet experience in their training. With few exceptions, women were excluded from progressing to the next stage of aviation – jet flight. As a result, when NASA announced the opportunity to fly in space, women were unqualified because they did not have jet experience.[73] This left high altitudes as spaces literally for men, who now also dominated jet and space aviation.

Recommended reading

Douglas, D. G. (2004) *American Women and Flight Since 1940* (Lexington: University Press of Kentucky).

Granger, B. H. (1991) *On Final Approach: The Women Airforce Service Pilots of W. W. II* (Scottsdale, AZ: Falconer Publishing Company).

Merryman, M. (1998) *Clipped Wings: The Rise and Fall of the Women Airforce Service Pilots (WASP) of World War II* (New York: New York University Press).

Meyer, L. (1996) *Creating GI Jane: Sexuality and Power in the Women's Army Corps during World War II* (New York: Columbia University Press).

Pisano, D. (2001) *To Fill the Skies with Pilots: The Civilian Pilot Training Program, 1939–1946* (Washington DC: Smithsonian Institution Press).

Stallman, D. A. (2006) *Women in the Wild Blue … Target-Towing WASP at Camp Davis* (Sugarcreek, OH: Carlisle Printing).

Weitekamp, M. A. (2004) *Right Stuff, Wrong Sex: America's First Woman in Space Program* (Baltimore: Johns Hopkins University Press).

Notes

1. Prior to World War II, according to the historian Joseph Corn, women pilots worked selling the safety of aviation to the American public. The WASP offer a continuation of this story, as they demonstrated the safety of certain aircraft to male Air Force pilots and utilized their femininity successfully to accomplish this assignment. J. Corn (1983) *The Winged Gospel: America's Romance with Aviation, 1900–1950* (New York: Oxford University Press). The Central Flying Training Command concluded that 'The WASPs were novelties'. 'History of the WASP Program: Central Flying Training Command', December 1944, Call # 223.072 V.1, IRIS # 00146288, USAF Collection, AFHRA, Maxwell AFB AL.

2. 'History of the WASP Program: Central Flying Training Command,' December 1944, Call # 223.072 V.1, IRIS # 00146288, USAF Collection, AFHRA, Maxwell AFB AL.

3. W. Chafe (1974) *The American Woman: Her Changing Social, Economic, and Political Roles, 1920–1970* (New York: Oxford University Press); D. Campbell (1984) *Women at War with America: Private Lives in a Patriotic Era* (Cambridge, MA: Harvard University Press); L. Rupp (1978) *Mobilizing Women for War: German and American Propaganda, 1939–1945* (Princeton: Princeton University Press).

4. S. B. Gluck (1987) *Rosie the Riveter Revisited: Women, The War and Social Change* (New York: Meridian) and S. M. Hartmann (1995) *The Home Front and Beyond: American Women in the 1940s* (New York: Twayne Publishers).

5. L. Meyer (1996) *Creating GI Jane: Sexuality and Power in the Women's Army Corps during World War II* (New York: Columbia University Press).

6. During World War II, the Army Air Force (AAF) did not discuss women pilots entering combat. S. Taylor (undated) 'Girl Pilots Train Like Cadets', The WASP Collection, MSS 250, Texas Woman's University, Denton, TX; *Women of Courage of World War II*, directed by K. Magid, Km Productions, 1993.

7. J. Cochran, 'Final Report on Women Pilot Program', The WASP Collection, MSS 250, Texas Woman's University, Denton, TX.

8. A very limited number of WASP flew outside the borders of the United States, including Canada, Puerto Rico, and Cuba. B. Howell Granger (1977) 'Evidence Supporting Military Service by WASP World War II', Call # K141.33–45, IRIS # 01097935, USAF Collection, AFHRA, Maxwell AFB AL. For discussion of a public

backlash, see: H. Williamson (1943) 'Hundreds of Women Training for Service as Ferry Pilots', *The Colorado Springs Evening Telegraph*, 28 April 1943, The WASP Collection, MSS 240c, Texas Woman's University, Denton, TX; 'Director of Women Pilots Asks Military Status for WASPs', War Department Bureau of Public Relations, 8 August 1944, The WASP Collection, MSS 250, Texas Woman's University, Denton, TX.

9. The WACs were also accused of becoming lesbians during their military service. Meyer, *Creating GI Jane*.

10. S. Myers (2014) '"A Weapon Waiting to be Used": The Women Airforce Service Pilots of World War II', PhD diss., Texas Tech University.

11. D. Pisano (2001) *To Fill the Skies with Pilots: The Civilian Pilot Training Program, 1939–1946* (Washington, DC: Smithsonian Institution Press), pp. 3–4, 76–7.

12. The first classes of women needed 200 hours of flying time, but this was later reduced.

13. Two women's pilot programmes were created in the autumn of 1942. They were combined and called the Women's Airforce Service Pilots (WASP) in July 1943. The original programme was entitled the Women's Auxiliary Ferrying Squadron (WAFS). The twenty-eight women who participated in this programme were required to have 500 flying hours. The second women's pilot programme, the Women's Flying Training Detachment (WFTD), accepted women with fewer flying hours, requiring 200 hours at first but later lowering it to thirty-five hours. 'Women Pilots with the AAF, 1941–1944', AAF Historical Studies No. 55, March 1946, The Eisenhower Presidential Library and Museum, Abilene, KS.

14. There is a significant body of literature on medical attitudes about women's bodies, including: J. Delaney, J. J. Lupton, and E. Toth (1976) *The Curse: A Cultural History of Menstruation* (New York: Mentor); B. Ehrenreich and D. English (1978) *For Her Own Good: 150 Years of Experts' Advice to Women* (New York: Anchor Press); A. Mangham and G. Depledge (2011) *The Female Body in Medicine and Literature* (Liverpool: Liverpool University Press); W. Mitchinson (2013) *Body Failure: Medical Views of Women, 1900–1950* (Toronto: University of Toronto Press).

15. J. Cochran, 'Final Report on Women Pilot Program', 1 June 1945, Jacqueline Cochran Papers, WASP Series, Box 12, The Eisenhower Presidential Library and Museum, Abilene, KS.

16. B. Howell Granger (1991) *On Final Approach: The Women Airforce Service Pilots of W. W. II* (Scottsdale, AZ: Falconer Publishing Company), p. 385.

17. S. Van Wagenen Keil (1979) *Those Wonderful Women in Their Flying Machines* (New York: Rawson, Wade Publishers), p. 175.

18. Letter, Adaline Blank to 'Sis' Edwina Blank, 21 July 1943, Adaline Blank Correspondence, July 1943–December 1943, MSS 300, Texas Woman's University, Denton, TX.

19. Anthropologist Mary Douglas provides a framework for understanding these medical concerns through her arguments about the body's orifices. M. Douglas (1991) *Purity and Danger: An Analysis of the Concepts of Pollution and Taboo* (London: Routledge).

20. 'Medical Consideration of WASPS', Jacqueline Cochran Papers, WASP Series, Box 15, The Eisenhower Presidential Library and Museum, Abilene, KS. See also: M. Mountain Clark (2005) *Dear Mother and Daddy: World War II Letters Home from a WASP* (Livonia, MI: First Page Publications), p. 21.

21. J. Cochran, 'Final Report on Women Pilot Program'.

22. A. B. Carl (1999) *A WASP Among Eagles A Woman Military Test Pilot in World War II* (Washington, DC: Smithsonian Institution Press), p. 83.

23. J. Cochran, 'Final Report on Women Pilot Program'.
24. 'Director of Women Pilots Asks Military Status for WASPs', War Department Bureau of Public Relations, 8 August 1944, The WASP Collection, MSS 250, Texas Woman's University, Denton, TX.
25. The review was based on statements via letters and interviews from 'AAF surgeons, commanding officers, flight safety officers, and other interested personnel at fields where WASPs were trained or stationed', medical records, statistical data from the Air Surgeon's office, and so on. See: J. Cochran, 'Final Report on Women Pilot Program'.
26. 'Medical Consideration of WASPS', Jacqueline Cochran Papers.
27. J. Cochran, 'Final Report on Women Pilot Program'.
28. 'Director of Women Pilots Asks Military Status for WASPs', War Department Bureau of Public Relations, 8 August 1944, The WASP Collection, MSS 250, Texas Woman's University, Denton, TX; 'Suggested report to be released in response to unfavorable reports to proposed militarization of the WASPs, 1943', Jacqueline Cochran Papers, WASP Series, Box 5, Militarization, The Eisenhower Presidential Library and Museum, Abilene, KS.
29. Series I – USAF Historical Studies, Box 15, The Eisenhower Presidential Library and Museum, Abilene, KS.
30. During each phase of training, the WASP flew more complicated aircraft as they moved from primary to basic and then to advanced training. They were given check rides by AAF officers and civilian pilots during each phase. 'Unsatisfactory' grades resulted in additional check rides and eventually 'washing out' of training, meaning she failed and would have to go back home. Letter, Adaline Blank to 'Sis' Edwina Blank, 21 July 1943, Adaline Blank Correspondence, July 1943–December 1943, MSS 300, Texas Woman's University, Denton, TX.
31. Malvina Stephenson (undated), 'WASPS – Heroines of Air War', The WASP Collection, MSS 250, Texas Woman's University, Denton, TX; Granger, *On Final Approach,* pp. 151–2, 398.
32. Dedi L. Deaton, WASP Staff Executive Historian, 'Supplementary History of the Women's Airforce Service Pilot Training Program', p. 37, The WASP Collection, MSS 250, Texas Woman's University, Denton, TX; *Fly Girls,* directed by Laurel Ladvich, Silverlining Productions and WGBH Boston, 1999.
33. J. Hascall Cole (1992) *Women Pilots of World War II* (Salt Lake City: University of Utah Press), p. 52.
34. Ibid., p. 75.
35. This certainly seemed to be the experience of many WASP, as evidenced in oral history interviews and their published personal accounts. For example, see: Carl, *A WASP Among Eagles,* p. 42.
36. 'Director of Women Pilots Asks Military Status for WASPs', War Department Bureau of Public Relations, 8 August 1944, The WASP Collection, MSS 250, Texas Woman's University, Denton, TX.
37. '319th AAFFTD Alphabetical Listing of Delinquencies and Demerits', The WASP Collection, MSS 250, Texas Woman's University, Denton, TX.
38. Cole, *Women Pilots of World War II,* p. 52.
39. Cole, *Women Pilots of World War II,* pp. 56–7, 26–8.
40. For example, see: 'The Guardian Angel: Class 43K, One Member's Autobiography', Ben R. Games Papers, Coll #98.0082, The Institute on World War II and the Human Experience, Florida State University, Tallahassee, FL.
41. Letter, Adaline Blank to 'Sis' Edwina Blank, 10 August 1943, Adaline Blank Correspondence, July 1943–December 1943, MSS 300, Texas Woman's University, Denton, TX.

42. Letter, Marjorie Osborne Nichol to her parents, 3 August 1944, Texas Woman's University.
43. Letter, Marjorie Osborne Nichol to her parents, 11 May 1944, Texas Woman's University.
44. Cole, *Women Pilots of World War II,* p. 56.
45. Letter, Jacqueline Cochran to Byrd Granger, 16 February 1943, Jacqueline Cochran Papers, WASP Series, Box 7, The Eisenhower Presidential Library and Museum, Abilene, KS.
46. For example, the women in the Navy, the Women's Auxiliary Volunteer Emergency Servicc (WAVES), published a newsletter called *Telewave.* See: *Telewave,* 15 April 1945, Dorothy 'Jane' Marshman Fredrickson Papers, Coll #07.0117, The Institute on World War II and the Human Experience, Florida State University, Tallahassee, FL.
47. Under the newsletter title *The Fifinella Gazette* was the heading 'All the News Is Safe to Print'. SEE: 'Note from the Editor', *The Fifinella Gazette,* 23 April 1943. In *The Avenger,* the editors explain the publisher association: '*The Avenger* is published by the *Sweetwater Daily Reporter* in the interests of personnel of Avenger Field and does not constitute an official Army publication.'
48. 'Life Under the Hood', *The Fifinella Gazette,* 1 March 1943, no. 2.
49. Keil, *Those Wonderful Women in Their Flying Machines,* p. 175.
50. 'Here Come the WAFS', *Time,* 7 June 1943, The WASP Collection, MSS 250, Texas Woman's University, Denton, TX.
51. Malvina Stephenson, 'WASPS – Heroines of Air War', undated, The WASP Collection, MSS 250, Texas Woman's University, Denton, TX; Granger, *On Final Approach,* pp. 151–2, 398.
52. Group Interview of WASP (Helen Wyatt Snapp, Marjorie Popell Sizemore, Doris Elkington Hamaker, Mary Ann Baldner Gordon, Mary Anna 'Marty' Martin Wyall) and WAFS Teresa James, Interview by Rebecca Wright on behalf of NASA, 18 July 1999; Joanne Wallace Orr, interview by Jean Hascall Cole for Texas Woman's University, 16 September 1991.
53. 'Zoot-Suits and Parachutes' to the tune of 'Bell Bottom Trousers', *WASP Songbook,* 8.
54. This was a WASP at Bryan Army Air Field in Bryan, TX. 'History of the WASP Program: Central Flying Training Command', December 1944, Call # 223.072 V.1, IRIS # 00146288, USAF Collection, AFHRA, Maxwell AFB AL. For resignations due to pregnancy, see: J. Cochran, 'Final Report on Women Pilot Program'.
55. Towing target display including a DVD of WASP Bev Beesemyer explaining her experiences at the Sweetwater Museum in Sweetwater, TX.
56. Jacqueline Cochran, 'Final Report on Women Pilot Program', 1 June 1945.
57. For an excellent study of Camp Davis, see: D. A. Stallman (2006) *Women in the Wild Blue … Target-Towing WASP at Camp Davis* (Sugarcreek, OH: Carlisle Printing).
58. The same is evident for women in other lines of work. P. Cooper (1992) *Once a Cigar Maker: Men, Women, and Work Culture in American Cigar Factories, 1900–1919* (Urbana: University of Illinois Press).
59. *Women of Courage of World War II,* directed by K. Magid, Km Productions, 1993.
60. For one example, see: 'The Girls Make Good: Women Pilots Overcome Both Masculine Tradition and a Tough Flying Chore', *National Aeronautics,* November 1943, WASP Collection.
61. 'The Girls Make Good: Women Pilots Overcome Both Masculine Tradition and a Tough Flying Chore', *National Aeronautics,* November 1943, WASP Collection.
62. 'Address by General H. H. Arnold, Commanding General, Army Air Forces, Before WASP Ceremony, Sweetwater, Texas', 7 December 1944, The WASP Collection, MSS 250, Texas Woman's University, Denton, TX.

63. 'Director of Women Pilots Asks Military Status for WASPs', War Department Bureau of Public Relations, 8 August 1944, The WASP Collection, MSS 250, Texas Woman's University, Denton, TX; Editorial, 'Words from a WASP', *New York World Telegram*, 17 April 1944, The WASP Collection, Gray Collection, Texas Woman's University, Denton, TX; Information about men's overseas preference taken from Carl, *A WASP Among Eagles*, Cole, *Women Pilots of World War II*; Granger, *On Final Approach*; A discussion about women being more suitable for tedious, repetitive work can be found in J. Light (2003) 'Programming', in N. Lerman, R. Oldenziel, and A. P. Mohun (eds) *Gender and Technology: A Reader* (Baltimore: Johns Hopkins University Press), pp. 299, 306.

64. 'Statement by Miss Jacqueline Cochran on Accomplishments of WASP Program', War Department Bureau of Public Relations, 19 December 1944, The WASP Collection, MSS 250, Texas Woman's University, Denton, TX; Jacqueline Cochran, 'Final Report on Women Pilot Program', 1 June 1945.

65. Corn argued 'this demeaning lady-flier stereotype … was pervasive'. Corn, *The Winged Gospel*, p. 76.

66. General Patrick Timberlake, interview, San Antonio, TX, 7 May 1970, AFHRA, Call #43828, IRIS #01103243, USAF Collection, AFHRA, Maxwell AFB AL.

67. World War II veteran pilot Lawrence Hunter utilized this term as the title of his memoir. L. Hunter (2000) *The Flying Prostitute* (Lincoln, NE: Writers Club Press), p. 103.

68. 'Sugar and Spice! B-26 Gentle as Lamb in Hands of WASPS', *The Martin Star*, February 1944, The WASP Collection, MSS 250, Texas Woman's University, Denton, TX; Granger, *On Final Approach*, 410–411; *Fly Girls*, directed by Laurel Ladvich, Silverlining Productions and Wgbh Boston, 1999.

69. General Patrick Timberlake, interview, San Antonio, TX, 7 May 1970, Call #43828, IRIS #01103243, USAF Collection, AFHRA, Maxwell AFB AL.

70. Corn, *The Winged Gospel*, p. 76.

71. 'History of the WASP Program: Central Flying Training Command', December 1944, Call # 223.072 V.1, IRIS # 00146288, USAF Collection, AFHRA, Maxwell AFB AL.

72. They also received recognition in the form of the Congressional Gold Medal in March 2010.

73. M. A. Weitekamp (2004) *Right Stuff, Wrong Sex: America's First Woman in Space Program* (Baltimore: Johns Hopkins University Press).

2

'Women don't want us anymore': Militarism and Masculinity in the Italian War

Lorenzo Benadusi

Although spurred by the development of gender studies, the relationship between masculinity and Fascism has long been the subject of historiographical analysis. Early studies focused on the various hypervirile characterizations of Mussolini, the *Duce:* Mussolini harvesting wheat, Mussolini in uniform or bare-chested, Mussolini the lion tamer, and Mussolini the ladykiller. Cinema has also long supplied representations of the Fascist male, including Pasolini's *Salò, or the 120 days of Sodom* (1975), Bertolucci's *Novecento* (1976), Scola's *A Special Day* (1977), and Bellocchio's *Vincere* (2009). In other words, the argument is so well known by now as to have become a commonplace caricature, as films such as Fellini's *Amarcord* (1973) and Benigni's *Life is Beautiful* (1997) have wittily shown us, and as Charlie Chaplin had already intuited in his grotesque parody of Mussolini in *The Great Dictator* (1940). Fascist masculinity has not, therefore, been an unstudied subject.

Contemporary historiographical scholarship on Fascism and questions of gender, has, however, added little to our understanding of the characteristics of the martial, virile Fascist male, and has often embellished, with rhetoric and too much psychoanalysis, well-established tropes. In particular, some American scholars have embraced a cultural approach that is overly attentive to language and representation. I am reminded, for example, of the constant search for a phallic reference, conscious or unconscious, in the bald head of the Duce or the billy-club, or the conviction that a publicity image of an infant resting in the palm of a hand conceals a message about the regime's authoritarian control over the sexuality of children. In a recent book on virile aesthetics and the representation of masculinity in Fascist art, one reads that the statues from the *Stadio dei marmi* are an expression of the anal fetishism of bodies which offer themselves to our gaze like prostitutes from their windows, the representation of nude male forms ambivalently shrouded in homoeroticism, because 'even without delving into the theme of anal eroticism, we might note that the naked buttocks are a source of pleasure for both men and women'.[1] These studies have paid particular attention to the literary and artistic production of intellectuals – such as D'Annunzio[2] – and have often read the provocations of the avant-garde movements too literally, imagining Fascist masculinity as a sort of incarnation of the super-male as theorized by F. T. Marinetti: seducer, rapist, and untiring lover.[3]

Moving beyond the discourse and focusing on behaviours and identities can help us to advance our historical understanding of the relationship between Fascism and masculinity. Initial applications of this approach can be found in the history of sport, the body, demography, and eugenics in which, through combining theoretical and empirical approaches, scholarship has begun studying the practices – the 'performances' of gender to use Judith Butler's concept – as much as the representations.[4] Little by little, and in part owing to the attenuation of the radicalism of the 1970s, and to the contributions of post-colonial studies and queer theory, scholarship has begun to call into question the repressive thesis used to read sex and gender under the regime. This new approach has succeeded in demonstrating how too rigid a scholarly vision of masculinity created a dichotomy between type and counter-type, between hegemonic and subaltern models, while in reality the practices and the definitions tied to masculinity were more nuanced. Indeed it is precisely the accentuation of the hypervirile characteristics of males that made gender identity even more labile, since the sheer existence of rules presupposes the possibility of breaking them, often leading to the coexistence of normative and transgressive behaviours. The subjectivities that come to the fore, even in dictatorial regimes, are therefore those negotiated through unstable forms of compromise. One sees this, for example, in the behaviour of the men based in the colonies compared with that of those at home,[5] in the attitudes expressed in Fascism towards homosexuality,[6] and more generally in the way in which the subtle encouragement of liberal and non-conformist forms of sexuality existed alongside the starkest of forms of repression, in particular with regard to blackshirt youths.

The image of Mussolini himself was never stable, but changed over time and according to his audience. The violent and resolute *squadrista* quickly transformed himself into the figure of the great statesman, and then the sportsman, and the fearless commander – thick, square-shouldered, austere, and authoritative. The anti-conformism of the young rebel was replaced with the moral rectitude of the mature family man, though within this official framework there is evident space for proud reminders of the sex drive of the Duce and his many female conquests. Moreover, the initial activism of the Fascist movement was also to be absorbed into a framework of bourgeois respectability promoted by the regime, even though these two drives gradually came to coexist. Not by chance was the model of virility expressed in an ambivalent manner: on the one hand, as an exaltation of strength, courage, the gratification of one's passions, camaraderie, machismo, and misogyny; and on the other, self-control, moderation, and respect for Catholic morality. This plurality of models gives us an idea of the difficulties encountered by Fascism in its attempt to carry out the integral politicization of existence, whether public or private, whether collective or individual. It also underlines the ability of Fascism to vary its proposals strategically depending on audience and context. This chapter explores the 'muddled mixture' of Fascist ideals of masculinity, both in representation and experience, and its juxtaposition with 'the feminine war'.[7]

War, Fascism, and masculinity

Masculine identity has been constructed on the strong nexus between combative ability and virility. Numerous anthropological and psychological studies have focused on this connection. However, with the exception of a few studies, it has not been widely investigated by historians, in particular in the context of the Second World War.[8] At the time of the Spanish Civil War, Virginia Woolf, in her essay *Three Guineas*, condemned the delay before people had begun reflecting on the terrible effects of the interference of politics into the private lives of people, and on the indissoluble connection between militarism and virility symbolized by the male figure who emerged from the ruins of the war in Spain:

> It is the figure of a man: some say, others deny, that he is Man himself, the quintessence of virility, the perfect type of which all the others are imperfect adumbrations. He is a man certainly. His eyes are glazed; his eyes glare. His body, which is braced in an unnatural position, is tightly cased in a uniform. Upon the breast of that uniform are sewn several medals and other mystic symbols. His hand is upon a sword. He is called in German and Italian Führer or Duce; in our own language Tyrant or Dictator. And […] it suggests that the public and the private worlds are inseparably connected; that the tyrannies and servilities of the one are the tyrannies and servilities of the other.[9]

The quotation suggests how the male body of the Duce was considered to be a source of gender identity and an example of the ideal man and soldier. Mussolini became the quintessential Italian male, the father of all Italian children, the husband and lover of all Italian women, and the commander of all Italian soldiers. The image of the Duce is expressed through a plurality of representations: Mussolini-aviator, Mussolini-skier, Mussolini-athlete, and Mussolini on horseback; there is almost no end to the masquerade. The superhuman coexisted with the common man; Mussolini was also represented as having remained close to his people providing a role model whom they could emulate.[10]

In the second half of the 1930s, when Fascism embarked on a series of foreign military endeavours, the role of the new wartime morality was to forge the 'new Italian', the 'Fascist Italian', from the generation that had fought the First World War, and, above all, from the new legions in training in the Party's youth organizations. Mussolini believed war, empire, and racism would mobilize and transform the Italian nation, making it truly Fascist within his lifetime.[11] With the formation of the empire and the implementation of the Fascist racial policy it became even more urgent to restore in 'all Italians that virile, martial, energetic and productive manner that had been typical of the Italian race throughout time'.[12] Only an imperialistic war could help break the old society's resistance to the new militarism, and make Italy the warrior nation that Mussolini demanded. Immediately after proclaiming Italy an Empire, he said:

> We made the Empire, we must make the imperialists. With the creation of the Empire, Fascism has to strengthen the renewal of the Italian way of life. [...] In all sectors of public and private life we must instil a new style, a new pride, a new discipline, a new Fascist sense of virility that is bold, martial and sporting.[13]

All of the various initiatives of Fascism would be characterized as battles: the demographic battle, the battle of the lira, the battle for grain. The military metaphor was much more than simple rhetoric; it was an effort to recreate the psychological tensions of war in peacetime. Dress, youth, and sport were militarized, and collective celebrations became mass military-style exhibitions. To put it succinctly, the aesthetics of politics became the aesthetics of war. There were problems implementing this in line with Catholic tradition, but as some recent studies have demonstrated, a pedagogical model of a virile, heroic Christianity was expressed through the myth of the *militia Christi*. Young Catholics could thus also present themselves in the guise of warriors.[14] The diffusion of the characteristics of the masculine model by Fascism was so great that it was almost impossible not to be conditioned by its influence. Whoever strayed from the ideal of the citizen-soldier by portraying a negative counterpart was to be isolated and corrected.

Within the totalitarian framework of the 'party-church' and the 'party-militia', commandments, catechisms, decalogues, rules, and behavioural guidelines served to define the duties of Fascists and distinguish them as true believers of the Fascist ideology.[15] The military lifestyle stood in opposition to that of the bourgeoisie, which was seen as an obstacle to the transformation of the state into barracks, to the elimination of the boundaries between private and public, and civil and military life. Fascism's attack on notions of peace and quiet, on inactivity and lack of strength, and its opposing exaltation of virility and militarism, constituted a rejection of bourgeois mentality. Since the *new man* had to be warrior-like, energetic, and courageous, with a strongly competitive spirit and endless vitality, it was inevitable that the passivity and lack of heroism ascribed to the bourgeoisie would come under attack.

With the onset of the Second World War the atmosphere grew even more severe and rigid. Exhibitions of amusement, luxury, and lust were inadmissible in the face of the poverty and hardship affecting the general public. The frivolous and dissolute lifestyle of the *gerarchi* (authorities of the Fascist regime) needed to be toned down to show solidarity with the civilian population who were suffering financial difficulties and with the soldiers who had committed themselves to fighting the war. The type of polemics that had arisen between draft-dodgers and the army during the First World War that had helped to sharpen the contrast between the battle front and the home front and to increase the resentment of the soldiers towards civilians had to be avoided at all cost. The regime's greatest concern was caused by the profligate 'moral pederasty' of those who continued to spend heedlessly in order to satisfy their desires but remained untouchable because of their social or political standing. The moral atmosphere had to be intensified, as the National Fascist Party (PNF) secretary Carlo Scorza tried to reiterate in his campaign against the feminization of men:

> Fascism must intervene with iron and fire, without exceptions. Therefore, it is absolutely necessary for all of the men — those who are really men — of the Fascist race to dedicate themselves to straightening the spine of the feeble-bodied and all of the descendants of Signor Brunetto Latini. We must reach the point at which bachelors and deserters of the marriage bed must live in shame and hide their condition: like impotent men do, treating it as a real physical defect.[16]

The tax on celibacy, the abolition of the formal 'Lei', the requirement that public employees dress in uniform and demonstrate their gymnastic abilities for the *gerarchi*, the introduction of the Roman salute and goose-step were all provisions intended to instil a martial and virile temperament in all (male) Italians. Observing the rhythmic march of the blackshirts, Mussolini observed with satisfaction the effects of this 'revolution of customs':

> When they march in the Roman step, their eyes shine, their mouths are rigid and linear and their faces acquire a new aspect which is not only that of a soldier, but rather the satisfied arrogance of a hammerer who smashes and crushes the head of his enemy.[17]

At the same time the regimentation of civil life involved in the antibourgeois campaign continued to create a clear sense of hostility in the population, so much so that Scorza himself sought to further exaggerate the contrast between the new Fascist man and the various counter-types who had begrudgingly accepted the interference of the party in their private lives. For the regime, these counter-types included those who were ill-suited to tough times, who spoke in a falsetto, or soft voice; who did not practise sport or were never soldiers; who were too soft or were not interested in war; who were averse to forms of discipline; and if they dated women were incapable of 'possessing' them. They were considered 'twisted, amoral, abnormal, moles, boils', a type of human who was useless and dangerous, who should be disposed of and forced to 'feel himself isolated, a reprobate, an outcast'. Once removed from circulation they were to be replaced with an ideal type, for whom 'the ethics and thought of Mussolini had become one in thought and nature': the prototypical Fascist of the first hour – politically active, married with children, a volunteer in Somalia, in the war in Spain against Bolshevism, and in the Second War World, who, after being wounded in Greece was forced 'to struggle again and wait to resume the place, which during his absence was cleverly occupied by those who did not act ... and who will never act'.[18]

The rejection of some of the ideological elements of Fascism tied to the heroic and military lifestyle was so widespread that it exasperated Mussolini himself, who became increasingly irritated with Italian men and determined to transform them into a population of warriors through war, ready 'to hate the enemy from the morning until the evening, all hours of the day and night', into 'brutes', 'barbarians', who were 'ruthless', and 'tough', 'without false sentimentalism'. The cruel image of the soldier assumed such an aggressive charge that it completely annulled even the slightest link with bourgeois respectability.[19]

Bourgeois respectability versus respectability in uniform

As early as 1961, George L. Mosse stressed the ambivalence of Nazism and Fascism in *The Culture of Western Europe*: both constituted political movements which aimed to preserve bourgeois traditions while at the same time disowning them.[20] Indeed, the totalitarian regimes tried to accommodate the contrasting drives at their centre: one destructive and the other conservative; activism alongside the safeguarding of tradition, order, and change. Mosse's formulation of the phenomenon as an antibourgeois revolution carried out by young members of the bourgeoisie effectively summarized this double standard of Fascism, the attempt to domesticate the revolutionary spirit through the evocation of bourgeois respectability.

The tension between the ideal of masculinity and family life – wrote Mosse – was common to all forms of Fascism: on the one hand the pact among men that was thought to determine the destiny of the State, and on the other the virtues of bourgeois family life that Fascism vowed to defend.[21]

Emilio Gentile correctly observed that Fascism sought to replace 'middle-class respectability' with a form of 'respectability in uniform' based on courage, militarism, strength, and virility. Gentile revealed how Mosse had overlooked these antithetical aspects of respectability in uniform and bourgeois respectability, leading him to equate the Fascist with the bourgeois ideal. The contradistinction between the two should not be overexaggerated, however, because it is precisely the dialectic and the coexistence of the two aspects which provides us with a better understanding of Fascism.[22] Gentile does not completely clarify the reasons for the failure of this attempted anthropological revolution. He underemphasizes the difficulties faced by the regime in its attempt to create 'a military man' who served the nation in his public and private life, difficulties which stemmed in part from a deep-rooted sense of bourgeois respectability. These are difficulties that would become particularly evident during the Second World War when the struggle between bourgeois respectability, considered indispensable for moulding the collective behaviour of Italians, and the totalitarian aspirations towards an anthropological revolution would come to the fore. The Italian public tended to be wary of an alliance with Germany and opposed to a militarization of society that extended into the private sphere – of subordinating their lives to the imperial aspirations of Fascism. Even the image of Mussolini as president of the Italians, the wise and responsible statesman, continued to have more influence than that of the Duce of Fascism, the fearless and resolved commander, as is evident from the fervid enthusiasm with which he was welcomed home after the Munich conference, praised as a saviour of peace.[23] Moreover, after the initial enthusiasm for entering the war, it became evident that there was a general unease and even an alarming increase in the number of attempts to evade military service.[24] As Giuseppe Bottai noted in his *Diario*: 'One feels the unease growing, fermenting in the souls of people. An obscure and profound marasmus. The myths and ideas giving form to this war are distorted into all sorts of forms; and in their distortion they become unclear, disappearing in a dim half-light which makes one shudder.'[25] The first signs of collapse came on the home front not the battle front, where to a great extent for the soldiers the values imposed by Fascism continued to nurture hopes of victory. For example, one reads in the writings of one young corporal: 'we were forged and hardened like the steel of our arms and like them we are inflexible. We are not afraid of death because victory will come to Fascist Italy.'[26] Ideological support for the war did not lessen despite the defeats suffered, but rather was nourished by the spiral of hatred born out of the conflict. In the face of the horror of the losses at the front, the Fascist ideal of masculinity remained a last resource from which soldiers drew the inspiration to continue fighting with even greater courage, to avenge those who had fallen, and justify the violence inflicted on their enemy. 'The rhythm of the Roman marching step' – wrote a volunteer in the Militia – 'was extraordinary, violent and powerful, as though all of those stones underfoot were the heads of the English and Americans, crushed by our faith and leonine courage.'[27] For those who had remained at home it was easier to recognize the course of the war, Fascism's responsibility for it, and the differences between the boastful propaganda of the regime and the sad reality of the facts.[28] As such, the transition from unease to disillusionment, and then to dissent, was rapid. With this realization even the heroic image of the new man proposed by the regime came to be seen as a sham. And so we begin to see the arrival at the front of characters such as Marmittone, the clumsy, bungling pacifist soldier created by Bruno Angoletta for the *Corriere dei Piccoli*, a popular boys' newspaper. He took the place of Dick Fulmine, a muscular hero who with the onset of war had become a combat soldier fighting on all fronts, at times a commando or submariner, at others a pilot or tank driver, who was ready to fight to defend the weak and bring criminals to justice.

Even the popular songs of the time had little to do with the warrior spirit desired by Fascism. For the most part, they were about themes related to love, longing for home and the family. Melancholy was the principal *leitmotif* and the great importance of feelings and emotional ties in the songs placed them in stark contrast to the image of wartime masculinity promoted by the regime – 'the separation from Fascism could not have been any more explicit'.[29] A retreat into the private sphere and a longing for one's family even appears in Marinetti's writings. An emblematic figure of violent and unrestrained virility, Marinetti responded to the call of Fascism, enrolling in the army when he was already over sixty, leaving behind, however, the uniform of the blood-thirsty, sex-hungry soldier for that of the charitable and fervent Catholic, the thoughtful husband and family man, believer in love and friendship.[30]

The Fascist wars themselves were likely to have had a great impact, causing a 'short circuit' between the ideal image of the soldier and the hard reality of the front. Engaging in real battle forced soldiers to change their perception, to reshape their identity, to change their values, and consequently to readjust their conception of masculinity, aggressiveness, comradeship, and combatant attitudes on the basis of their different experiences. This is not to deny that Fascist ideology provided some individuals with the conviction that through the values of courage, honour, and sacrifice, victory remained possible; it was the betrayal of those ideals that led to the disastrous defeat.

The questioning of Fascist virility: the feminine war

It was the nature of the war that lent it a new gender connotation: the involvement of civilians, and for the first time of such a large number of women, made the Second World War, quintessentially, a feminine war. As Ernesto Galli della Loggia observes, in comparison to the masculine and monosexual character of the First World War, the Second was manifold in nature, with a 'profoundly heterosexual' character.[31] In addition, it gave rise not only to a process of female emancipation, but to a potential inversion of gender roles. Democracy itself – with its egalitarian quality, its recognition of rights – questioned forms of dictatorial chauvinism. In fact, there is no doubt that in comparison with what we could define as the completely chauvinist character of Fascism – with an aesthetic precariously balanced between the image of phallic vigour and the funerary, with its preference for hierarchy and the cult of the leader – democracy, for the very fact that it presents itself through antithetical characteristics, belongs to a more 'feminine' perspective.[32] So after the Armistice of 8 September 1943, the struggle for democracy assumed an egalitarian potential also from the point of view of gender differences. Not surprisingly, Fascism had accused liberalism of 'over-reflecting a feminine sensibility, the kind that grows out of a civilization in decline, on the brink of anarchy' and had singled out democracy as a dangerous and degenerative form of social levelling and emasculation.[33]

During the war, the army also offered men various visions of masculinity. The figure of the compassionate and peaceful warrior coexisted alongside the fearless and violent combatant.[34] The years spent in battle threatened the rigid canon of virility imposed by the regime: fear, discouragement, exhaustion, desperation, cowardice, along with a general lack of heroism, aggressivity, and combativeness, created a clear contrast between the ideological intensions of the regime and reality. In particular the veterans of the Eastern Front returned with the signs of their suffering inscribed on their bodies and minds. Upon returning to their families, who sought to alleviate their distress, the men appeared exhausted, depressed, emaciated, sick, and mutilated. One doctor from a hospital in Liguria described the state of his patients:

> There are numerous survivors, even among the officers, who have been unable to sleep for days, so great has been the shock to their nervous system. Seconds after beginning to close their eyes they awake with a start, their faces contracted. They think they have heard their fellow soldiers who, immobilized from the freezing of their limbs, cry out to them, begging them not to leave them to die from exposure or abandon them to the torture that the enemy would inflict on them if taken prisoner.[35]

It was precisely the bond between soldiers that altered the virile *squadrista* form of camaraderie, attenuating its violent and misogynistic aspects. At the front, the men were presented with alternative models of masculinity and experienced more intimate and less rigid forms of friendship, forming polymorphous ties amongst them, often based on solidarity, affection, protection, and looking out for one another.[36] However, it is significant that in Italy during the Second World War these aspects were either not openly expressed or remained an unspoken subtext. Note in fact Paul Fussell's argument:

Compared with the passionate writing in the Great War, the convention in the Second is that love is strenuously heteroerotic. From the Second War there seem to be none of those poems fantasizing loving 'lads' that the lonely imagination threw off in Flanders and Picardy. References to homosexuality are so rare as to engender special notice and comment. If we do hear now and then of such minority sexual compensations, they seem largely limited to the PoW camps, with their extreme circumstances of deprivation.[37]

Whether or not Fussell's reductionism is to be believed, trench warfare, with its male character, was diminished during the Second World War. The once trench-bound soldier who had existed largely in a single-sex community was now in constant contact with women and civilians, the fluidity of warfare less conducive to the formation of stable homosocial bonds. The Second World War broke the masculine paradigm of war and delegitimized the war itself. The nexus war/masculinity, nation/virility, began to crack with the birth of a post-heroic society.

From July 1943 to 1945 with the Anglo-American occupation in the south and the Nazi–Fascist occupation in the north the difference between the new model of masculinity personified by handsome American soldiers, the liberators, and that of the barbaric German soldiers, the oppressors, became even more evident.[38] The image of the bad German also helped to foster that of the good Italian, further propagating the stereotype of the Italians as '*brava gente*'.[39] Every violent and inhuman aspect of the conflict, including crimes, rapes, and torture, was attributed to the Germans, erasing in an instant twenty years of the ceaseless ideological exaltation of strength and the attempted formation of the tough and virile new man. This contrast was also echoed in representations of the partisans and the Fascists of the Republic of Salò.

In Fascism's attempt to reaffirm its identity, the wartime climate, already difficult, deteriorated still further and erupted in brutality and cruelty. The Fascist symbol of death was once again flaunted as it had been in the days of *squadrismo* but now it was accompanied by an air of gruesomeness and ferocity hitherto unknown. It was this transformation of values, this estrangement from the life of the rest of the country and loss of consensus, that inverted the image of the Fascists, transforming them into a hateful internal enemy, despised and stereotyped as inhuman monsters. As Marco Tarchi rightly comments, 'in the vortex of bombings, retaliations, ambushes and police round-ups that dot the difficult months of Mussolini's republic, many of the Fascist volunteers gradually, and angrily became aware that people saw them as *abnormal*; the same people who had been united in their consensus now became fearful and, at times, openly hostile'.[40] The desperate awareness of the population's hostility is clearly expressed in the official chant of the Black Brigade – the Fascist paramilitary groups, organized by the Fascist Party during the Italian Social Republic (RSI):

Women don't want us anymore/ because we wear black shirts/ They say we are good for the prisons/ they say we are good for chains/ To love a Fascist is not a good idea/ better a weakling without a flag/ one who'll save his skin/ one without blood in his veins!

Leaving aside the question of the accuracy of this famous song by Mario Castellacci – which according to the accounts of some volunteers was not entirely reflective of reality – the unscrupulous behaviour and violent extremism of the young RSI members created a hostile reaction in people which became clear from the behaviour of women towards them: 'On the one hand there was a complete refusal of any contact and on the other a reaction of sympathy and a willingness to pass time together in town without fear of being seen together.'[41] In any case, the collapse of Fascist ideals marked the tragic end of the myth of the blackshirts as conquerors and seducers, and as the highest expression of masculine attractiveness and living symbols of virility; now the women who had loved them, conquered by their explosive virility, were giving them the cold shoulder. In addition, alongside the model of the citizen-soldier stood now that of the woman soldier, that of the Women's Army Auxiliary Corps, 'toughened by military discipline and a sense of duty and sacrifice toward her "betrayed" country, who set aside—deferring to more serene and less tragic times—her natural maternal mission for the more urgent task of saving Fascism'.[42] These women may only have been charged with non-combatant roles, but theirs was hardly a model in line with that of woman as 'spouse and mother exemplary'. These were women soldiers without weapons, heroines and citizen activists modelling the unconfessed desire to fight and die alongside men.

On the other side of the barricade, the partisans tried to recover the heroic image of virility, emphasizing, however, the characteristics of volunteerism and altruism which had been obscured by the uniformity and conformism of Fascism. As such, their masculine models were heterogeneous.

> A masculine model—wrote Anna Bravo—that was a muddled mixture, in which the heroic met the comic, the planned with the unplanned, one which included different types, from the popular hero and the armed gentleman to the faithful combatant and the rocambolesque picaro—not without echoes of the regime's influence, nor with concern for friction between one or another concept of masculinity.[43]

Regardless of whether the images connoted a combatant figure or not, the partisans were represented as attractive men whose attractiveness stemmed from both their outward appearance and their interior morality. For example, Moretto, the protagonist in Mario Rigoni Stern's short story *Un ragazzo delle nostre contrade,* had a 'strong physique and was tall and good looking', moreover 'he was always happy and kind, and all of the women in the *contrada* [locality] were in love with him'.[44] The attractiveness had less to do with demonstrations of strength than with their humanity, and even with the innocence of these young 'bandits', whose 'large dark eyes' illuminated their 'clear and pure' gazes.[45] They too, when faced with women's involvement in the liberation, often remained anchored to a rigid and chauvinistic model that attributed the use of arms to men alone. Although the civil war favoured female military participation, the use of violence by women continued to appear a violation of gender roles and an exceptional and abnormal behaviour. In the memories of all the partisan woman – 'the ferocious few' as described by Jean

Bethke Elshtain – the violence committed is a theme that remains in the background, considered as a regrettable temporary necessity, or as simple self-defence.[46] In contrast, for men, the use of arms continued to represent a rite of passage to virility and the male community, as is expressed in the experiences of Italo Calvino's character Pin, the young protagonist of *The Path of the Nest of Spiders*.[47]

With the military defeat, even for those Italians who had sat out the end of the civil war in their *House on the Hill* after 8 September 1943, coming to terms with twenty years of dictatorship meant questioning the virile and bellicose figure of Mussolini.[48] Moreover, as Sergio Luzzatto has stressed, the body of the Duce, a constant metaphor for the political body, became a metaphor for the fate of the country during the dramatic events of the civil war.[49] According to Giorgio Fenoalta, only then did it become evident that the regime was intrinsically weak and that its leader was 'no more of a masculine leader than any other man: in fact, he was a little less of one', because he concealed all of his cowardly and feminine traits.

> And now your Duce, broad-chested and wiggling, eager for applause and admiration, fearful of his fate, cowardly and cruel was no more than a pansy: yet his big, prominent jawbone, to which physiognomist ascribe a certain meaning, had been enough to awaken the physical and mental inferiority complex of an entire population, whose profile could be found in any psychoanalytical handbook, and to earn him that reputation of force which no one actually deserved less than him.[50]

In his 1945 satirical pamphlet *Eros e Priapo*, the Italian writer Carlo Emilio Gadda ridiculed the Fascist obsession with virility by hyperbolizing it: 'For everything then was male and bellicose: even broads and wet nurses, and the tits of your wet nurse and the ovary and the fallopian tubes and the vagina and the vulva. The virile vulva of the Italian woman.'[51]

The image of the citizen-soldier steadily gave way to a less martial, less aggressive vision of a man. For example, the male characters in the neorealist films were the first to represent simple and fragile people, whose weak and emaciated bodies showed the signs of poverty and hardship. After the Second World War, the image of the charming Italian seducer may have remained a constant, but the most accentuated features of Fascism's hegemonic masculinity came to be seen as ridiculous.[52] Nonetheless, at the same time the fascination with Fascism has remained strong in the Italian military forces, in the neo-Fascist movements, and more recently in skinhead culture.[53] Fascist masculinity casts a long shadow.

Recommended reading

Benadusi, L. (2012) *The Enemy of the New Man: Homosexuality in Fascist Italy* (Madison: Wisconsin University Press).

Bravo, A. (ed.) (1991) *Donne e uomini nelle guerre mondiali* (Rome-Bari: Laterza).

Fussell, P. (1989) *Wartime: Understanding and Behavior in the Second World War* (New York: Oxford University Press).

Goldstein J. S. (2001) *War and Gender* (Cambridge: Cambridge University Press).

Herzog D. (2009) *Brutality and Desire: War and Sexuality in Europe's Twentieth Century* (New York: Palgrave).

Imbriani, A. M. (1992) *Gli italiani e il Duce: Il mito e l'immagine di Mussolini negli ultimi anni del fascismo, 1938–1943* (Naples: Liguri).

Mangan, J. A. (ed.) (2000) *Superman Supreme: Fascist Body as Political Icon* (London: Frank Cass).

Mosse G. L. (1996) *The Image of Man: The Creation of Modern Masculinity* (New York: Oxford University Press).

Pavone, C. (2013) *A Civil War: A History of the Italian Resistance* (London: Verso).

Spackman, B. (1996) *Fascist Virilities: Rhetoric, Ideology, and Social Fantasy in Italy* (Minneapolis: University of Minnesota Press).

Notes

1. J. Champagne (2013) *Aesthetic Modernism and Masculinity in Fascist Italy* (New York: Routledge), p. 4.
2. For a critique of the idea that D'Annunzio's conception of masculinity inevitably assumes the political consequences suggested by psychological accounts of Fascism's appeal, see D. Duncan (2006) *Choice Objects: The Bodies of Gabriele D'Annunzio*, in *Reading and Writing Italian Homosexuality: A Case of Possible Difference* (Ashgate: Aldershot), pp. 17–40.
3. On the relationship between Futurist and Fascist virility see B. Spackman (1996) *Fascist Virilities: Rhetoric, Ideology, and Social Fantasy in Italy* (Minneapolis: University of Minnesota Press).
4. J. A. Mangan (ed.) (2000) *Superman Supreme: Fascist Body as Political Icon* (London: Frank Cass); D. G. Horn (1994) *Social Bodies. Science, Reproduction, and Italian Modernity* (Princeton: Princeton University Press); C. Ipsen (1996) *Dictating Demography. The Problem of Population in Fascist Italy* (Cambridge: Cambridge University Press).
5. G. Stefani (2007) *Colonia per maschi. Italiani in Africa orientale: una storia di genere* (Verona: Ombre Corte).
6. L. Benadusi (2012) *The Enemy of the New Man: Homosexuality in Fascist Italy* (Madison: Wisconsin University Press).
7. For 'muddled mixture' see A. Bravo (1991) 'Simboli del materno', in *Donne e uomini nelle guerre mondiali*, cit., p. 121 (see text referenced at note 43).
8. D. H. Morgan (1994) *Theater of War: Combat, the Military, and Masculinities*, in H. Brod, M. Kaufman (eds), *Theorizing Masculinities* (Thousand Oaks: Sage Publications); E. J. Leed (1993) 'Violenza, morte e mascolinità', *Ventesimo Secolo*, vol. 9, 243–72; P. Highgate (ed.) (2003) *Military Masculinities: Identity and the State* (London: Praeger); J. S. Goldstein (2001) *War and Gender* (Cambridge: Cambridge University Press).
9. V. Woolf (2006) *Three Guineas* (New York: Harcourt), p. 168.
10. See S. Gundle, C. Duggan, and G. Pieri (2013) 'The Cult of Mussolini in Twentieth-Century Italy', *Modern Italy*, vol. 18, no. 2, 111–15.
11. See M. Knox (1984) 'Conquest, Foreign and Domestic, in Fascist Italy and Nazi Germany', *Journal of Modern History*, vol. 1, no. 44, pp. 1–57; and (2000) *Common Destiny. Dictatorship, Foreign Policy, and War in Fascist Italy and Nazi Germany* (New York: Cambridge University Press).
12. National Fascist Party (1940) *Il secondo libro del fascista* (Rome), p. 49.
13. B. Mussolini (1938) 'Eventi di portata storica. Ora la Rivoluzione deve incidere profondamente sul "costume". Il popolo ha l'orgoglio di sapersi mobilitato permanentemente per le opere di pace e quelle di guerra', *Il Popolo d'Italia*, 10 June.

14. See F. De Giorgi (2002) 'Linguaggi militari e mobilitazione cattolica nell'Italia fascista', *Contemporanea*, vol. 2, April, pp. 253–86 and A. Ponzio (2005) 'Corpo e anima: sport e modello virile nella formazione dei giovani fascisti e dei giovani cattolici nell'Italia degli anni Trenta', *Mondo Contemporaneo*, vol. 3, pp. 51–104.

15. See E. Quaresima (1940) *I doveri del fascista. Precetti di Mussolini* (Bologna: Cappelli). Regarding Fascist decalogues and catechisms see C. Galeotti (2000) *Mussolini ha sempre ragione: I decaloghi del fascismo* (Milan: Garzanti); and Id. (1999) *Credere, obbedire, combattere: I catechismi del fascismo* (Rome: Stampa alternativa).

16. Brunetto Latini was a writer of the thirteenth century, famous for being placed by Dante Alighieri in the circle of sodomites in Hell. C. Scorza (1943) *Le direttive al Partito* (Bergamo: Ufficio Stampa e Propaganda), p. 29.

17. B. Mussolini (1945) *Storia di un anno. Il tempo del bastone e della carota* (Milan: Mondadori), p. 163.

18. C. Scorza (1942) *Tipi... Tipi... Tipi...* (Florence: Vallecchi), pp. 15–20, 145–52; see also T. Buzzegoli (2007) *La polemica antiborghese nel fascismo, 1937–1939* (Rome: Aracne).

19. On the aggressive and warlike image of the fascist see M. Isnenghi (2001) *Il volto truce dell'Italiano Nuovo*, in *Immagini e retorica di Regime* (Milan: Motta Editore), pp. 17–20.

20. G. L. Mosse (1961) *The Culture of Western Europe* (Chicago: Rand McNally); on these aspects see L. Benadusi (2014) 'A Fully Furnished House: The History of Masculinity', in L. Benadusi and G. Caravale (eds), *George L. Mosse's Italy. Interpretation, Reception, and Intellectual Heritage* (New York: Palgrave Macmillan), pp. 29–46.

21. G. L. Mosse (1995) 'Estetica fascista e società: alcune considerazioni', in A. Del Boca, M. Legnani, M.G. Rossi, (eds) *Il regime fascista. Storia e storiografia* (Rome-Bari: Laterza), p. 112.

22. See E. Gentile (2002) 'L''uomo nuovo' del fascismo. Riflessioni su un esperimento totalitario di rivoluzione antropologica', in E. Gentile., *Storia e interpretazione del fascismo* (Rome-Bari: Laterza), pp. 235–64; L. Benadusi (2012) 'Borghesi in Uniform: Masculinity, Militarism, and the Brutalization of Politics from World War I to the Rise of Fascism', in G. Albanese and R. Pergher (eds) *In the Society of Fascist. Acclamation, Acquiescence and Agency in Mussolini's Italy* (New York: Palgrave), pp. 29–48.

23. See A. M. Imbriani (1992) *Gli italiani e il Duce. Il mito e l'immagine di Mussolini negli ultimi anni del fascismo, 1938–1943* (Naples: Liguri).

24. S. Colarizi (2009) *L'opinione degli italiani sotto il regime, 1929–1943* (Rome-Bari, Laterza); P. Corner (2006) 'L'opinione popolare e il tentativo di effettuare la militarizzazione della società italiana sotto il fascismo', in P. Del Negro, N. Labanca, A., and Staderini (eds) *Militarizzazione e nazionalizzazione nella storia d'Italia*, (Milan: Unicopli), pp. 197–205.

25. G. Bottai (1982) *Diario, 1935–1944* (Milan: Rizzoli), 10 April 1942, p. 301.

26. Cit. in M Avagliano, M. Palmieri (2014) *Vincere e vinceremo! Gli italiani al fronte, 1940–1943* (Bologna: il Mulino), p. 77.

27. Avagliano and Palmieri, *Vincere e vinceremo!*, p. 126.

28. G. Rochat (2011) 'Parole di guerra alla prova dei fatti, 1940–1943', in P. Del Negro and E. Francia (eds) *Guerre e culture di guerra nella storia d'Italia* (Milan: Unicopli), pp. 167–77; M. Dominioni (2006) 'Da esercito aguerrito e invincibile ad armata di straccioni. Esaltazione e delusione nel soldato italiano in Africa orientale', in N. Labanca and G. Rochat (eds) *Il soldato, la guerra e il rischio di morire* (Milan: Unicopli), pp. 237–50.

29. P. Cavallo (1994), 'Cantare e recitare al tempo delle bombe', in P. Ortoleva and C. Ottaviano (eds) *Guerra e mass media* (Naples: Liguori), p. 163.

30. F. T. Marinetti (1988) 'Ricostruire l'Italia', in M. Verdone, *Teatro del tempo futurista* (Rome: Bulzoni); see also M. Harmanmaa (2000) *Un patriota che sfidò la decadenza. F. T. Marinetti e l'idea dell'uomo nuovo fascista, 1929–1944* (Helsinki: Academia scientiarum fennica).

31. E. Galli della Loggia (1991) 'Una guerra femminile? Ipotesi sul mutamento dell'ideologia e dell'immaginario occidentali tra il 1939 e il 1945', in A. Bravo (ed.) *Donne e uomini nelle guerre mondiali* (Rome-Bari: Laterza), pp. 3–27.

32. Galli Della Loggia, p. 23.

33. G. Mazza (1939) *Il paradosso dei sessi* (Milan: Alfieri), p. 18.

34. J. B. Elshtain (1995) *Women and War* (Chicago: University of Chicago Press).

35. Cit. in S. Antonini (1999) *Catene al pensiero e anelli ai polsi: Censura di guerra in Liguria 1940–1944* (Genoa: De Ferrari), p. 212.

36. M. Foucault (1997) 'Friendship as a Way of Life', in Id., *Ethics: Subjectivity and Truth* (London: Penguin Press), pp. 135–40.

37. P. Fussell (1989) *Wartime. Understanding and Behavior in the Second World War* (New York: Oxford University Press), p. 109.

38. A similarity can be noted here with the construction of temperate masculinity analysed by Sonya Rose. See S. O. Rose (2004) 'Temperate Heroes: Concepts of Masculinity in Second World War Britain' in S. Dudink, K.Hagermann, and J. Tosh (eds), *Masculinities in Politics and War: Gendering Modern History* (Manchester: Manchester University Press).

39. F. Focardi (2013) *Il cattivo tedesco e il bravo italiano: La rimozione delle colpe della seconda guerra mondiale* (Rome-Bari: Laterza); A. Osti Guerrazzi (2010) *Noi non sappiamo odiare. L'esercito italiano tra fascismo e democrazia,* (Turin: Utet); A. Del Boca (2005) *Italiani, brava gente? Un mito duro a morire* (Vicenza: Neri Pozza).

40. M. Tarchi (1993) '"Esuli in Patria": I fascisti nella Repubblica italiana', in E. Pozzi (ed.), *Lo straniero interno* (Florence; Ponte alle Grazie), p. 186.

41. Interview with the volunteer of the Waffen-SS Alessandro Scano, cit. in N. Guerra (2012) *I volontari italiani nelle Waffen-SS. Una storia orale* (doctoral thesis, University of Turku), p. 112; see also F. Alberico (2010) 'Identità e stereotipi di genere nella memorialistica di Salò', in Id. (ed.), *Identità e rappresentazioni di genere in Italia tra Otto e Novecento* (Genoa), pp. 97–116.

42. M. Fraddosio (1999) 'La militanza femminile fascista nella Repubblica sociale italiana', *Storia e problemi contemporanei*, vol. 24, pp. 1107–08.

43. A. Bravo (1991) 'Simboli del materno', in *Donne e uomini nelle guerre mondiali*, cit., p. 121.

44. M. Rigoni Stern (2005) *Un ragazzo delle nostre contrade*, cit. in G. Pedullà (ed.) *Racconti della Resistenza* (Turin: Einaudi), pp. 228, 226.

45. P. Chiodi (1975) *Banditi* (Turin: Einaudi), p. 31.

46. J. B. Elshtain (1995) *Woman and War,* (Chicago: University of Chicago Press); P. R. Willson, (1999) 'Saints and Heroine. Re-writing the History of Italian women in the Resistance', in T. Kirk and A. McElligott (eds), *Opposing Fascism: Community, Authority and Resistance in Europe* (Cambridge University Press, New York), pp. 180–98; D. Gagliani, (ed.) (2006), *Guerra, resistenza, politica. Storia di donne* (Reggio Emilia: Aliberti); P. Gabrielli (2007) *Scenari di guerra, parole di donne. Diari e memorie nell'Italia della seconda guerra mondiale* (Bologna: il Mulino).

47. See E. Sinigaglia (2007) 'Quel gusto aspro: grandezze e miserie della figura maschile nel romanzo italiano di Resistenza e di guerra', in E. Dell'Agnese, E. Ruspini (eds) *Mascolinità all'italiana* (Turin: Utet), pp. 35–64; P. Gabrielli (2008) *Tempio di virilità. L'antifascismo, il genere, la storia,* (Milan: Franco Angeli).

48. C. Pavese (1968) *The House on the Hill* (New York: Grosset & Dunlap); see also R. Liucci (1999) *La tentazione della 'Casa in collina': Il disimpegno degli intellettuali nella guerra civile italiana, 1943–1945* (Milan: Unicopli).

49. S. Luzzatto (2006) *The Body of Il Duce* (New York: Metropolitan Books).

50. G. Fenoalta (1943) *Sei tesi sulla guerra con note per i fascisti onesti* (Florence: Barbèra), p. 39.

51. C. E. Gadda (1967) *Eros e Priapo* (Milano: Garzanti), p. 73, as translated in Spackman (1996) *Fascist Virilities*, cit., p. 1.

52. See B. Pozzo (2013) 'Masculinity Italian Style', *Nevada Law Journal*: vol. 13, no. 2, pp. 585–618; J. Reich (2004) *Beyond the Latin Lover: Marcello Mastroianni, Masculinity, and Italian Cinema* (Bloomington, Indiana University Press); K. Ravetto (2001) *The Unmaking of Fascist Aesthetics* (Minneapolis, University of Minnesota Press).

53. S. Sontag (1980) 'Fascinating Fascism', in *Under the Sign of Saturn* (New York: Farrar) and J. T. Schnapp (1996) 'Fascinating Fascism', *Journal of Contemporary History*, vol. 2, April, pp. 235–44.

3

Sanctuary or Sissy?
Female Impersonation as
Entertainment in the British
Armed Forces, 1939–1945

Emma Vickers and Emma Jackson

In June 1945, the first official naval production of the Second World War, *Pacific Showboat*, opened at the Lyric Theatre in Hammersmith. Some of the revue's performers were men, specifically naval personnel, performing as women. The producer of the show called it 'a sensation' and claimed that 'People fought for tickets, especially the queers who were mad about us.'[1] This popular enthusiasm was not confined to *Pacific Showboat*. Following the end of the war there were countless glowing newspaper reports that detailed revues performed by ex-service personnel in drag. In Hull and Derby for example, the local press extolled the 'clever',[2] 'deceptive',[3] 'seductive … [and] realistic'[4] performers and called the shows 'good fun'.[5] At the Stoll theatre in London, in July 1945, a group of airmen who were all former inmates of Stalag Luft III delivered 'quality' impersonations, with two of the men being described by a reviewer writing for the *Observer* as 'especially persuasive in their maiden meditation'.[6]

Following the end of the Second World War, revues such as *Pacific Showboat*, *Soldiers in Skirts, Forces Showboat, Misleading Ladies*, and Ralph Reader's *Gang Show* (which had also run successfully during the war) capitalized on the appetite of audiences for ex-servicemen in drag. Over time, and owing to the popularity of the shows, most servicemen were quickly replaced by professional artists but the premise of the shows remained the same.[7] In an attempt to explain this popular fervour, Lawrence Senelick emphasized the British public's insatiable appetite for drag shows populated by servicemen, in part because they 'borrowed from the prestige of patriotic war work … [and] combined nostalgia for the camaraderie of the conflict with an avidity for glamour in a grey, heavily rationed world'.[8] This chapter will consider how the populace of post-war Britain acquired their affection for ex-servicemen in drag through an examination of men in the British armed forces who informally cross-dressed to entertain their colleagues during the Second World War. It will focus in particular on how those performances were decoded by those who viewed them.

Female impersonation in the British armed forces

Men donning female clothing as a means of entertainment has a long and celebrated history, both in music halls and in celebrations and events such as university rag weeks. For working-class men and women in particular, bawdy drag acts were an important cultural trope. In the armed forces, female impersonation undertaken by personnel for their colleagues dates back to at least the eighteenth century.[9] During the First World War, entertainment in the trenches took many forms but men often mimicked civilian drag performances. It was estimated by the historian J. G. Fuller that 80 per cent of the divisions that served in active war theatres during the war had an established concert party attached to them.[10]

During the Second World War, service personnel found it necessary to supplement the official entertainment that was provided and formed their own concert parties, often with a female impersonator at the helm. Numerous organizations were set up specifically to entertain the troops, including Stars in Battledress, the Army Welfare Players, and the Entertainments National Service Association (ENSA). The latter, ENSA, was the biggest and most active wartime organization. Founded in 1939 by Basil Dean and Leslie Henson, and with logistical support from the Navy, Army and Air Force Institutes (NAAFI), ENSA staged over 2 million concerts during the Second World War. However, it could not deliver performances in sufficient quantity, especially to units stationed overseas and in areas considered to be dangerous, and there was too much variation in the quality of what it could deliver.[11] Not even the appearance of a stellar performer could satisfy all audiences. Patrick Barry, a veteran of Bomber Command, singled out Vera Lynn in particular as having a detrimental impact on his morale.

> They were terrible; they made you weep all the time. Songs like 'We'll Meet Again' and 'The White Cliffs of Dover', they were disheartening, they made you feel rotten, you know. We just thought let's get the war over, let's get back to civvy street. It was good of her [Vera Lynn] to do it but it didn't do anything for morale, imagine it, you're waiting to go to war and she's coming along singing songs like that, Christ almighty.[12]

ENSA's close links with the War Office and the church also meant that entertainment was, more often than not, conservative and restrained. According to one performer, ENSA 'was just after dinner stuff. What the troop wanted was tits and tinsel.'[13]

In contrast, unofficial concert parties made use of local talent and were free to deliver material that suited the tastes and temperament of each individual unit, whether that was a 'straight' play or a colleague dressed in female clothing reciting a 'blue' song. The maintenance of morale was essential, and unofficial performers based within their units frequently knew how best to keep it up.

One performer known as 'Tommy', who was called up in 1944 and served with the Royal Air Force (RAF) in Burma, was cajoled into singing and dancing for his colleagues because 'ENSA hadn't hit that part of the world'. He went on: 'I had a fair voice … they started inviting me into the officers' mess. I'd perch on top of the piano with my legs crossed doing Helen Morgan numbers, singing "You'll Never Know" or "The Man I Love" from the bottom of my heart.'[14] Later on in the war he joined his unit's band and performed as Carmen Miranda in full drag.

As this chapter goes on to explore, unofficial performances frequently included elements of female impersonation. This should not, however, be taken to suggest that female impersonation was absent from official offerings but that there were limits on how frequently such performers could appear and the kind of material that was deemed acceptable. Billy Wells served in the RAF and toured with ENSA as a female impersonator and the duos Bartlett and Ross, Ford and Sheen, and Barden and Moran all performed for the organization as drag artistes.[15] Clearly these performers supplemented the unofficial entertainment laid on by individual units rather than the other way round. Moreover, female impersonators who performed for their units were not under the duress of the War Office or ENSA, or subject to the limitations imposed on artists when it came to performing in dangerous zones.

'My girl back home': female impersonation as entertainment

Men performing as women formed a large part of the unofficial entertainment laid on by theatrical subunits, whether organized as part of an evening's entertainment or merely as a means of passing the time. Richard Buckle, an officer in the army, amused his colleagues by dressing as a prepubescent girl and singing an 'obscene' song called 'My Little Pussy'. The comedy of the officer's routine lay in the unsubtle double entendre created by his prepubescent persona and the vulgar content of the song that he performed. To a contemporary audience, this is a disquieting juxtaposition, not least because it hints at paedophilic desire, yet it fell within a comedic trope very familiar to the men, exemplified, for example, by Donald McGill's bawdy seaside postcards.[16] This genre of humour also survived well past the war, an obvious example being the *Carry On* films that began in 1958. Moreover, however sexually suggestive and discomforting the performance might appear to a modern-day observer, its favourable impact on Buckle's colleagues was indisputable. He proudly claimed that his performance 'boost[ed] the morale of the Central Mediterranean Force and expedite[d] an Allied Victory'.[17] Similarly, along with the men in his unit, R. C. Benge would create ad hoc officers' messes and nominate some of the batmen to serve as waiters. Wearing cosmetics and christened with female names, the 'waiters' would serve the officers with vermouth – or whatever was available – in a bucket. Such parodies 'provid[ed] color to an existence which would otherwise have been emotionally drab'.[18] Benge believed that these performances contributed to the *esprit de corps* of his unit and provided welcome respite from the tedium and destruction of daily life. In this sense drag allowed men to escape the reality of war and break away from many of the 'restrictive social conventions that usually governed everyday life'.[19]

There are obvious questions here of exploitation and abuse of rank which resonate quite profoundly when Benge's vignette is understood in the context of unofficially sanctioned sexual contact between batmen and officers, some consensual and some not, and in the context of men being forced to wear cosmetics and female clothing as a shaming tactic. However, taken at face value, Benge's anecdote demonstrates the important function served by such performances in cementing kinship and in providing officers and other ranks with a clear indication that playful manipulation of gender identity was welcome.

Although some performers, like Buckle, relied on parody and exaggeration of the female form, known as mimicry, others sought to emulate women as closely as possible, thereby challenging the fundamental premise of drag, which is that the audience is aware the 'women' before them are actually men. Arguably, mimicry was the least disruptive of gender identities, and the easiest type of performance for audiences to decode as there could be no doubt that the impersonation was just that, an impersonation. However, as Bloomfield argues, authenticity was actually preferred by personnel, and in this spirit some performers went to great lengths in their preparation.[20] The dressing room scene shown in Figure 3.1 depicts Stoker A. J. Barnes in a makeshift bra, cami knickers, and half a face of makeup, while behind him a colleague appears to be having powder applied to his face. Such was the preparation by some performers that the men in this dressing room scene would have been considered amateurish. Indeed, newspaper articles from the time outline how female impersonators were entertaining their colleagues 'expertly' and testimony from performers themselves reveal detailed preparatory regimes.[21] Keele, whose career in army concert parties spanned both world wars, described how he would prepare for a female role: '[H]alfway down my chest, to be technical, I used to put a dark red line and then shave that line off so the side on was slightly pink, and then put a little darker one down the centre … from a distance it looked like the cleavage of a woman.'[22]

Performances themselves frequently involved men emulating women as authentically as possible, not only in terms of aesthetics but also female gestures and movement. The author of a review of 'The Boy Comes Home', a 'straight' comedy play written by A. A. Milne (whose most famous creation was Winnie the Pooh) wrote appreciatively about the authenticity of the army personnel playing the female parts: 'The part of Aunt Emily, played by W. R. Briggs, showed a keen understanding of feminine roles. His movements, particularly his hand movements, are a joy to watch. Mrs Higgins (Aubrey Gracie) was the boisterous overbearing cook, and Mary, the Maid, (Richard Maynard) the typical timid domestic.'[23] What is interesting here is the admiration shown towards these female impersonators for their authenticity; there is no discomfort, just appreciation and a sense of beguilement that the performers are able to mimic the femininity of women so seamlessly. It is also interesting to note that although the play was labelled as a gentle comedy it offered a

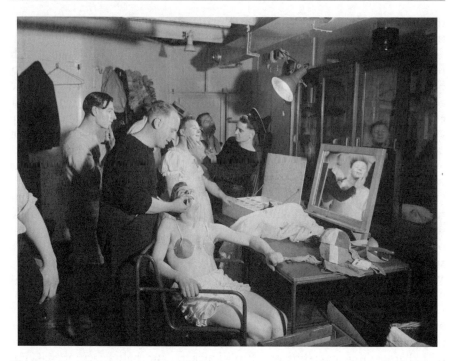

Figure 3.1   J. A. Hampton, Christmas Entertainment in the Home Fleet, 18 December 1942.[24]
© *Imperial War Museum.*

serious commentary on the challenges of returning from military service at the end of the First World War.[25]

There can be no doubt that female impersonators reflected a range of gendered stereotypes. In a programme reporting one camp's concert party, there were accounts of a farce taking to the stage in 'Lord Babs', a play written by Keble Howard and adapted into a film in 1932. The author of the review reported that cast member John Bradbrook 'went off at a tangent in this show and played a feminine part – [the] Countess of Sawbridge. A Blue-blooded old bitch, always thrusting her ever-ready-to-be-shocked modesty in front like a whitlow.'[26] Another actor, Charles McDowall, was said to be able to 'play large parts or small, as producers demand, and his buxom Bible-quoting, whiskey-gulping Nurse Rounce was very effective'. The review went on to say that Ivor Lipscombe's performance as Clara, 'the secret wife-cum-parlour-maid, and later Baby's nurse, gave the quietly efficient female impersonation'.[27] There is nothing in the author's account of the performance to suggest that audiences objected to these parodies of women. Indeed, they were enjoyed for their accuracy and for their evocation of female relatives and acquaintances. For men away from home, such constructions were familial *and* familiar and would have played an important role in entertaining servicemen and bonding them together in shared memories of home.

This was, however, not the only style of impersonation. Some performers went to great lengths to inject glamour and overt female sexuality into their acts. Charles Pether was one such performer. Pether was a postman and a female impersonator in the RAF. In the absence of anybody 'vivacious', and mindful that as an effeminate and androgynous young man he 'stuck out like a sore thumb' in his unit, Pether volunteered to take part in his unit's concert parties. He did not perform in 'straight' dramatic performances and instead delivered ad hoc performances for his colleagues, usually in the form of bawdy songs, which he delivered with as much Hollywood glamour as possible. 'I used to strut on the stage and I made costumes out of nothing, out of parachute silk, mosquito netting. I used to cut my plimsolls ... cut the top part off where the shoe laces would be then someone in the workshop would silver them for me ... I adored it.' Pether's pièce de résistance was a song called 'The naughtiest girl in the forces':

I'm the naughtiest girl in the forces
The fellows declare I'm a lad,
The things that I show to our youngest M.O.
I wouldn't never show to my dad,
I'm a devil for going on courses
I know all the tricks of the trade,
And I'm always the one for a bit of clean fun,
For I'm out every night on a raid

There isn't a single station to which I haven't been
With signs of acclamation the sentries let me in
When I appear the air men cheer, my charm undoes all locks
The only place I never grace is in the married blocks.[28]

Although Pether's character stopped short of challenging the fidelity of the married blocks, he was frequently followed back to his quarters after his performances, which suggests that the suspension of disbelief continued off stage and into the dressing room. By counting how many men were queuing outside his door following each performance, Pether was able to gauge just how convincing his impersonation had been. Not every individual performed as authentically as Pether on stage and off it, but there could be no doubt that Pether's colleagues wanted to interact not only with his female character but also with the male body underneath it. This goes beyond the suspension of disbelief and hints more at a conscious expression of queer desire. Another example of a queer man involved in unofficial female impersonation is Dennis Prattley, a naval rating who spent much of his wartime service in drag entertaining his matelots and fulfilling the role of a sexual surrogate. For him, and for his sexual partners, the line between onstage and offstage persona was deliberately unclear, and he was frequently informed that he reminded his sexual partners of their 'girl back home'.[29]

In this way, some servicemen were proactive in taking female impersonation to the limits of possibility and their colleagues were more than happy to reimagine them as women both on- and offstage. Dennis Boast, a British private who served with the Second Battalion Royal Norfolk Regiment, described how men in his camp believed that the impersonators 'were women in their own right'.[30] This view is reinforced by Maurice Driver who asserted that he and his colleagues 'were quite prepared to treat these people as being women ... as ... in their acting roles we took them to be what they purported to be' and went on to say that 'to [their] women starved lives, they looked absolutely great ... they were wonderful'.[31] As performers, these men were integral to their units. Fred Rolleston, a British private who served with the Second Battalion Royal Norfolk Regiment, reminisced about a time when a general reinforced the importance of the job being done by the division's entertainers, including men who performed as female impersonators: 'The job we were doing was absolutely vital to the well-being of the division, that after all the time we'd been in the concert party, they'd now consider ourselves as untrained soldiers.'[32] This meant that Rolleston and his fellow performers were unofficially exempt from service on the front line. Dennis Prattley was also deemed to be indispensable to his ship. His success as a drag queen while serving in the navy seemed to suggest that he could make a career of it. However, when he tried to leave the navy, he was denied dismissal. After three appointments with naval psychiatrists, three declarations of homosexuality, and three outright refusals, Prattley gave up trying and resigned himself to the fact that the navy would retain him until the end of the war for the sake of his ship's morale and as an acknowledgement of his abilities and experience.[33]

There is, of course, a duality in the way that audiences read and interpreted male bodies performing as women. Some were evidently comfortable with their colleagues performing as women, and were able to 'get into' the shows, even to the point of expressing desire for the men underneath the costume. Maurice Driver for example claimed the impersonators 'excited hearts',[34] and highlighted how the lack of female interaction throughout the duration of the war meant that he was 'ripe ... for ... getting into the show, [and] getting into the theatre'.[35] Other men found female impersonation challenging because it blurred the binaries between male and female: colleague and attainable woman. This blurring is summed up by a remark made by the editor of a journal circulated within an Allied prisoner of war camp in Italy. The day after a drag performance given by Private Jones, the editor remarked that the soldier had given 'an excellent representation of flowering womanhood; so excellent in fact that it made you want to go into the lavatory and think'.[36]

In this sense, while performances could be comforting, their reliance on (and exploitation of) homosocial relations could be unsettling. To claim, as does Laurel Halliday in reference to the Canadian armed forces, that men viewing other men dressed as women did not sexualize their bodies is too reductionist.[37] There were clearly those, like the men who queued outside Charles Pether's quarters, who were motivated by curiosity and desire, not just for the 'surface' characters that had been portrayed but for the body underneath the masquerade. Indeed, the suspension of disbelief could travel far beyond the stage.

Why were some men able to immerse themselves in this way? Joshua Goldstein's concept of women as a 'metaphysical sanctuary' to fighting men is perhaps one way of understanding why. Drag, and particularly mimesis, evoked and reintroduced a female element into a segregated institution. Performances such as those provided by the male actors in 'The Boy Comes Home' emulated traditional gender roles and provided familiar and therefore comforting evocations of mothers, sisters, and female partners which did not disrupt conventional understandings of gender but actually worked to restore and reinforce those understandings. Servicemen in drag were, to quote S. Schacht and L. Underwood, 'symbolic representatives of the cultural ideals associated with the feminine and women'.[38] Moreover, such performances were part and parcel of peacetime entertainment; if anything, they allowed men more of an opportunity to play around with performance in the safety provided by their friends and colleagues and away from the gaze of family, church, and workmates. That some men could perform authentically with limited access to female clothing and makeup was largely admired for its resourcefulness, regarded as an extension of the wartime philosophy of 'make-do-and-mend'. Crucially, too, by entrenching female impersonation as a form of entertainment, the services were demarcating very specific boundaries on behaviour that was, for most men, temporary, not least because it was bound to a stage and limited to a specific time frame, but also owing to the fact that the majority of men fulfilled official roles as part of their operational units. This emphasis on the transitory nature of performance helped to neutralize any threat that might have been posed by female impersonation. So, while drag could have real subversive potential and frequently narrated the proximity of homosociability and same-sex desire, it was also profoundly normative in terms of how it presented sex, gender, and sexuality. It is also interesting that the versions of femininity invoked by female impersonators could be viewed by audiences as more enjoyable than that of female performers themselves.

In this sense, female impersonators could be powerful brokers of morale, and their accurate renderings of femininity demonstrated a determination to be better women than women themselves. Moreover, the effective incorporation of these men and their performances into contemporary renderings of martial masculinity confirms what Sonya Rose describes as 'the assimilation to masculinity of what, in other contexts and articulations, might be considered soft, feminine traits'.[39] Such assimilation suggests that performers could play around with a multiplicity of potential identities in what was otherwise a deeply gendered, inflexible, and traditional institution. It also questions the rigidity and singularity of martial masculinity in the British armed forces during the Second World War.

'Poofy and gay': same-sex desire and female impersonation

The final theme that this chapter will explore is same-sex desire. Various historians and academics have concluded that male to female cross-dressing, both on and off the stage, was, by 1939, linked unproblematically to same-sex desire and more importantly, identity. For example, Marybeth Hamilton believes that, in the 1930s, 'this form of theatre was stigmatized as "queer in itself"'.[40] Boxwell claims that the high-profile trial, in 1870, of the theatrical cross-dressers Boulton and Park helped to solidify the connection between 'homosexuality, the world of theatre and transvestism', a claim that both Harry Cocks and Alan Sinfield decisively unpick.[41] Finally, Lesley Ferris argues that, by 1939, female impersonation was 'thoroughly demonized. Impersonators were no longer seen as performers – they were performing homosexuals.'[42] By 1939, there is some evidence to suggest that there was indeed a connection between same-sex identity and in-service theatre. In the navy during the Second World War, impromptu theatrical performances were known colloquially as 'Sod's Operas' because of the performers that flocked to take part. Seemingly, there was never a shortage of volunteers for the female parts. Charles Stringer, who served in the navy, overheard one man claiming, 'it's the only opportunity to be myself'.[43]

Such an association between female impersonation and same-sex desire was not lost on some. Sidney James Harper, who served in the Far East and the Pacific, expressed disdain at the 'absolutely hairy-arsed ... [and] ridiculous' acts performed by his unit, and lamented that that such men were 'on the wrong side of the tracks'.[44] Similarly, RAF pilot George Biggs described the cross-dressing performances that he witnessed as 'poofy' and 'gay', and recounted a situation where a female impersonator was forced to 'get undressed and get in bed before [the other soldiers] ... [and] put [his] head under a pillow, [so he was not allowed to] look at them. They didn't want [him] lying in bed watching them undress.'[45] This seems to suggest that some men felt distinctly vulnerable when the gaze was reversed and was experienced outside of the 'safe' confines of the stage. Moreover, it is clear that some audience members found the alignment of on- and offstage personas threatening, not least because that alignment breached the temporariness of the onstage performance. This alignment was a choice rather than a given, and would have depended on the extent to which individuals felt able to perform their gender identity off stage.[46] For Biggs, the lack of authenticity, or poor gender blending, was perhaps more the issue than the same-sex desire that he decoded from the performances. This is confirmed by Terry Gardener, who served in the Royal Navy and spent much of his service life in drag. After the war he joined the revue *We Were in the Forces*, and remarked that 'the general idea of the first show was to put men into dresses to make them look dreadful, [for comic effect] but that soon started to change because the audiences like the prettiest ones best'.[47]

This tension is most interesting when it is narrated by ostensibly heterosexual men performing female parts. Tommy Keele, a British non-commanding officer claimed that he 'always hated playing a girl, [as those playing] ... all these girls parts ... were nearly all poofs, they were nearly all Nancy's [sic] ... pansy bloody noises all the time ... all those sissy sort of sounds coming from them'.[48] Keele went on to say that he was afraid of being 'lumped' as a sissy, a comment which suggests that there was a much firmer cultural association between same-sex desire and female impersonation by the middle of the 1940s. Men like Keele could parry accusations of queerness by proclaiming their disdain for the 'poofs and Nancy's [sic]' and lamenting the requirement to play the female roles too frequently. Others could be protected from accusations of queerness by recourse to the wartime necessity of finding men who would play female roles because of the absence of women.[49]

So, while there was, by 1939, a much stronger cultural connection between male bodies in female clothing and queer sexuality, it would be unwise to overstate its knowability, first because of the strong theatrical tradition of dames in Britain and second, because the war upended the pre-war cultural association between drag and same-sex desire. The Second World War provided men with a safe space where they could experiment with dress and performance in the quest for entertainment and in the spirit of wartime deprivation. There were obviously some queer men who used performance as a means of exploring and expressing their sexuality and gender identity and who played around with the boundary between onstage and offstage. However, to claim that this was hankered for by all performers is too reductionist. Moreover, each audience member decoded cross-dressing performances subjectively and brought their own meanings and subtexts to bear on what they saw. The connection between queer identity and cross-dressing was not explicitly problematized unless it was disruptive to morale and detrimental to efficiency. When we do hear of men such as Biggs protesting at the presumed queerness of female impersonators and protecting his body from the gazes of other men, this in no way reflects an institutional discomfort with same-sex desire, but rather, a subjective one.

Conclusion

Between 1939 and 1945, cross-dressing performances were sanctioned by officials within the armed forces as essential to the maintenance of morale. These performances did not permanently destabilize gender boundaries but actually reinforced them through the active production of femininity. So while cross-dressing may have, in some cases, provided magnified, almost carnivalesque parodies of women, and in others, exceptionally sincere and authentic portrayals, they were performances that were familiar and unsurprising. Another contradiction is that while performers were able to 'queer' their environment, their performances were seen as necessary because of the absence of women and because they fell into a celebrated tradition of men taking female parts. Rather than emulating women these men were emulating a theatrical tradition of men playing female parts. Finally, by entrenching female impersonation as a form of entertainment, the services were demarcating very specific boundaries of temporary behaviour, behaviour that was bound to a stage and limited to a specific context and time frame. Cross-dressing performances in the context of the British armed forces did not pose a threat to the established order, civilian or military, because they were bound to specific perimeters. When such activity occurred *out* of those boundaries, it could be perceived as more of a threat, not least to the comfort of the audience.

Recommended reading

Boxwell, D. A. (2002) 'The Follies of War: Cross-Dressing and Popular Theatre on the British Front Lines, 1914–18', *Modernism/modernity*, vol. 9, no, 1, pp. 1–20.

Eldridge, S. (2014) '"We Girls" Female Impersonators in POW Entertainment on the Thailand-Burma Railway During the Second World War', *Popular Entertainment Studies*, vol. 5, no. 1, pp. 74–99.

Fuller, J. G. (1990) *Troop Morale and Popular Culture in the British and Dominion Armies, 1914–1918* (Oxford: Clarendon Press).

Halliday, L. (2003) 'A Lovely War: Male to Female Cross-Dressing and Canadian Military Entertainment in World War II' in Schacht, S. and Underwood, L., (eds) *The Drag Queen Anthology: The Absolutely Fabulous but Flawlessly Customary World of Female Impersonators* (London: Routledge) pp. 19–34.

Hamilton, M. (1993) 'I'm the Queen of the Bitches', in L. Ferris, (ed.) *Crossing The Stage: Controversies on Cross-Dressing* (London: Routledge).

Kirk, K., and E. Heath (1984) *Men in Frocks* (London: Gay Men's Press).

Mackay, R. (2003) *Half the Battle: Civilian Morale in Britain During the Second World War* (Manchester: Manchester University Press).

Rachamimov, I. (2006) 'The Disruptive Comforts of Drag: (Trans) Gender Performances among Prisoners of War in Russia, 1914–1920', *The American Historical Review*, vol. 3, no. 2, pp. 1–23.

Senelick, A. (2000) *The Changing Room: Sex, Drag and Theatre* (New York: Routledge).

Vickers, E. (2012) *Queen and Country: Same-Sex Desire in the British Armed Forces, 1939–1945* (Manchester and New York: Manchester University Press).

Notes

1. Ronnie Hill, quoted in A. Senelick (2000) *The Changing Room: Sex, Drag and Theatre* (New York: Routledge) p. 367.
2. Author unknown (1946) 'Tivoli Variety', *Hull Daily Mail*, 21 May.
3. Author unknown (1946) 'Follies' Bright Show' *Hull Daily Mail*, 18 June.
4. Author unknown (1946) 'Around The Shows: Ex-Forces "Lovelies" Are Good Fun', *Derby Evening Telegraph*, 1 October.
5. Ibid.
6. J. C. T. (1945) 'Back Home', *Observer*, 22 July, p. 2.
7. K. Kirk and E. Heath (1984) *Men in Frocks* (London: Gay Men's Press), p. 18. In wartime and post-war cinema female impersonation was an established trope. Take for example *You're in the Army Now* (1941) and *Abroad with Two Yanks* (1944), both of which involved servicemen in drag. The British film *Skimpy in the Navy* (1949) starred Vic Ford and Chris Sheen, two of the most famous female impersonators in Britain at that time.
8. Senelick, *The Changing Room*, p. 367.
9. See S. Eldridge, (2014) '"We Girls" Female Impersonators in POW Entertainment on the Thailand-Burma Railway During the Second World War', *Popular Entertainment Studies*, vol. 5, no. 1, pp. 74–99, here p. 75.
10. J. G. Fuller, (1990) *Troop Morale and Popular Culture in the British and Dominion Armies, 1914–1918* (Oxford: Clarendon Press), p. 188. See also J. Bourke (1996) *Dismembering the Male: Men's Bodies Britain and the Great War* (London: Reaktion Books), p. 233, D. A. Boxwell (2002) 'The Follies of War: Cross-Dressing and Popular Theatre on the British Front Lines, 1914–18, *Modernism/modernity*, vol. 9, no. 1, pp. 1–20 and I. Rachamimov (2006) 'The Disruptive Comforts of Drag: (Trans) Gender Performances among Prisoners of War in Russia, 1914–1920', *The American Historical Review*, vol. 3, no. 2, pp. 1–23.
11. Groups like Stars in Battledress and the Army Welfare Players went some way in addressing this shortfall. The former consisted of a group of servicemen with performance skills who, unlike ENSA, could perform closer to and on the front because they had been trained to defend themselves if they came under attack. Importantly, they were not subject to the collective censorious power of Dean and the War Office.

12. Patrick Barry interviewed by Emma Jackson, 6 January 2013. It may not have pleased Lynn to know that the comedian Dick Emery created a parody character called 'Vera Thin' while he was working as an entertainer in Ralph Reader's Gang Show. See A. J. Woodward, 'Dick Emery' at https://www.woodysnet.co.uk/people/dick-emery/, date accessed 18 July 2015.

13. Patrick Nicholson (1976) 'A Matter of Morale', *Sunday Times Magazine*, 16 August, cited in Bloomfield, 'Veterans Cross-Dressing Revues', p. 4.

14. Cited in Kirk and Heath (1984) *Men in Frocks*, pp. 14–15.

15. Author unknown (n.d.) 'It's Behind You – Bring On Those Wonderful Dames!', http://www.its-behind-you.com/damesarticle.html, date accessed 17 July 2015.

16. See A. Calder-Marshall (1966) *Wish You Were Here: The Art of Donald McGill* (London: Hutchinson).

17. R. Buckle (1981) *The Most Upsetting Woman* (London: Collins), p. 195.

18. R. C. Benge (1984) *Confessions of a Lapsed Librarian* (London: Scarecrow Press), p. 51.

19. C. Johnson (2007) 'Camp Life: The Queer History of "Manhood" in the Civilian Conservation Corps, 1933–1937', *American Studies*, vol. 48, no. 2, pp. 19–36, here 29.

20. See Bloomfield, 'Veterans Cross-Dressing Revues'.

21. Author unknown (1941) 'The Soldiers' "Sing-Song"', *The Times*, 15 April.

22. Imperial War Museum Sound Archive (hereafter IWMSA) 9428, interview with Tommy Keele, Reel 9.

23. National Army Museum (hereafter NAM) 9307-222-7, *Theatre Article*, date unknown.

24. Imperial War Museum Department of Photography A13436, J.A. Hampton, Christmas Entertainment, 18 December 1942. © Imperial War Museum.

25. See http://www.readbookonline.net/readOnLine/37786/, date accessed 18 July 2015.

26. NAM 9307-222-7, *Theatre Article*, date unknown.

27. NAM 9307-223-14, 'Lord Babs', Theatre Willenberg, date unknown.

28. Transcript of interview with Charles Pether, 3bmtv, *Conduct Unbecoming*, Channel 4 (1996), p. 8.

29. Dennis Prattley, Timewatch, *Sex and War*, BBC2 (1998). For a discussion of homosex between men during the Second World War see E. Vickers (2012) *Queen and Country: Same-Sex Desire in the British Armed Forces, 1939–1945* (Manchester and New York: Manchester University Press).

30. IWMSA, 17535, Dennis Boast, Reel 5.

31. IWMSA, 27064, Maurice Driver, Reel 12.

32. IWMSA, 17764, Fred Rolleston, Reel 7.

33. Dennis Prattley, Timewatch, *Sex and War*, BBC 2 (1998).

34. IWMSA 27064, Maurice Driver, Reel 12.

35. Ibid., Reel 12.

36. Wellcome Library, RAMC 466/49, Captain Mustarde, 'Adjustment and maladjustment within the camp', talk at Psychiatrists conference, 7–8 October 1944.

37. L. Halliday (2003) 'A Lovely War: Male to Female Cross-Dressing and Canadian Military Entertainment in World War II' in S. Schacht and L. Underwood (eds) *The Drag Queen Anthology: The Absolutely Fabulous but Flawlessly Customary World of Female Impersonators* (London: Routledge), pp. 19–34.

38. S. Schacht and L. Underwood (2004) Introduction to special edition of the *Journal of Homosexuality*, vol. 46, no. 3–4, pp. 1–17.

39. S. O. Rose (2004) 'Temperate Heroes: Concepts of Masculinity in Second World War Britain' in S. Dudink, K. Hagermann, and J. Tosh (eds) *Masculinities in Politics and War: Gendering Modern History* (Manchester: Manchester University Press), p. 192.

40. M. Hamilton (1993) 'I'm the Queen of the Bitches', in L. Ferris, (ed.) *Crossing The Stage: Controversies on cross-dressing* (London: Routledge), p. 108.

41. A. Boxwell (2002) 'The Follies of War: Cross-Dressing and Popular Theatre on the British Front Lines, 1914–18' *Modernism/Modernity*, vol. 9, no. 1, p. 10.

42. Hamilton, 'I'm the Queen of the Bitches', p. 119.

43. E-mail from C. Stringer to Emma Vickers, 29 November 2005.

44. IWMSA, 23376, Sidney James Harper, Reel 5.

45. George Biggs interviewed by Emma Jackson, 3 January 2013.

46. Ibid.

47. Kirk and Heath, *Men in Frocks*, p 19

48. IWMSA, 9428, Tommy Keele, Reel 9.

49. See S. Eldridge, '"We Girls"'.

Part 2
Conformity and Disruption on the Home Front

4

Conspicuous Consumption in Wartime? Welsh Mining Communities and Women in Munitions Factories

Ariane Mak

A miner's wife:
There was a woman in the shop the other day.
'Hope that war doesn't stop yet', she says.
'Why now?' says I.
'I've got a husband and three girls working at the factory', she says.
'You've got no one in the army, not like I have got' I says.
'Then you'd be different, whatever'.
It was wicked![1]

The consequences of women's employment during the Second World War have attracted considerable scholarly attention but many dimensions of the impact of wartime employment practices remain unexplored. Focusing on the towns of Blaina and Nantyglo, two mining settlements situated deep within the South Wales Valleys between Brynmawr and Abertillery, this study explores the impact of new employment patterns on the gender order of Welsh mining communities.

Three dimensions will thus be closely interwoven in this chapter: a history of the Second World War, a gender history, and a history of working-class consumption. This chapter makes a contribution to a gendered history of the working classes, which shifts from institutional labour history to a study of spending and money practices. In its focus on conspicuous consumption and respectability it is indebted to Paul Johnson's influential studies of the working-class saving and spending patterns, but it departs from the latter on two important points: the periodization of the analysis and the types of sources used.[2]

First, an explanation of the periodization of this analysis. While several richly detailed studies of working-class consumption in the Victorian era and the interwar years have been published, there has been no equivalent for the Second World War, in spite of the important disruptions affecting consumption habits.[3]

It appears that the history of rationing, which has been remarkably reinvigorated in recent years, has tended to overshadow that of consumption in the wider sense.[4] Similarly, popular attitudes to consumption have tended to be narrowly understood and studied as attitudes to the black market or to upper-class profiteers. This gap in the history of working-class consumption is all the more surprising as it would allow an exploration of the connection between the inter-war years and the debates in the 1950s and 1960s on the affluent society, debates which have been revived by historians today.[5]

Second, an introduction to the approach and sources used. The contention of this chapter is that in this field a gender perspective which foregrounds community produces rich empirical and theoretical insights. Indeed, while miners have long been considered by historians as 'archetypal communitarians', women have not played a significant part in the various paradigms put forward.[6] It is in the studies of labour and industrial relations, where the literature on the mining industry has been so abundant, that women have started to be studied. Indeed, following the 1984–85 miners' strike, accounts of the involvement of women in mining strikes have started to appear.[7] But useful as these are to show the pivotal role of women in these struggles, as Nancy M. Forestell has pointed out, 'the social dynamics of daily existence and sustenance have been obscured in these works'.[8] Little scholarly attention has been paid to the everyday nego-tiation of gender relations in mining communities and to the effect of wars on the gender orders of mining settlements.[9]

Some historians have underlined the difficulty of a community study-based approach in view of the fact that 'the early social surveys were based on local government administrative units', stating that 'it was not until after the Second World War that an anthropological approach to the social survey broke down this rigid analytical framework'.[10] While the first phase of community studies in Britain has indeed commonly been taken to run from the end of the Second World War until the late 1960s, a few pioneering surveys seem to have been overlooked and remain superficially exploited so far. Yet two of these surveys focus on the mining communities of Blaina and Nantyglo, and by covering the years before the war as well as the wartime period, they provide a fascinating insight into local responses to wartime changes in terms of the attitudes to consumption and to closely connected changing understandings of gendered respectability.

The first study, *Portrait of a Mining Town*, is a monograph written by Philip Massey in 1937.[11] Based on first-hand observations and eighty-three interviews of two to three hours each, the study provides a very detailed picture of Blaina during the Depression. The second one is a Mass Observation (MO) fieldwork investigation led by Mollie Tarrant and based on several long stays in Blaina and Nantyglo between 1941 and late 1943.[12] The manuscript, prefaced by Leonard Woolf, was never published. Both Massey and Tarrant chose to adopt the 'anthropological approach to the social survey' so rare before the end of the 1940s in Britain. Philip Massey's study was the first part of a larger project which attempted to 'survey typical corners of Britain as truthfully and penetrat-ingly as if our investigators had been inspecting an African village'.[13] Similarly, MO is well known for its project to set up 'an anthropology of ourselves'.[14] And while British anthropology was Tom Harrisson's prime model of inquiry, the Blaina and Nantyglo survey was also undertaken with the Lynds' Middletown studies in mind.[15]

In terms of a gendered analysis of the Second World War, such material offers a situated study of masculine and feminine respectabilities in the making. These ethnographical studies enable the historian to step out from a history of discourses, disconnected from experiences. On the contrary men and women's experiences are described and grounded in the interpretations and judgements expressed by various members of the community. Masculine and feminine respectabilities are not studied as fixed entities but as ongoing processes, subject to changing practices and assessments, and eventually to breaching episodes such as the one analysed here.

The central contention of this chapter is that the sudden focus on consumption embodied the fears of the mining towns which were faced with a perceived threat to their community's gender order. This chapter begins by exploring the issue of wage differentials, and shows how these changes in earnings shook family and village hierarchies and threatened to modify the map of respectable manhood. With wages rising unequally and the fairness of these discrepancies called into question, spending and saving in the community were closely monitored and judged. Morality issues came to the fore with unremitting discussions and gossip about women's lack of respectability stemming from their habits of consumption. The crystallization of the community's fears on the issue of conspicuous consumption will be analysed, through the case study of clothes consumption and sartorial immorality – as inflected by gender.

Wartime wages: 'A temporary loss of balance in the community'

The role the Depression plays in Welsh history has been compared to that of the famine in Irish history.[16] The two Monmouthshire towns of Blaina and Nantyglo were part of the 'Head of the Valleys' communities where pits had been worked out and steel works had closed down, and which suffered the highest level of unemployment.[17] For over fifteen years, since the closure in 1921 of seven collieries which had employed over 4,800 men and boys, between 70 per cent and 75 per cent of the male population was consistently unemployed. Blaina in particular came to epitomize the bleakness of depressed areas in the interwar period, with its record figure of 93 per cent unemployed in 1932.[18] It was also of Blaina that the Prince of Wales had famously said, 'Something will and something shall be done' at the time of his tour around areas in South Wales that were economically depressed. This chapter thus explores an exemplary case where the consequences of wartime jobs and salaries on local communities were particularly sharp.

On the eve of the war, Philip Massey estimated the number of unemployed in Blaina and Nantyglo to be 1,300 to 1,400 – around 51 per cent of the 2,720 insured workers aged 16 to 64 recorded in July 1936.[19] Following the transference of youth to the Kent coalfield, to Bristol and mainly to the Midlands, the district's population had fallen from 16,488 in 1921 to 12,280 in 1936. Coal was at the time virtually the only source of employment, with 90 per cent of the men in work in 1937 being colliery workers. [20] There were 780 men and boys working at the Beynon Colliery and the West Blaina Red Ash Colliery, and the rest travelled to the Rose Heyworth Colliery in Abertillery. The opportunities for work for Blaina women were very limited; as in the rest of the South Wales coalfields, they would generally be shop assistants, teachers or work in domestic service.[21] Once again, the Nantyglo and Blaina district had the lowest rates of women's employment of the South Wales coalfields, with only 11 per cent of the female population over twelve recorded as employed by the 1921 census. As a point in comparison the British average at this time was 33 per cent.[22]

It was the war which brought full employment in Blaina and Nantyglo, and led to deep changes in the micropolitics of power in the towns. The rearmament campaign led to the construction of three Royal Ordnance Factories at Glascoed, Hirwaun and Bridgend which employed 60,000 workers in 1942, and to a number of other war factories. In 1941, at the start of the MO survey, a very large section of the Blaina population travelled daily to the Royal Ordnance Factory at Glascoed and to the Northern Aluminium Company at Rogerstone.

Table 4.1 highlights the gradual absorption of the unemployed into the munitions industry in the first years of the war in Blaina.

The number of Blaina and Nantyglo women employed in war work was remarkable. Some 600 women from the district were working in munitions factories or in other types of war factory in 1941. The Labour Exchange records indicate that there were about 532 women working in munitions at Usk; about seventy working in aluminium works at Rogerstone; a small number of girls (between fourteen and eighteen years of age) at the silk factory at Brynmawr; and some thirty women working permanently away from the district at Bridgend, a filling factory which produced detonators and fuses for mortar bombs.[23] According to Mollie Tarrant, the MO investigator, a large number of war workers were married, most were young, but there was a wide age range, and many women were in their forties and fifties.

In 1941, 600 formerly unemployed men had gone to construction works at the Royal Ordnance Factory at Usk and to the aerodrome at Hereford, as well

Table 4.1 Unemployment in Blaina, Blaina Labour Exchange Records – MO manuscript.

	Number of registered unemployed
August 1937	1,176
August 1939	1,000
August 1940	400
August 1941	77
March 1942	16
April 1942	6

as into munitions factories. Moreover, 925 men and boys were still employed in 1943 at the three collieries: 600 men and 150 boys at Beynon colliery, 120 men and 30 boys at West Bargoed Level, 20 men and 5 boys at the Major Red Ash Colliery.[24] These were virtually the same miners who were in work during the Depression. Under the Essential Works Order, they were now tied to the mining industry and prevented from leaving their positions of employment. In July 1943, 1,300 men and 200 women were in the services.[25]

When the war started, the small towns of Blaina and Nantyglo thus shifted from relying almost entirely on coalmining as a source of work to a dual segmentation: miners on the one side and munition workers on the other.[26] One of the important consequences of the changes in the employment structure was that of an increased wage differential in the community. While a labourer or a packer in the mines would earn between £3 12s. and £3 15s. a week, a munitions worker would earn a minimum average wage of £5 a week to which overtime could be added.

In other words, it was not unusual to find two neighbours whose weekly pay displayed a £2 difference. This was most striking in Blaina, where the homogeneity of living conditions in the town before the war had been underlined by Philip Massey.[27] Blaina and Nantyglo were almost wholly working class, with only a bare handful of people who could be considered middle class: teachers and retired teachers, some shopkeepers, people from the gas and electricity boards. And even these members of the community usually lived in the same sort of houses as the manual workers, many of them being former manual workers or sons of manual workers. The central line of division then was between employed miners and miners on the dole. Yet even among them the income gap was not marked, as miners' average weekly earnings were of £2 10d., so in many cases only about 15s. more than the allowances of the unemployed.[28] Colliers who worked at the coalface on piecework and who were amongst the most respected miners in the community, were the only kind of coal workers who would earn in average £3. 14s. In 1937, as in 1942, they formed only a sixth of Blaina and Nantyglo's miners.

But alongside the strong sense of community described by Massey, some of his interviews with Blaina inhabitants in 1937 highlighted that 'there is a certain amount of snobbery among those who have kept in regular work'.[29] Indeed, the miners who had experienced long-term unemployment since 1921 were those less fit to work or less skilled.[30] In other words, they were considered as the less respectable miners of the community.

Yet these were precisely the men who were employed in munitions factories in 1942, and thus earned much more than the most respected and skilled miners. The MO investigation of 1942 shows how exasperated Blaina mine workers were by the comparison they could easily make between wages in the mines and wages in the munitions trades. Not only were wage differentials now substantial, they were also in stark contradiction to the former village order, and questioned a sense of respectable working-class masculinity. Indeed, as evidenced by one of the best study of mining communities, 'the work a miner does and the wage he receives both express concretely his status as a man and as a member of his profession'.[31]

Miners' manliness was closely associated with the physical and dangerous work undertaken in the mines as well as with the physical strength it required. In contrast, it was contended that no particular physical effort was demanded of munitions workers. Moreover, many of the munitions workers were former unemployed miners, deemed unfit to work in the mines at the end of the 1930s since they were hampered by all kinds of debility and illnesses. Yet, they were now making their fortunes in Royal Ordnance factories.

Miner, M45D:[32]

I here should be a standardization of wages for war, irrespective of the job. Every man should have £5 a week. There should be more contentment and more heart in the job. This colliery employs 700, about 230 principals. Of these, there aren't more than 20 averaging £6 a week. I know a man whose work on one face brought him in £4 5s. He left underground work prior to the Essential Works Order coming in because of heart trouble. Now he's at Glascoed earning £9 10s. He said he was having it for nothing!

Few men in factories get under £6 or £7. These buggers are getting £6 for nothing. Why should we work![33]

Blaina miners deemed the munitions workers' new found prosperity particularly unjust in view of the easy tasks they were supposedly undertaking compared with the toughness of miners' jobs. While many war workers emphasized the danger of their work, boasts of former miners claiming they were now getting money 'for nothing' were not rare and were bound to emphasize this sense of injustice. This was further instilled by the complaints of other former miners about the unmanliness of factory work: 'It's no work for a man in the factory'; 'Up there, we're all a "set of little ladies in pinafores".'[34]

Furthermore, as the MO investigator stressed, the comparison between what a man could earn in the pit, after years of experience, and what others could earn in the munitions factories with hardly any training or experience, struck observers. Suddenly these previously unemployed, or unemployable, were earning more (a minimum wage of £4 5s.) than the most skilled colliers, who had a minimum weekly wage of £3 18s. 5d.

Mining lodge delegate, M50D:

Skilled men in the mines are getting less than they would in any other kind of outside work. They should have at least £2 more.[35]

Miner, M45D:

Look now, what I'm getting. £3 it is, and I got the same for years. My brother, younger than me he is, he brings home £6. I could weep for it![36]

The wage differential led to a crisis of respectable masculinity in Blaina, as 'the wage structure, with its differentials for skill and danger, has been built in such a way that a man's status as a strong and skilled worker, and as a man worth his pay, is conveyed by what shows on the pay-note'.[37] In other words, the two main criteria identifying miners' manliness were under attack: physical endurance and technical skills. The high earnings of munitions workers were seemingly gained without merit, and especially when ostentatiously exhibited, were much resented:

Miner, M40D:

We're getting nothing like we should have. Look now, what the munitions workers get. Much more than we do. And I'll tell you what it is, see. *It's the men from here on munitions work that never worked before at all.* People that's never earned nothing, getting £5 a week or more.

There's one I would tell you. He never would work. Last week he showed me his note for over £8. 'Keep it dark', he said. But he showed it to everyone. And I'd got £4 that same week. Not fair, is it?[38]

This crisis of respectable masculinity was heightened by women's work which challenged a coalfield society deeply fractured until then along the line of gender. Indeed, what Blaina's miners seem to have resented even more strongly was the elevated economic and social position of the female munitions workers, which threatened to undermine their own status. Although the vast majority of female industrial workers only earned between 50 and 70 per cent of the rates paid to men within the factories, the earnings of the munitions' workers appeared high in comparison with the low wages paid within the mining industry.[39] As Tables 4.2 and 4.3 show, the weekly wage of an unskilled female munitions worker was roughly equivalent to that of a semi-skilled and skilled surface worker, and could be marginally higher than some underground workers.[40]

Many miners viewed women's newfound economic gains as a serious affront to their manliness. As early as November 1940, a Welsh deputy had warned the House of Commons that South Wales was on the verge of witnessing a 'cultural

Table 4.2 Blaina miners' wages.

Classes of Miners	Wages in 1937	Wages in April 1942
Labourers	£2. 10s. 8d.	£3. 12s. 8d.
Assistant repairers & Packers	£2. 18s. 6d.	£3. 15s. 4d.
Repairers & Engineers	£2. 18s. 6d.	£4. 6s. 0d.
Colliers	£2. 16s. 7d. (minimum)	£3. 18s. 5d.

Table 4.3 Wages of Blaina women working in munitions factories.[41]

Type of shift	Women's wages in munitions factories
Day shift	£2. 4s. 9d.
Afternoon shift	£3. 0s. 0d.
Night shift	£3. 12s. 0d.

revolution', as young girls, 'who had once been regarded as a liability in the miners' homes, were now the main bread-winners'.[42] It was this perceived loss of balance in the micropolitics of mining settlements which was at the heart of the 1942 wave of strikes in the British coalfields. In the first three weeks of May 1942, 86 disputes arose across the coalfields, involving 58,000 men. They started in South Wales before extending to the English coalfields. The Mineworkers Federation was asking for a general rise of 4s. a shift and a national minimum weekly wage of £4 5s. 0d. And the comparison with the women munitions workers' wages was a central argument in the wage debates which eventually led to the Greene Award of June 1942. It awarded a 2s. 6d. increase per shift for every adult miner, and more importantly, it implemented a national minimum wage of 83s./week for underground workers and 78s./week for surface workers, bringing them closer to the munitions workers' minimum wage.[43] The most important colliery in Blaina, Beynon colliery, took part in the strikes in May 1942.

Indeed, in Blaina, too, family hierarchies were deeply shaken, as evidenced by the testimonies collected by Mollie Tarrant. A Blaina man reported of one of his friend for instance: 'Last week his daughter, she's on munitions, brought home more than he did. He felt very put out about it.'[44] Especially with overtime, it was not rare for wives working in war factories to earn consistently higher wages than their husbands. The following account from a miner's representative sheds light on the resulting tensions created in some Blaina households:

> A man for six days underground works like a slave. At the end of the week, he gets a matter of £3 15s. In some houses, where the wife is an ordnance worker, she'll bring home between £4–£5. Then you have the psychological effect in the house. These problems do arise here. I know two cases where the woman brings home more than the man. In one case, they've parted.[45]

To circumvent this sensitive issue, astute wives came up with clever manoeuvres. Such was the case of a 38-year-old Blaina woman working at the Rogerstone Northern Aluminium Company and whose husband was a miner earning £4 3s. per week:

> I've been in there six weeks now, and I like it very much...Whether there's any feeling about the munitions workers getting more wages, all depends upon how you deal with things. Now I might sometimes get a little more than my husband. But what I do is to come in, and I just put my wages up on the mantelpiece. I don't say how much I've got. If I did, my husband would just say, 'Alright, you don't go out to work then.'[46]

By not mentioning the amount in her pay packet and putting it directly on the mantelpiece, this munitions worker was careful to avoid any open threat to her husband's primary breadwinner-status – and to her job. This demonstrates how problematic the earnings of munitions workers, which were not pin money wages anymore, could prove to be in the patriarchal setting of the mining homes. The women's diagnosis of the troubles arising in other households is also quite enlightening: 'In some houses, there may be women who'd say, I've earned all this, I've got a right to so and so. And then it'd be all up.'[47] The earning and spending of 'their' money by munitions workers appears to be at the heart of the discontent in Blaina's households.

Conspicuous consumption in wartime? Sartorial immorality and respectable femininity

In Blaina and Nantyglo, gossip on and appraisals of the amount spent by each and everyone were relentless. The aim of this chapter is less to evaluate the degree to which spending had in fact increased in the community, than to analyse why this issue came to the fore at such a time and how it affected the contours of respectable femininity. In these mining towns where one of the greatest wartime concerns was the disparity between miners' and munitions workers' wages, apparently irresponsible spending was much resented:

> A miner's wife:

> These munitions workers are bound to miss their money after the war. They'd be wise to look after it now, but they're not doing it, and I'll tell you for why, the half of them are not used to having it. I feel in my mind that they'll go to any depths after the war to have what they're getting now. Why, there are girls getting more than my husband do have![48]

> A Blaina housewife F45D:

> These girls wouldn't be having the money they are if it was peacetime. It's not right. They don't know how to use it properly. They spend far too much.[49]

After years of Depression and in anticipation of rainy days, the miners' wives were outraged by the lack of financial prudence demonstrated by the female munitions workers, and especially – but not exclusively – that of young unmarried girls. The excessive spending these 'Welsh Mams' witnessed shocked their sense of thrift.[50] Moreover, the hostility towards reckless spending was reinforced by the national emphasis on saving as an important contribution to the war effort. Propaganda campaigns were launched promoting Savings Groups, National Certificates, Defence Bonds and Trustee Savings Banks.[51] As Ross McKibbin has shown, the result was an intense disdain for anyone indulging in excessive spending.[52]

But how much spending was there really in Blaina? Tarrant drew four conclusions from a comparative analysis of Blaina's miners and munitions workers' family budgets in 1937 and in 1942. First, it was evident that far fewer families lived up to the limits of their income. Second, the amount of spending did not appear to have increased very much, as for many families the priority was to make arrear payments and pay off their debts. Third, two sectors of spending had, however, increased generally amongst Blaina's population and a little more in munitions workers' families than in miners' families: that of food, despite rationing, and that of housing goods. The MO survey showed that munitions workers and miners' wives to a lesser degree had in fact been inclined during the first years of the war to replace things their homes had been lacking for years. The local draper explained for instance that there was a great demand for towels, tea-towels and tablecloths. Moreover, while munitions workers spent more at that time than miners it was also because around 90 per cent of them had been unemployed for years. The MO investigator describes households that had reached rock bottom, and where furniture could now gradually be replaced.

Finally, and very surprisingly as compared with pervasive accusations of reckless spending, Blaina and Nantyglo were actually amongst the small towns saving the most in the area. The efficiency of the local school's Savings Group was noted by Tarrant and the encouragements of the War Savings secretary duly reported: 'The average per head is £3. 12s. In another mining district over the mountain, it's only 5/-. People here have really done extraordinary well as far as savings are concerned.'[53] And women munitions workers, most of whom had never had anything to spare, did take part in the national effort towards saving:

M40D:

> I hear women talking in the trains. More than once I've heard one turn to the other and say 'How much are you saving?' The answer is often £1, or 30/- or even 'the whole of it'. Of course, the idea of saving has been put over very effectively at the factory. 60–80 per cent of people must be saving there. They've got saving stamps and when a certificate is due to anybody, they get it in an envelope with a special label, so that everybody can see it. The people who get the envelopes get a little publicity you see.[54]

Why, then, were accounts of munitions workers' reckless spending so numerous? Was it because excessive spending by a minority acquired disproportionate importance? The contention of this chapter is that what was particularly resented was the *ostentatious* manner in which spending was perceived in the community. Thorstein Veblen's famous concept of 'conspicuous consumption', as unnecessary spending in view to gain a reputable status in the community appears particularly fruitful here.[55] One needs to be careful in the use of this concept as in *The Theory of the Leisure Class* it is predominantly taken in the context of the upper middle class. But Veblen shows how both conspicuous leisure and conspicuous consumption as a means of showing financial strength are in vogue as far down the social hierarchy as it remains possible. It can be applied rightly in pre-war Blaina and Nantyglo where there was virtually no middle class but rather two 'classes' of miners distinguished by whether they were employed or not. Ostentatious spending was thus seen in 1942 as deep reminders of the reversal of fortune and of the break in the traditional hierarchies. Conspicuous consumption – or, more rightly, that which was perceived as such – was thus particularly dreaded and resented in wartime, as shown for instance by this miner's testimony:

M40D:

> Where a man and wife are both working, as a result, they're having an income which is dangerous. A butcher said to me the other day that he was very fed up. He was hoping everybody would be put on soldier's pay. 'You should have my

experience', he said, 'to be behind this counter. The other day a woman bounced in and in the presence of others asked for a turkey. Then she asked if I thought that'd be sufficient for her. And I knew that she hadn't had a Sunday joint for 10 years!'

The miner's wife has to follow on after that customer … I think that in some cases, this extra money has led to a temporary loss of balance.[56]

In Blaina and Nantyglo fears of conspicuous consumption such as these were common and widespread. They arose precisely from the fact that such spending threatened to reveal the 'temporary loss of balance' which seemed to occur in the mining villages. In what was now understood by some as a competitive parade for acquisition, the miner and his wife saw themselves losing for the first time. A miner told Mollie Tarrant, for instance, 'The munitions workers are spending more than the miners. You see more £1 notes flying round on Saturday night than you used to see shillings before the war.' Indeed, the difference between the munitions worker's and the miner's pocket money was nowhere more obvious than in the public houses. In a culture where 'pints sustained masculinity', the numerous drinks bought by munitions workers did nothing to relieve the sense of injustice of miners.[57]

A 65-year-old lodge delegate at one of the collieries confided in the investigator: 'My wife has to compete with workers getting higher wages. Naturally there's a certain amount of jealousy.'[58] This symbolical undermining of the miner's wife's status challenged more generally the miner's and his household's reputation and contributes to an explanation of why women as shoppers were the focus of close scrutiny. As has indeed been stressed by Daniel Wight, in some extent 'husbands established their status vicariously through the consumption of their wives'.[59]

Therefore to equate excessive spending with immorality was also, and perhaps more importantly, a defensive move against the breakdown of the traditional hierarchies. In other words, in these small mining towns, there seems to have been a shift in the primary criteria used to construct hierarchies and assess respectability in the community. There was a shift of focus from wealth status based on earnings (and linked to physical strength and skills in the past) to spending and saving attitudes. The pay packet had traditionally been the 'symbol of power' precisely because it was connected with skills and strength,[60] but to many miners the 'easy money' made by munitions workers meant that this connection no longer held true. The primary locus for respectability thus shifted to consumer habits, with an emphasis on restraint from excessive and conspicuous consumption.

This connection between spending and respectability was certainly not new in mining districts. Indeed, several historical studies have explored the way credit worthiness was ascertained through gossips assessing respectability and consumption habits. But what is surprising is that this obsession with inappropriate spending came to the fore precisely at a time where it should have faded, should credit be solely considered. Indeed, the war saw a marked shift to cash purchase in Blaina and Nantyglo and a substantial decrease in the multiple means of credit purchase. The unremitting accusations of ostentatious spending did arise from this traditional background but came to the fore because of the resentment for what was readily labelled as conspicuous consumption and the threat it posed to the micro hierarchies of the community. As long as consumption differentials were not publicly displayed, the micropolitics of power in the mining districts could be protected and the 'temporary loss of balance in the community' concealed.

Interestingly, Mark Benney, in his chronicle of a Durham coalfield between 1944 and 1945, described mining communities as being almost entirely devoid of conspicuous consumption. To him, the uniformity of colliery housing, house furnishings and living standards was such that there was less conspicuous consumption in a mining village than in other communities in the country. Consequently, according to him, 'a sharp increase in wages, as happened last year [1944], does not produce the phenomenon, so repellent to middle class wives, of working women wearing fur coats'.[61] While working women in Blaina did not start to wear fur coats during the war either, ostentatious spending could be perceived in micro differentials of consumptions, precisely because of the uniformity of colliery living standards. In that sense, the situation in these mining settlements was close to that depicted by Lady Bell, when she said of Middlesbrough that most people were 'living under conditions in which the slightest lapse from thrift and forethought is necessarily conspicuous'.[62] In Blaina and Nantyglo where women had had to mend their clothes for years, the wartime purchase of two new dresses was sufficient to be labelled as conspicuous consumption. And indeed, clothing expenditure as the most visible form of consumption became a focal point of attention in this community on the look-out for conspicuous consumption, and it constitutes a paradigmatic example of the hostility and projections towards ostentatious spending.

Thornstein Veblen stated that 'At no other point is the sense of shabbiness so keenly felt as it is if we fall short of the standard set by social usage in this matter of dress. It is true of dress in even a higher degree than of most other items of consumption, that people will undergo a very considerable degree of privation in the comforts or the necessaries of life in order to afford what is considered a decent amount of wasteful consumption.'[63] As a matter of fact, unnecessary clothing spending and accusations of sartorial immorality appear unremittingly in Mollie Tarrant's notes. These accusations were directed against both men and women munitions workers, but more particularly against the young women. Indeed, for years, Blaina women had no money to spare except for the barest necessities. The MO survey found that as earnings increased, married women tended to buy items for their homes, which had been gradually emptied by the Means Test, while younger munitions workers tended to spend more on new clothes, especially as, until June 1941, they were one of the rare items that were not rationed. This spending, readily labelled as ostentatious, was perceived as demonstrating these women's lack of respectability.

Housewife, F25D:

You can easily see people have been spending more on clothes since the war. Women you'd know had only one pair of shoes for Sundays and weekdays at one time, now they might have half a dozen. The money the munitions workers spend on their clothes before coupons come in![64]

The woman who runs the only up-to-date dress shop for women in Blaina:

> It's ridiculous. The amount of spending that's going on among those young munitions workers. Of course, you can't do anything about it, but sometimes I feel I'd like to refuse to serve them.[65]

The association between working-class women's purchase of finery and their moral degradation is a topos of the middle-class social and political debates.[66] But clothing purchases were a focal point of complaint within Blaina's working-class community. This obsession appears to lie in the fact that they are an important marker of social status and a very effective means of social display, the most notable example being that of Sunday best, a habit which was even more prevalent in South Wales.[67] And in a small town where the micropolitics of power were felt to be on the verge of losing their equilibrium, they became crucial. For mining families who were used to being part of the most respected stratum of Blaina's society, 'keeping up with the Joneses', was critical. Let us take the example of a particular mining family. The household comprised a collier, one of the most respected types of miners, a housewife, with a son and daughter under twenty. The only earnings in the family were the miner's weekly £3 15s. This is what the wife told Mollie Tarrant:

> I don't have no money for my own clothes. They have to go on for years. But I've just paid off the last instalment of a suit for my boy. 6 guineas it cost me! But he didn't have nothing decent, and the other people there did, and you know how it is![68]

The Second World War thus led to an important shift in who 'the Joneses' were. And sartorial consumption became the focus of neighbourhood talk and angry whispering since it threatened to reveal the transformations occurring in the traditional order of the mining community.

Conclusion

In wartime Blaina and Nantyglo, conspicuous consumption was tracked by a community on the lookout. This analysis has shown that the root of this fear and resentment against ostentatious consumption lay in the fact that it was perceived as a threat to the micro hierarchies of the mining settlements. For miners, the high earnings of munitions workers disrupted the traditional connections between pay packet, skills, strength and masculinity. They also challenged the gender order of the households as well as that of the mining community at large. An overt display of wage differentials was thus to be equated with a lack of respectability, and respectable masculinities and femininities renegotiated. For many in Blaina and Nantyglo, the mining communities were witnessing a gender crisis and a 'loss of balance'.

This entrenched belief and fear sheds a new light on the historical debate on the impact of the Second World War and women's employment on gender roles. Historians have aptly questioned the supposedly revolutionary impact of the war, stressing the reinforcement of traditional gender roles which took place in many sectors, as well as the rapid return to post-war normalcy. It seems important to shed light, however, on the way social actors themselves perceived these changes as they occurred during the war, without any knowledge of their possible outcome.

By unveiling the tensions and conflicts within these mining settlements, this study also contributes to a demythologized reappraisal of working-class 'communities'. Historians such as Joanna Bourke have indeed pointed out how problematic this concept was, because of its resonance within two discourses: the backward-looking romanticism embedded in many working-class autobiographies and oral histories, and the political symbol the class consciousness 'community' has traditionally stood for in historical studies.[69] According to her, these imprints have resulted in systematically positive depictions of communities which tend to overlook conflicts. Tensions and suspicions within communities need to be subjected to the same level of critical inquiry as neighbourhood solidarity and reciprocity have been.

Recommended reading

Dennis, N., F. Henriques, and C. Slaughter (1956) *Coal Is Our Life: An Analysis of a Yorkshire Mining Community* (London: Eyre & Spottiswoode).

Hinton, J. (2013) *The Mass Observers: A History, 1937–1949* (Oxford: Oxford University Press).

Hywel, F. and D. Smith (1998) *The Fed: A History of the South Wales Miners in the Twentieth Century* (Cardiff: University of Wales Press).

Johnson, P. (1985) *Saving and Spending: The Working-class Economy in Britain 1870–1939* (Oxford: Clarendon Press).

Mak, A. (2015) 'Spheres of Justice in the 1942 Betteshanger Miners' Strike: An Essay in Historical Ethnography', *Historical Studies in Industrial Relations*, vol. 36, pp. 29–57.

Massey, P. (1937) *Portrait of a Mining Town* (London: Fact).

Roberts, B. (1998) 'The "Budgie Train" : Women and Wartime Munitions Work in a Mining Valley', *Llafur: Journal of Welsh Labour History*, vol. 7, no. 3–4, pp. 143–52.

Tarrant, M. (1944) *Blaina and Nantyglo: A Mining Town Survey 1938-44* (unpublished).

Veblen, T. (1899) *The Theory of the Leisure Class: An Economic Study in the Evolution of Institutions* (New York: Macmillan).

Wight, D. (1994) *Workers Not Wasters: Masculine Respectability, Consumption and Unemployment in Central Scotland: A Community Study* (Edinburgh: Edinburgh University Press).

Williams, M. A. (2002) *A Forgotten Army: Female Munitions workers of South Wales, 1939–1945* (Cardiff: University of Wales Press).

Notes

All the Mass Observation quotations in this article are reproduced with permission of Curtis Brown Group Ltd, London on behalf of The Trustees of the Mass Observation Archive. I wish to thank Laura Downs and Alain Cottereau for their sharp comments, as well as the editors of this book, Corinna M. Peniston-Bird and Emma Vickers for their thoughtful suggestions. The research presented in this chapter was recently complemented by fieldwork conducted in Blaina and in Blaenau Gwent more generally. Twenty-three interviews were conducted in July and September 2015 on the issues examined in this chapter as well as on wartime strikes. Although they could not be included here, they have greatly contributed to my understanding of the dynamics at play in Blaina and Nantyglo and will be at the heart of a future publication. I wish to take this opportunity to express my sincere thanks to Ceri Thompson, Peter Strong, John Evans, Martin Parfitt, Eifion Lloyd Davies, Rev. Pam Griffiths, and David Selway who played key roles in this ongoing research.

1. Mass Observation Archives (MOA), TC64/1/D. Blaina and Nantyglo Survey, p. 141.

2. P. Johnson (1985) *Saving and Spending. The Working-class Economy in Britain 1870–1939* (Oxford: Clarendon Press); P. Johnson (1988) 'Conspicuous Consumption and Working-Class Culture in Late-Victorian and Edwardian Britain', *Transactions of the Royal Historical Society,* vol. 38, 27–42.

3. See also M. Finn (1996) 'Women, Consumption and Coverture in England, c. 1760–1860', *The Historical Journal,* vol. 39, no. 3, pp. 703–22; M. Finn (1998) 'Working-Class Women and the Contest for Consumer Control in Victorian County Courts', *Past & Present,* vol. 161, no. 1, pp. 116–54; S. O. Rose (1992) *Limited Livelihoods: Gender and Class in Nineteenth-century England* (Berkeley: University of California Press); J. Benson (1996) 'Working-Class Consumption, Saving, and Investment in England and Wales, 1851–1911', *Journal of Design History,* vol. 9, no. 2, pp. 87–99; M. Daunton (2007) *Wealth and social history of Britain* (Oxford: Oxford University Press).

4. I. Zweiniger-Bargielowska (2000) *Austerity in Britain: Rationing, Controls and Consumption. 1939–1955* (Oxford: Oxford University Press).

5. J. K. Galbraith (1958) *The Affluent Society* (Toronto: New American Library). J. H. Goldthorpe (1969) *The Affluent Worker in the Class Structure* (London: Cambridge University Press). For recent works on this issue see in particular *Contemporary British History*'s special issue on 'Contesting Affluence'; S. Majima and M. Savage (eds) (2008) 'Contesting Affluence: An Introduction', *Contemporary British History,* vol. 22, no. 4, pp. 445–55.

6. David Gilbert uses this expression to warn against the dangers and limitation of such a model: D. Gilbert (1995) 'Imagined Communities and Mining Communities', *Labour History Review,* vol. 60, no. 2, pp. 47–110. For a thorough discussion of the concept of 'community' in mining studies, see in particular: H. Barron (2010) *The 1926 Miners' Lockout: Meanings of Community in the Durham Coalfield* (Oxford and New York: Oxford University Press).

7. See for instance A. V. John (1984) 'A Miner Struggle? Women's Protests in Welsh Mining History', *Llafur: Journal of Welsh Labour History,* vol. 4, no. 1, pp. 72–90; R. Jones (1991) 'Women, the Community, and Collective Action: The "Ceffyl Pren" Tradition', in A. V. John (ed.) *Our Mothers' Land: Chapters in Welsh Women's History, 1830–1939* (Cardiff: University of Wales Press), pp. 17–41; J. J. Gier-Viskovatoff and A. Porter (1998) 'Women of the British Coalfields on Strike in 1926 and 1984: Documenting Lives Using Oral History and Photography', *Frontiers,* vol. 19, no. 2, pp. 199–230.

8. N. M. Forestell (2003) 'The Miner's Wife: Working class femininity in a masculine context 1920–1950' in K. McPherson, C. Morgan, and N. M. Forestell (eds) *Gendered Pasts: Historical Essays in Femininity and Masculinity in Canada* (Toronto: University of Toronto Press), pp. 139–57, here pp. 139–40.

9. With some notable exceptions such as: N. M. Forestell (2003) 'The Miner's Wife'; V. G. Hall (2001) 'Contrasting Female Identities: Women in Coal Mining Communities in Northumberland, England, 1900–1939', *Journal of Women's History,* vol. 13, no. 2, pp. 107–31.

10. F. Bédarida (1982) 'La vie de quartier en Angleterre: enquêtes empiriques et approches théoriques', *Le Mouvement Social,* vol. 118, pp. 9–21, here p. 12–8.

11. P. Massey (1937) *Portrait of a Mining Town* (London: Fact).

12. Mass Observation Archives (MOA), TC64/1/D. Blaina and Nantyglo Survey. Mollie Tarrant had also been in charge of various MO investigations in Portsmouth, and from 1949 on she was at the head of the organization alongside Len England. See B. Roberts (1998) 'The "Budgie Train" : Women and Wartime Munitions Work in a Mining Valley', *Llafur: Journal of Welsh Labour History,* vol. 7, no. 3–4, pp. 143–52 and B. Roberts (2002) 'Shopping, Saving and Spending in Wartime: The Experience of a Welsh Mining Valley', *Family and Community History,* vol. 5, no. 1, pp. 19–31.

13. Massey, *Portrait of a Mining Town,* p. 4.

14. On the history of Mass Observation and the methods used, see J. Hinton (2013) *The Mass Observers: A History, 1937–1949* (Oxford: Oxford University Press) and L. Stanley (2001) 'Mass-Observation Fieldwork's Methods' in P. Atkinson (ed.), *Handbook of Ethnology* (London: Sage), pp. 92–108.

15. R. S. Lynd and H. M. Lynd (1929) *Middletown: A Study in Modern American Culture* (New York: Harcourt Brace & World).

16. W. A. Gwyn (1982) *The Welsh in Their History* (London: Croom Helm), p. 104.

17. Thompson, S. (2006) *Unemployment, Poverty and Health in Interwar South Wales* (Cardiff: University of Wales Press).

18. MOA, TC64/1/D. Blaina and Nantyglo Survey, p. 45 and S. Thompson (2006) *Unemployment, Poverty and Health.*

19. Massey, *Portrait of a Mining Town,* p. 29.

20. Apart from the collieries, a Nantyglo crusher employed about twenty, a clay mine about thirty, and a foundry about a dozen.

21. S. R. Williams (2005) '"The only profession that was around": Opting for Teaching in the South Wales Valleys in the Interwar Years', *Llafur: Journal of Welsh Labour History,* vol. 9, no. 2, pp. 45–58; S. Bruley (2012) '"Little Mothers": Adolescent Girls and Young Women in the South Wales Valleys between the Wars', *Llafur: Journal of Welsh History,* vol. 18, no. 3, pp. 126–44.

22. It should, however, be stressed, following Chris Williams' warning, that the census failed to record remunerative work undertaken by women on a temporary, seasonal, or informal basis: taking in other people's washing and sewing, taking in lodgers, selling food, and so on. See C. Williams (1998) *Capitalism, Community and Conflict: The South Wales Coalfield 1898–1947,* (Cardiff: University of Wales Press), pp. 63–5.

23. MOA, TC64/1/D. Blaina and Nantyglo Survey, p. 47. On female munitions workers in South Wales, see M. A. Williams (1995) *'Where is Mrs. Jones going?': Women and the Second World War in South Wales* (Aberystwyth: Canolfan Uwchefraydiau Cymreig a Cheltaidd); M. A. Williams (2002) *A Forgotten Army: Female Munitions workers of South Wales, 1939–1945* (Cardiff: University of Wales Press).

24. National Archives (NA) BT64/3399. Reports on Nantyglo and Blaina, 1943. Location of industry – Surveys, by Board of Trade Regional Controllers.

25. NA BT64/3399. Reports on Nantyglo and Blaina, 1943. Location of industry – Surveys, by Board of Trade Regional Controllers.

26. The expression of 'munition worker' used in Blaina and Nantyglo included any war worker working in any factory.

27. Massey, *Portrait of a Mining Town*, pp. 33–4.
28. Massey, p. 30.
29. Massey, pp. 36–7.
30. In her study of the effect of unemployment in Brynmawr, a city just two miles from Blaina, Hilda Jennings showed the preponderance of men over forty years of age in long-term employment in 1929, and stresses at the other end of the age scale the considerable number of boys from fourteen to eighteen years of age who had never had even temporary employment. H. Jennings (1934) *Brynmawr, A Study of a Distresses Area* (London: Allenson & Co), pp. 137–8.
31. N. Dennis, F. Henriques, and C. Slaughter (1956) *Coal Is Our Life: An Analysis of a Yorkshire Mining Community* (London: Eyre & Spottiswoode), p. 74.
32. According to MO's code M50D reads 'a man of around fifty year-old, from the unskilled working class' (A meaning 'upper class'; B 'middle class'; C 'artisan or skilled working class'; D 'unskilled working class').
33. MOA, TC64/1/D. Blaina and Nantyglo Survey, p. 54.
34. MOA, TC64/1/C. Blaina and Nantyglo Survey, miscellaneous.
35. MOA, TC64/1/D. Blaina and Nantyglo Survey, p. 54.
36. MOA, TC64/1/D. Blaina and Nantyglo Survey, p. 55.
37. MOA, TC64/1/D. Blaina and Nantyglo Survey, p. 65.
38. MOA, TC64/1/D. Blaina and Nantyglo Survey, p. 50.
39. H. Wilson (1945) *New Deal for Coal* (London: Contact). For a comparative analysis of the origins of wage discriminations in the metalworking industries, see L. Downs (1995) *Manufacturing Inequality: Gender Division in the French and British Metalworking Industries, 1914–1939* (Ithaca, NY: Cornell University Press).
40. See also M. Heinemann (1944) *Britain's Coal: A study of the mining crisis* (London: Victor Gollancz).
41. Overtime work should be added to these figures. These are the figures for the munitions factory at Usk. According to the investigator they are roughly equivalent to that of the Rogerstone factory.
42. *Western Mail*, 21 November 1940, quoted by M. A. Williams, (1995) 'Where is Mrs. Jones going?', p. 6.
43. On the 1942 miners' strike and the Greene award, cf W. H. B. Court (1951) *Coal* (London: Longmans); B. Supple (1987) *The History of the British Coal Industry*, vol. 4 (Oxford: Clarendon Press); F. Hywel and D. Smith (1998) *The Fed: A History of the South Wales Miners in the Twentieth Century* (Cardiff: University of Wales Press). For an example of using a Mass Observation survey to analyse a miners' strike, see: A. Mak (2015) 'Spheres of Justice in the 1942 Betteshanger Miners' Strike: An Essay in Historical Ethnography', *Historical Studies in Industrial Relations*, vol. 36, pp. 29–57.
44. MOA, TC64/1/D. Blaina and Nantyglo Survey, p. 60.
45. MOA, TC64/1/D. Blaina and Nantyglo Survey, p. 59.
46. MOA, TC64/1/C. Blaina and Nantyglo Survey, miscellaneous.
47. MOA, TC64/1/C. Blaina and Nantyglo Survey, miscellaneous.
48. MOA, TC64/1/D. Blaina and Nantyglo Survey, p. 116.
49. MOA, TC64/1/D. Blaina and Nantyglo Survey, p. 115.
50. While the archetype of the Welsh Mam depicts a powerful matriarch whose central role is that of guardian of the household budget, historians have stressed that, as is true of the miner's financier in general, the myth overemphasizes the powers of the miner's wife. See, for instance, C. Williams (1998) *Capitalism, Community and Conflict*, p. 68.
51. See for instance C. Madge (1943) *War Pattern of Saving and Spending*, (Cambridge: Cambridge University Press), pp. 41–52.

52. R. McKibbin (1998) *Classes and Cultures: England 1918–1951* (Oxford: Oxford University Press), p. 177; M. Cohen (2012) *The Eclipse of 'Elegant Economy': The Impact of the Second World War on Attitudes to Personal Finance in Britain* (Farnham, Surrey; Burlington, VT: Ashgate Publishing), p. 44.

53. MOA, TC64/1/D. Blaina and Nantyglo Survey, p. 142.

54. MOA, TC64/1/D. Blaina and Nantyglo Survey, p. 109.

55. T. Veblen (1899) *The Theory of the Leisure Class: An Economic Study in the Evolution of Institutions* (New York: Macmillan).

56. MOA, TC64/1/D. Blaina and Nantyglo Survey, p. 58.

57. On the links between pub drinking, earning capacity, and masculinity, see D. Wight (1994) *Workers Not Wasters: Masculine Respectability, Consumption and Unemployment in Central Scotland: A Community Study.* (Edinburgh: Edinburgh University Press), p. 163.

58. MOA, TC64/1/D. Blaina and Nantyglo Survey, p. 54.

59. D. Wight (1994) *Workers Not Wasters: Masculine Respectability, Consumption and Unemployment in Central Scotland: A Community Study* (Edinburgh: Edinburgh University Press), p. 77.

60. McIvor, A. (2013) *Working Lives: Work in Britain Since 1945,* (Basingstoke: Palgrave Macmillan), p. 90; D. Wight (1994) *Workers Not Wasters: Masculine Respectability, Consumption and Unemployment in Central Scotland: A Community Study* (Edinburgh: Edinburgh University Press).

61. M. Benney (1946) *Charity Main: A Coalfield Chronicle* (London: Allen & Unwin), p. 172–3. It should also be noted that Mark Benney studied mining villages with no possibility of employment in war factories.

62. Lady Bell (1907) *At the Works: Study of a Manufacturing Town, Middlesbrough* (London: Edward Arnold), p. 52 quoted by P. Johnson (1988) 'Conspicuous Consumption and Working-Class Culture in Late-Victorian and Edwardian Britain', *Transactions of the Royal Historical Society,* vol. 38, p. 40.

63. T. Veblen (1899) *The Theory of the Leisure Class: An Economic Study in the Evolution of Institutions* (New York: Macmillan), p. 109.

64. MOA, TC64/1/D. Blaina and Nantyglo Survey, p. 115.

65. Ibid.

66. M. Valverde (1989) 'The Love of Finery: Fashion and the Fallen Woman in Nineteenth-Century Social Discourse', *Victorian Studies,* vol. 32, no. 2, pp. 169–88.

67. Pilgrim Trust (1938) *Men without work: A report made to the Pilgrim Trust* (Cambridge: Cambridge University Press), p. 308.

68. MOA, TC64/1/D. Blaina and Nantyglo Survey, p. 116.

69. J. Bourke (1994) *Working Class Cultures in Britain, 1890–1960: Gender, Class and Ethnicity* (London: Routledge), p. 137.

5

Gender and Nazi Espionage: Hildegard Beetz, the Ciano Affair, and Female Agency

Katrin Paehler

In mid-1944, Ernst Kaltenbrunner, the head of the Reich Security Main Office (RSHA), Heinrich Himmler's main instrument of racial and political surveillance and policing, received a troubling report. An agent on a long-term assignment had subverted her task, assisted her target, and harmed the objectives of the office. Kaltenbrunner, however, scoffed at the report; he 'upheld Frau Beetz' and reasoned that the report was 'motivated by personal jealousy against [a] competitor'.[1] As a rule, Kaltenbrunner was nothing but suspicious, but in this case he trusted his own assessment more than anything else. Did the fact that the agent in question was a young woman sway his opinion? Did gender matter?

The conventional version of Hildegard Beetz's story runs as follows. In autumn 1943, Office VI – the political foreign intelligence service of the RSHA – tried to acquire the papers of the recently deposed Italian Foreign Minister Galeazzo Ciano. These documents, in particular Ciano's diaries, were rumoured to be damaging to German Foreign Minister Joachim von Ribbentrop. The leadership of the RSHA and Office VI had long wanted to topple Ribbentrop and to replace him with a high-ranking member of its organization, thereby taking over the leadership of the *Auswärtiges Amt*, the German Foreign Office, and bringing it into Himmler's universe. Banking on Ciano's reputation as an accomplished womanizer, Beetz, a young and pretty secretary and translator attached to the embassy in Rome, was sent to Ciano. A love affair developed, and Beetz became the intermediary between the imprisoned Ciano and Office VI personnel. Office VI hatched a plan to spring Ciano from prison and to exchange his life and freedom for his diaries, but it fell through. Ciano – found guilty of treason by the Italian Republic of Salò, led, under German overview, by his father-in-law Benito Mussolini – was executed. In love with Ciano and dismayed by the course of events, Beetz assisted his widow Edda, Mussolini's daughter, in her escape to Switzerland, fully aware that she carried with her the prized diaries. Beetz thus snatched a success from Office VI and made possible the diaries' eventual transfer into US hands and their use at the Nuremberg trials. Thereafter, Beetz slipped into oblivion. Put pointedly: Beetz was a secretary who became a bit player in a scheme masterminded by her male superiors; her greatest asset was her looks; and she defied her superiors for love. It is an irresistible tale of espionage, sex, and Nazism that accorded with available post-war statements and confirmed received knowledge about both Nazi Germany and women.

Hildegard Beetz's recently declassified (and voluminous) Central Intelligence Agency (CIA) files tell a different story. Carefully contextualized, they make it possible to advance a far more nuanced rendition of Beetz's life and activities – in Nazi Germany and beyond.[2] Beetz was anything but a smitten secretary who found herself in a situation beyond her control; rather, she was a professional woman of great agency and determination. In this chapter, I will highlight three issues in particular. First, Beetz had a pre-Ciano career in intelligence. Secondly, Beetz held a prominent and, thus far, completely unacknowledged role in the formulation of Office VI's plan to spring Ciano from prison. Indeed, there is much indication that she, maybe in cooperation with Ciano, came up with it and persuaded her superiors of its logic and potential benefits. Lastly, Beetz's activities, especially after Ciano's execution, were less those of a double agent or of a woman in love with a dead man, but rather those of a woman negotiating divided loyalties and gendered expectations. Indeed, the comparative abundance of primary sources allows for insights into the role Nazified gender expectations as well as traditional gender expectations played in Beetz's personal as well as in her professional life and makes it possible to study how, when, and why Beetz was able to use those expectations to her advantage. Ultimately, these inquiries go beyond the individual case and suggest the need to broaden the view on women in Nazi Germany to include a 'Nazi New Woman' – a professional, modern woman at home in the political system and using to her fullest advantage its racist and imperial designs.

This chapter then intertwines its arguments into various, interconnected historiographies. It stands as a much-needed corrective to the traditional view of Beetz's role in the Ciano affair; it complicates the story of Office VI activities in Italy and beyond; and it asks broader questions about the role other woman in subaltern positions might have played in and for Office VI.[3] This case study also contributes to the growing body of scholarship that focuses on women's agency and their active roles in state policies, for example in the Germanization of the Nazi East or in the Holocaust.[4] Women were clearly not restricted to the domestic sphere's 'emotional work', based on traditional and fixed gender roles, which stabilized the system.[5] Rather, they – and the men with whom they lived and worked – interpreted gendered roles and expectations within concrete situations. Indubitably, these experiences and negotiations also influenced post-war gender relations. Finally, this chapter stands as a reminder that assumptions about gendered roles and activities tend to blind even best-intentioned researchers to realities hidden in plain sight.[6] Beetz's CIA files make writing her story easier, yet it was not impossible before.

Childhood and youth

In the summer of 1945, US interrogators took Hildegard Beetz into custody in Weimar and interrogated her extensively. Asked also to write a *Lebenslauf*, a long-form résumé, she produced a fluently written, English-language document that offers an insight into her background in her own – written – voice. Born in 1919 near Weimar, Hildegard Burckhardt grew up in a conservative, middle-class environment. She described her father, a member of the air force who became a teacher after the First World War, as an admirer of the military who nevertheless accepted Germany's defeat, but longed to see Germany 'great and proud again'. Until his death in 1935, he appears to have been the primary influence on her and was committed to her education; the family moved to Weimar to allow Beetz to study languages in high school. Indeed, her father enrolled her into a boys-only *Realgymnasium*, as this particular university-track high school had the best curriculum for modern languages.

In 1934 Beetz joined the *Bund Deutscher Mädel* (BDM). Even though her parents objected to it, she 'liked it, especially the idea of a community without social classes'.[7] She devoted much time to it and was selected for a leadership course in 1937; however, her evaluation noted that she displayed 'too much opposition'.[8] As Dagmar Reese has shown, *Gymnasiastinnen* were most involved with BDM, as they had the social and cultural background and the free time to do so, and thereby reproduced Germany's traditional class structures. However, professional BDM leaders tended to come from lower social strata, for these women had fewer other options.[9] Young women of Beetz's background could afford a contrary streak, as witnessed in her negative evaluation. Beetz had more options available to her than simply becoming a professional BDM leader.

A career woman

Beetz had planned to train as a translator and she remained on track even when money became tight after her father's death. After fulfilling her *Pflichtjahr* (Duty Year) requirement, she enrolled in an Italian programme in Leipzig, finishing the accelerated course in August 1939.[10] She had planned to study French subsequently in Lausanne and had procured the required permits and currency. Thereafter, she expected to 'begin to work and take care of myself so that my mother should have to pay only for my brother's studies'.[11] Hildegard Beetz was anything but a damsel in distress, which was a position neither her parents nor the BDM had encouraged. Rather, she was a determined young woman who took her education seriously and was planning to embark on a career based on her specialized skills.

With the German invasion of Poland in September 1939, her plan to study in Switzerland fell through and heeding her mother's wish, she looked for employment in her hometown. The local *Arbeitsamt*, employment office, 'assigned [her] to SD-Abschnitt Weimar' (*Sicherheits Dienst* – that is Security Service). Sworn to secrecy, she worked as a mail clerk.[12] Beetz does not provide many details, but it is likely that she worked in the local branch of the domestic intelligence service.[13] She had, in effect, been directed towards a young woman's job; it was also a position for someone with less specialized knowledge. But then Weimar was presumably not a place in dire need of a 20-year-old woman fluent in English, French, and Italian. Unhappy with the atmosphere in the office and her position, Beetz took charge. She approached her boss, a certain *SS-Sturmbannführer* Hermann, informing him that she was 'good with languages and wanted to use them'. Beetz was soon transferred to the RSHA headquarters in Berlin, where she worked for Office VI, the political foreign intelligence service. She translated reports from Italian agents and was also in charge of reading Italian and Vatican newspapers, translating those articles that showed 'certain anti-German tendencies'.[14] Beetz's role in Berlin thus straddled the line between translation and analysis and is indicative of her linguistic and analytical abilities.

In June 1941, Beetz was posted to Rome as the secretary to Guido Zimmer, the Main Representative of Office VI, the political foreign intelligence service in the RSHA. Zimmer was supposed to untangle for Office VI the highly problematic intelligence situation in Rome but he failed spectacularly. Zimmer, along with Beetz, was soon recalled. Beetz returned to Rome with the new Main Representative, Helmut Looss, in June 1942. He was soon recalled as well, but Beetz stayed on, officially as a secretary to the police attaché at the German Embassy, Gestapo member *Obersturmbannführer* Herbert Kappler. In her *Lebenslauf*, Beetz made it clear that she deemed both Main Representatives ill-suited for their positions. She noted that she had warned Zimmer against the very blunder that led to his recall and stressed that Looss was 'simply not interested in the work and, therefore, let me do everything'. Even before Looss' return to Germany, then, Beetz's work went beyond the secretarial. And as no replacement for Looss was sent to Rome, Beetz commented: 'I worked alone until August 1943.'[15] Put differently, in 1943, Hildegard Beetz – ostensibly a secretary – functioned as Office VI's Main Representative in Rome. Figure 5.1 captures an image of Beetz in this period.

German historians of gender have coined the term *Handlungsräume* to describe scopes for action open to women in subaltern positions.[16] Beetz had them, used them, and did not apologize for them after the war. In Beetz's *Lebenslauf*, her professional pride, her annoyance with Zimmer and Looss, and her self-assuredness as someone intimately involved with intelligence-gathering efforts are all palpable. But are her accounts reliable? Beetz is likely to have given a somewhat guarded rendition of her early life and career up to the Ciano affair but the comparative frankness of her statements is noteworthy. She acknowledges, for example, both the appeal of the BDM and her commitment to its ideals, without hiding behind her youth. The negative evaluation she received during the 1937 leadership course, on the other hand, is not part of her original *Lebenslauf* but only mentioned in the later Addendum drawn up during her vetting process for employment with US intelligence in post-war Berlin. Beetz thus provides an intriguing glimpse into the normalcies of Nazi Germany, as experienced by a racially and socially privileged young woman. Her account also highlights her agency, her quest for a career, and her fiscal

Figure 5.1 Hildegard Beetz, winter 1943.
Reproduced courtesy of the copyright holder, Hilde Purwin.

responsibility as a daughter and sister. Most striking is her rendition of her exchange with *SS-Sturmbannführer* Hermann in Weimar. Unhappy with the office atmosphere, she had voiced her case on professional grounds, arguing that she was overqualified to sort mail – and she won it. What emerges from Beetz's own narrative is a modern young woman whose specialized skills moved her from provincial Weimar to the *Reichshauptstadt* Berlin to a dream posting in Rome.[17]

Beetz's US interrogators were somewhat perturbed by her candid rendition of events and used their assumptions about young women's roles in Nazi Germany to make sense of it. The Addendum to her *Lebenslauf* subtly reconfigures her narrative. It, for example, notes that there was no work requirement for women in 1939 but acknowledges Beetz's wish to earn a living; stresses that Beetz was 'assigned' to the SD without knowing anything about it; emphasizes her youth and lack of work experience; and intimates that *SS-Sturmbannführer* Hermann abused the 'oath' by not releasing her outright.[18] The Beetz of the Addendum appears much younger, much more fragile, and much less qualified than the Beetz depicted in her own words. In the rendition of her interrogators, much of Beetz's agency goes missing. Conversely, these assumptions about female roles in Nazi Germany also allowed for her interrogators to ignore what was right in front of them: the one person who knew most about Office VI and a fair amount about the Gestapo's day-to-day activities in Rome. There is no indication that she was ever asked about these issues in any detail.

Beetz and the Cianos

In August 1943, in the aftermath of the coup against Mussolini in July, all female personnel were recalled from Italy; gender overrode qualification. However, Beetz was soon assigned as a translator-hostess to former Italian Foreign Minister Ciano and his family who were under thinly veiled house arrest in southern Germany. Ciano, who was married to Mussolini's daughter Edda, had served as her father's foreign minister since 1936. He was one of the architects of the so-called Rome–Berlin Axis but, unlike his father-in-law, had been less inclined to involve Italy heavily in Germany's war. In February 1943, Ciano was dismissed from his position and, in July 1943, he voted to depose Mussolini. In the eyes of Mussolini, his supporters, and the Germans, Ciano had thus sided with the traitors. In the unstable situation after the ousting of *Il Duce*, Ciano feared arrest by the new Italian government and, after seeking the counsel of one of Himmler's men in Rome, Office VI arranged for the family's escape from the city.[19]

Office VI had little interest in Ciano personally but rather in his papers: records of political conversations; a collection labelled 'Germania'; and his personal-political diaries whose existence, tone, and some of its content, including damning material on Ribbentrop and snide remarks on Hitler, were well known.[20] Ciano saw these hidden papers – and his threat to publish them abroad or refrain from publication – as his bargaining tool and life insurance. As the publication of the diaries or of memoirs by Ciano abroad would have created an embarrassment, Hitler had, as Propaganda Minister Josef Goebbels noted in his diary, no intention of allowing Ciano to leave.[21] Office VI engaged in a different calculus. For years, it had attempted to remove Ribbentrop and to gain dominance over or swallow the *Auswärtige Amt*.[22] Ciano's diaries would be the needed ammunition, as Beetz put it after the war, 'to unseat Ribbentrop and put a candidate of their own – Schellenberg [the head of Office VI] was mentioned – into his place.'[23] As the Cianos' designated translator-hostess, Beetz held a central role in the scheme: she was to gain Ciano's confidence and learn about 'his views on the political affairs before, during, and after the fall of Mussolini'.[24] Beetz had become an intelligence operative.

Gender clearly played a role in her assignment. Her superiors must have seen her youth and looks as assets in the game afoot. Yet she was fluent also in Italian. In addition, it appears that Beetz's new husband facilitated her entry into Ciano's circle. In June 1943 she had married a German air force captain and member of the General Staff acquainted with Ciano.[25] Moreover, Beetz possessed what, by 1943, passed as a serious background in intelligence. She was in her fourth year with Office VI and had effectively run its Roman operations.

In October 1943, Ciano was transferred from Germany to prison in Verona in the new Italian Republic of Salò, headed – under German oversight – by his newly liberated father-in-law.[26] He was to stand trial for treason and the death penalty seemed likely. Ciano's transfer to Verona had been arranged by two of Ribbentrop's men active in the Republic of Salò and caught Office VI unawares, or so Beetz's post-war interrogations suggest. As the *Auswärtige Amt* and

Office VI were at cross-purposes when it came to Ciano, this development is unsurprising. Beetz, faced with her charge having been spirited off, took matters into her own hands. She flew to Berlin, met with her immediate superior, *SS-Sturmbannführer* Wilhelm Hoettl, and received new orders. She was to 'make contact with Ciano in prison and find out from him where he had hidden the papers'. Beetz travelled to Verona, presented her credentials to the local representative of the RSHA, Karl Harster, and began visiting Ciano in prison on 6 November. In the coming weeks, Beetz had virtually unrestricted access to Ciano, who was aware of her role – 'she is a spy, but she is mine' – but played coy with official visitors. Beetz provided Hoettl with detailed, if presumably not always complete, reports on her visits with Ciano.[27]

In her interrogations, Beetz claimed that the plan to have an SS/SD commando team spring Ciano from prison and spirit him to Switzerland in exchange for his diaries, commonly ascribed to Hoettl and others, largely originated with her and, to some extent, with Ciano. The idea of a diaries-for-life trade had certainly been in the air but, according to Beetz's statement, it was she who pushed it in the right places, moving an idea towards an actual plan. There was no German need to execute Ciano. He did not matter. His diaries did. This was particularly true of Office VI's wish to use them against Ribbentrop. On 4 December, Beetz met with Hoettl in Berlin to discuss her ideas; he asked her to put them in writing for the head of the RSHA Ernst Kaltenbrunner. This Beetz did.[28]

On 2 January 1944, Beetz met with Kaltenbrunner, Harster, and Hoettl in Innsbruck to discuss details. The four agreed on the following. One: Ciano was to disclose the location of the Italian Foreign Office materials as a sign of good faith. Two: Ciano was to be sprung from prison and brought to Switzerland with his family, accompanied by Beetz. Three: he would hand the diaries to Beetz. Four: he would receive money, for he had few assets short of the diaries. Kaltenbrunner did not sign the agreement but promised to adhere to it, even against Hitler's wish.[29] Beetz was playing with the proverbial 'Big Boys' who were, indeed, following her lead. Her plan was carefully thought out, carefully implemented, cognizant of her office's ultimate goals, and, if successful, would allow Beetz to kill two birds with one stone: save Ciano and put his diaries into the hand of her office.

On 3 January, Beetz met with Edda Ciano to inform her of the agreement and to deliver a secret letter from Ciano. Beetz subsequently retrieved the Italian Foreign Office documents or at least part of them.[30] A friend of Edda Ciano's hid another part; it remains unclear whether Beetz knew. Increasingly drawn into double-dealings, Beetz still fulfilled her tasks: she handed the documents to Harster, who had them flown to Berlin. Beetz had scored a tremendous success.[31] And then, things fell apart. Beetz's focus had been the task at hand: get Ciano's diaries. She was not a male, career SD official 'working towards the Führer', as Ian Kershaw has phrased it, and it was owing to that mentality that everything that had been planned, collapsed.[32] Recollections diverge but either Hitler came to know of the plan by a third party; was asked by either Himmler or Kaltenbrunner – or both – for approval and said no; or the SD men came to the conclusion that Hitler would not approve if he knew

and shelved the plan on their own. Kaltenbrunner's earlier bravado notwith-
standing, the plan was dropped. [33] For career-minded men, Hitler remained the
ultimate point of reference.

Beetz, whose focus had been on Ciano and his papers and not on Hitler's
approval, was blindsided by the developments. When Edda Ciano appeared in
Verona with the diaries as planned, Beetz prevented her from handing them
over, informed Edda Ciano that the deal was off and urged her to make a run
for Switzerland. Allan Dulles, the OSS Station Chief in Berne, likened Beetz's
decision to that of a double agent.[34] That oversimplifies it: even when she let
go of Edda Ciano and the diaries, Beetz did not completely undermine her
office. Rather, she left Edda Ciano with one more desperate play for her
husband's life; in subsequent days, Edda Ciano tried to blackmail her father, the
Duce, and the German authorities – Hitler as well as Harster in Verona – by
threatening the diaries' publication if her husband were executed.[35] In the end,
it did not change anything. The trial against Ciano and others commenced on
8 January; death sentences were handed down on 10 January; and, badgered
by German officials close to Ribbentrop, Mussolini decided against clemency.
The executions took place a day later. Beetz spent the night before Ciano's
execution, which she later described as the 'most terrible night of my life', in
prison at his side.[36]

There have always been suggestions that Ciano and Beetz had an affair, the
argument running along its own gendered logic, for only an intimate relationship could possibly explain her activities. Beetz always denied this, but few have
listened to the nuances in her statements. She noted, for example, that in
autumn 1943, she was a newlywed, much in love with her husband, and did not
fall in love with Ciano. Yet she also allowed that she felt something 'more
intense than simple sympathy, something that arose from my heart'. Years later,
she also added that she believed that Ciano had been betrayed by the Germans
and, noting that she 'was then a little naïve; [she] felt an obligation to repair
the wrong'. Eventually, she settled on trying to explain her situation by settling
on 'I loved him, certainly, but it is not true that I made love to him'. Edda
Ciano, for her part, allowed for the possibility that Beetz had been 'slightly in
love with Galeazzo' but also noted, maybe with an eye towards the alleged
affair: 'Frau Beetz was what she was, but she never betrayed me.'[37] Ultimately,
the argument that Beetz and Ciano must have had an affair mostly shows that
many have looked for Beetz's motivations in scurrilous places while ignoring
both Edda Ciano's comments and Beetz's own narration of her life.

In this entire scheme, which had little to do with foreign intelligence and a
lot to do with infighting among German agencies, Beetz was the only person
with her eyes on the alleged prize. If Office VI's goal was to depose Ribbentrop
by using the diaries against him, then letting Ciano go was the most efficient
way of going about it. Beetz followed this route with dogged determination.
However, her superiors had their careers in mind and were eagerly 'working
towards the Führer'. The Führer, in turn, supported Ribbentrop. Their wish to
dispose of Ribbentrop thus collided with their eagerness to please Hitler, creating a circle that could simply not be squared. Beetz neither shared nor was she
able to appreciate this predicament; as a woman working in a subaltern position,

and unlikely ever to move beyond it, 'working towards the Führer' was not part of her mindset. Thus, she found herself blindsided when her supervisors jettisoned a plan that made all the sense in the world. After the war Beetz claimed to have complained to Kaltenbrunner about his failure to live up to his earlier promises. The head of the RSHA, in return, subtly reminded Beetz of hierarchical realities and her gender: he sent her a bouquet of roses.[38]

Divided loyalties

The quest for the diaries did not end with Ciano's execution. In the next months, Beetz found herself on assignments in Switzerland, all of them related to Edda Ciano and the diaries. Beetz dealt with various, increasingly mutually exclusive, issues: to fulfil the demands of her office; assist Edda Ciano; and avoid charges of treason. Her activities grew increasingly frantic, and gender and gendered roles loomed large. Her gender made possible, for example, her quick deployment in Switzerland. Given the cover of a substitute secretary at the German consulate in Lugano, she received a Swiss visa and an eventual renewal without much trouble. She only ran into difficulties when she tried to renew the visa a third time.[39]

Her initial mandate was straightforward: first, she was to make contact with Edda Ciano and ensure that she would not make public 'the way the RSHA had allowed her husband's execution although he had kept his part of the bargain; second, she was to attempt to discover the hiding place of the remaining Ciano papers'. Unable to make personal contact with Edda Ciano, Beetz tried her best to keep her quiet. At one point Beetz drew up a letter to Edda Ciano that she claimed included her late husband's last words and thoughts. As Beetz's sympathetic US interrogators put it: 'it is plain that the thoughts—whether actual or not—were nicely calculated to keep Edda silent, as the RSHA desired.'[40] Beetz did not give up on her Office VI tasks.

At other points, Beetz attempted to assist Edda Ciano and those around her. When Höttl asked Beetz to embark on her new mission, she made it contingent on the release of a friend of Ciano's from a Gestapo prison, arguing that he would be of use when it came to making contact with Edda Ciano. She gained his release; he was smuggled into Switzerland where he was, however, promptly interned. As Beetz needed him to contact Edda Ciano, she tried to raise his bail among prominent Italians in the country. At a later point, she tried to arrange for a certain Lancelot de Garston, rumoured to be with the British Intelligence Service, to buy the diaries from Edda Ciano and to publish them. This, too, would have met the initial objective of Office VI to – 'smear Ribbentrop' – if not gain Hitler's praise, and help Edda Ciano's finances. De Garston refused.[41] Beetz had clearly not given up on being of use to the remaining Cianos either.

Beetz also experienced pressure. In spring 1944, a certain Pater Guisto Pancino, Edda Ciano's confessor, arrived in Switzerland. He had been sent by Mussolini, and he, too, was tasked to find out the diaries' whereabouts. Pancino was also on Office VI's payroll. Beetz grew increasingly concerned that he would learn about the roles she had played over the last few months. Fear of treason charges loomed large.[42] Around this time Beetz asked one of her Italian contacts, Susanna 'Suni' Agnelli, for poison; the chemistry student delivered. Ray Mosely reports that Agnelli asked Beetz why she did not simply stay in Switzerland, effectively defecting. Beetz responded that she had to go back for her husband's sake, 'fighting on the Russian front'.[43] Beetz's explanations had much to do with her relationships – she feared for her husband and her younger brother, and noted that she was her mother's main support. This shines an interesting light on gender and the female operative in danger: Beetz prized her responsibility as a wife over her safety and assumed, accurately, that her husband would be held responsible for her actions.

On the other hand, gendered assumptions saved her from harm. In late spring 1944, Pancino reported that Edda Ciano had the diaries with her in Switzerland and that Beetz had helped her escape to Switzerland. The SD Office in Verona subsequently put together a report for Kaltenbrunner. The head of the RSHA remained, however, Beetz's champion. He 'upheld Frau Beetz, considering that Pancino's report was motivated by personal jealousy against his competitor and by his desire to eliminate her as a German outsider'. Kaltenbrunner clearly could not believe that the pretty young secretary had taken the leadership of the RSHA, and him personally, for a ride. Beetz, for her part, 'dismissed Pancino's reports as unworthy of credence…'.[44] Beetz kept her cool and Kaltenbrunner believed the steadfast secretary, to whom he had given the princely sum of 10,000 marks for a job well done a few weeks earlier, over the Italian priest.[45]

Yet her brush with treason charges rattled Beetz; in its aftermath she made a show of 'finding' additional papers of Ciano's in Ramiola. She had presumably known about their whereabouts for months. And with that, Beetz had delivered to her office everything but Ciano's diaries.[46] These were the crown jewels of Ciano's papers, but the rest was not paltry either. Even when assisting both Cianos and while withholding crucial information from her office – she might have known the hiding places of various of Ciano's paper as early as autumn 1943 – Beetz was a tremendously effective operative. And she came on a secretary's pay.

By late summer 1944, the quest for the diaries petered out.[47] Beetz spent the remainder of the war in Germany, summarizing and translating the materials she had acquired and keeping copies of some materials for herself. These copies were her gift to her interrogators when US military intelligence came knocking in early summer of 1945. This would eventually launch her into her second career in intelligence and ultimately into her third in journalism.

Conclusion

Hildegard Beetz was clearly neither an innocent abroad nor a smitten secretary who became an accidental double agent for the love of a dead man. Rather, she was a smart and assertive woman with valuable professional skills, determined to make something out of herself. Nominally the secretary, she was a central player in Office VI's Roman operations in the early 1940s, while also living the dream of a foreign posting. Nazi Germany's New Order gave her opportunities and she made the best out of them. Similarly, her post-war interrogations show her as fundamental not only in the execution of the activities surrounding

Ciano and his diaries but also in their formulation. They also provide much detail about SD activities after Ciano's execution. Beetz's interrogations are, however, not simply a minor corrective to those of her male superiors. There is much reason to regard her testimony as more trustworthy and gender plays a central role.

Beetz's known and proven activities, her gender, assumptions about gender roles in Nazi Germany, and the gendered realities of the post-war period provided her with advantages during her interrogations. As a woman who officially had held a subaltern position and had helped Edda Ciano and the diaries reach Switzerland, she had little reason to worry about Allied inquiries. She was seen as having assisted the Allies and although she fell under the 'automatic arrest' category established by the Allies, she was on its outer margins. And while she would need post-war employment, especially with her husband in a Prisoner of War camp, she must have realized that her linguistic and secretarial skills – and not her background in espionage – would be her ticket. Unlike her male counterparts, she was not auditioning for a job in espionage and trying to put her best, and least truthful, foot forward. She could afford to tell much more than her male superiors. And tell she did, making the best out of a situation, again. Last but not least, her charmed US interrogators sanded off her statements' few remaining edges by making them conform to their understanding of gendered roles in Nazi Germany – and by not asking many questions that went beyond her role in the Ciano affair.

Gender and gender relations were central to Beetz's assignments. They defined her possibilities as a handler in Rome and as an operative in Verona and in Switzerland as well as her restrictions in those roles. Looking closely and evaluating her statements and those of others carefully, a woman of much greater agency, involvement, grit, and cunning than commonly acknowledged emerges. She used these traits to everybody's benefit: hers, her Office's, and the Cianos'. Thus, Beetz and gender relations need to be written into the story of the Ciano diaries, as she was in many ways the driving force behind developments. Interesting insights come to the fore with a focus on professional women in Nazi Germany. Where and how did they fill their positions differently from their male counterparts and superiors? In Beetz's case, she focused on the task at hand – separate Ciano from the diaries – and did not share her male superiors' obsession of 'working towards the Führer'. This made Beetz both extremely efficient on a small scale and fundamentally clueless on a grand scale.

The focus on women in subaltern positions of potential influence – secretaries, clerks, paper pushers, and the amorphous office girls – does provide valuable insights into the professional and personal experiences of theorized 'new Nazi women'. These modern, professional women who, seeing 'a professional opportunity and a liberating experience', as Wendy Lower has phrased it in the context of women involved in the crimes of the Holocaust, also formed the backbone of Germany's bureaucracy. And sometimes women did more than that. It becomes possible to gain an understanding of their lives and experiences and the benefits they could gain while serving the Nazi empire, experiences that they brought with them into the post-war lives. Last but not least, these women provide an alternative window into organizations, bureaucracies, and their day-to-day operations that are still shrouded in mystery. It is, after all, the secretary who runs the place and knows where the bodies are buried. Indeed, chances are that she was the only one who knew where to find the shovel in the first place.

Recommended reading

Cutler, R. W. (2009) 'Reminiscence. Three Careers, Three Names: Hildegard Beetz, Talented Spy', *International Journal of Intelligence and Counterintelligence*, vol. 22, no. 3, pp. 515–35.

Kohlhaas, E. (2015) 'Revision of Life/History. From National Socialist Co-Perpetrator to Expellee Official—Gertrud Slottke', in D. A. Messenger and K Paehler (eds), *A Nazi Past: Recasting German Identity in Postwar Europe* (Lexington: University of Kentucky Press), pp. 249–70.

Lower, W. (2013) *Hitler's Furies:. German Women in the Nazi Killing Fields* (Boston, MA: Houghton Mifflin Harcourt).

McGraw Smyth, H. (1975) *Secrets of the Fascist Era: How Uncle Sam Obtained Some of the Top-Level Documents of Mussolini's Period* (Carbondale: Southern Illinois University Press).

Mosely, R. (1999) *Mussolini's Shadow. The Double Life of Count Galeazzo Ciano* (New Haven, CT: Yale University Press).

Paehler, K. (2008/2009) 'Creating an Alternative Foreign Office: A Reassessment of Office VI of the Reich Main Security Office', *Journal of Intelligence History*, vol. 8, no. 2, pp. 27–42.

Paehler, K. (forthcoming) *The Third Reich's Intelligence Services: The Career of Walter Schellenberg* (New York: Cambridge University Press).

Notes

1. Appendix D to FR 75, SS Stubaf Dr. Klaus Huegel @ Dr. Hübner, Appendix D, Operations 'Felicitas' and 'Roderich,' 28 May 1946, NARA, RG 263, ZZ-16, Box 5, Beetz, Hildegard, vol. 3. (Hereafter 'Appendix D'.)
2. The files can be found at NARA, RG 263, ZZ-16 and ZZ-18; they also cover her later association with US intelligence entities and her career in journalism. This chapter is part of a larger project on Beetz in which I am engaged. On Beetz but with substantial issues: R. W. Cutler (2009) 'Reminiscence. Three Careers, Three Names: Hildegard Beetz, Talented Spy', *International Journal of Intelligence and Counterintelligence*, vol. 22, no. 3, pp. 515–35.
3. Compare: K. Paehler, *The Third Reich's Intelligence Service: The Career of Walter Schellenberg* (working title; forthcoming with Cambridge University Press), chapters 6 and 7. For a glimpse of other female RSHA staffers, for example: Politisches Archiv des Auswärtigen Amts (PAAA), Berlin, R 100803-100808 [Auslandsreisen/ Auslandsreisen des SD].
4. E. Harvey (2003) *Women and the Nazi East: Agents and Witnesses of Germanization* (New Haven, CT: Yale University Press); W. Lower (2013) *Hitler's Furies. German Women in the Nazi Killing Fields* (Boston, MA: Houghton Mifflin Harcourt); E. Kohlhaas (2015) 'Revision of Life/History: From National Socialist Co-Perpetrator to Expellee Official—Gertrud Slottke' in D. A. Messenger and K. Paehler (eds), *A Nazi Past: Recasting German Identity in Postwar Europe* (Lexington: The University of Kentucky Press), pp. 249–70.

5. See: A. Grossmann (1991) 'Feminist Debates about Women and National Socialism', *Gender & History*, vol. 3, no. 3, pp. 350–8.

6. Compare: G. Tsouvala,(2015) 'Women Members of the Gymnasium in the Roman East (*IG* IV 732)' in John Bodel and Nora Dimitrova (eds), *Ancient Documents and Their Context. First North American Congress of Greek and Latin Epigraphy (2011)* (Leiden/Boston: Brill), pp. 111–23.

7. Untitled Document, no date, NARA, RG 263, ZZ-16, Box 5, Beetz, Hildegard vol. 3. (Hereafter: Untitled Document.)

8. Addendum to *Lebenslauf* by H.B., 28 May 194[6], NARA, RG 263, ZZ-16, Box 5, Beetz, Hildegard vol. 3. (Hereafter: Addendum.) This document was compiled by US intelligence while Beetz was being vetted for work with them in spring 1946.

9. D. Reese (2006) *Growing Up Female in Nazi Germany* (Ann Arbor: The University of Michigan Press), chapter 3.

10. W. Schneider (2001) *Frauen unterm Hakenkreuz* (Hamburg: Hoffmann und Campe), pp. 67–8. From 1938 on, young women had to complete a year of farm or domestic service before entering the workforce. While there is a debate in the literature as to which women actually fulfilled this duty, anecdotal evidence suggests that most middle-class women regarded the *Pflichtjahr* als '*selbverständlich*: it went without saying'. See E. H. Tobin and J. Gibson (1995) 'The Meanings of Labor: East German Women's Work in the Transition from Nazism to Communism', *Central European History*, vol. 28, no. 3, pp. 307–11.

11. Untitled Document.

12. Untitled Document.

13. For a local study, see: C. Schreiber (2003) '"Eine verschworene Gemeinschaft." Regionale Verfolgungsnetzwerke des SD in Sachsen', in M. Wildt (ed.), *Nachrichtendienst, politische Elite, und Mordeinheit. Der Sicherheitsdienst des Reichsführers SS* (Hamburg: Hamburger Edition), pp. 57–85.

14. Untitled Document.

15. Untitled Document. On Italy more broadly: Paehler, *Intelligence Service*, chapter 6.

16. K. Heinsohn, B. Vogel, and U. Weckel (eds) (1997), *Zwischen Karriere und Verfolgung: Handlungsräume von Frauen im nationalsozialistischen Deutschland* (Frankfurt: Campus).

17. Compare: Lower, *Furies*, pp.10–14; 30.

18. Addendum.

19. R. Mosely (1999) *Mussolini's Shadow: The Double Life of Count Galeazzo Ciano* (New Haven, CT: Yale University Press), p.184; see also Paehler, *Intelligence Service*, chapter 7.

20. H. McGraw Smyth (1975) *Secrets of the Fascist Era. How Uncle Sam Obtained Some of the Top-Level Documents of Mussolini's Period* (Carbondale: Southern Illinois University Press), pp. 56; 68.

21. Quoted – and misdated by a year – in L. Charlesworth and M. Salter (2006) 'Ensuring the After-Life of the Ciano Diaries: Allen Dulles' Provision of Nuremberg Trial Evidence', *Intelligence and National Security*, vol. 21, no. 4 , p. 574, note 67. I thank Gerhard L. Weinberg for running down the reference to the Goebbels' notation for me. J. Goebbels, *Memoiren* Part II, Band 9, pp. 570–2.

22. On the long conflict see, Paehler, *Intelligence Service*, chapter 7.

23. RSHA/Death Ciano.

24. SCI Detachment Weimar, L.E. de Neufville, The RSHA and the Death of Count Ciano, Source: Interrogation of Frau Hildegard Beetz, 14 June 1945, NA, RG 263, Entry ZZ-18, Box 9, File: Beetz, Hildegard, Vol. 1, 2 of 2. (Hereafter: RSHA/

Death Ciano.) See also: Edda Ciano, *My Truth* (1977) as told to Albert Zarca, translated from the French by Eileen Finletter (New York: William Morrow and Company), p. 203.

25. RSHA/Death Ciano.

26. Plans for the family to move to a German-allied or German-friendly country, while leaving behind Ciano's papers to Office VI, had not come to pass; Edda Ciano subsequently left Germany. Her husband and children stayed behind. Moseley, *Shadow*, p. 192.

27. RSHA/Death Ciano; Appendix D; Moseley, *Shadow*, pp. 201–5. A number of Beetz's progress reports are found in her CIA file

28. RSHA/Death Ciano. Beetz to Hoettl, 27 December 1943, NARA, RG 263, ZZ-18, Box 9, Beetz, Hildegard, vol. 1, 1 of 2.

29. RSHA/Death Ciano. For a slightly different timeline, see: Moseley, *Shadow*, pp. 213–14.

30. As is customary in Italy, Edda kept her maiden name – her father's – after her marriage. Non-Italian literature, however, refers to her as Edda Ciano; I follow this custom.

31. RSHA/Death Ciano; Moseley, *Shadow*, pp. 214–15; Smyth, *Secrets*, pp. 37–9.

32. I. Kershaw (1999) '"Working Towards the Führer." Reflections on the Nature of the Hitler Dictatorship' in C. Leitz (ed.), *The Third Reich* (Oxford: Blackwell Publishers), pp. 249–52.

33. RSHA/Death Ciano; see also: Moseley, *Mussolini's Shadow*, p. 216; Smyth, *Secrets*, pp. 39–40; Ciano, *Truth*, p. 230. Headquarters 12th AG, SCI Detachment to Chief, CIB, G-2, 12th AG, Hildegard Beetz, nee Burckhardt, SD Executive and Agent, 18 June 1945, NARA, RG 263, Entry ZZ-16, Box 5, File: Beetz, Hildegard, Vol. 3. (Hereafter: Beetz/SD Executive/Agent.)

34. Moseley, *Shadow*, pp. 215–17; Ciano, *Truth*, p. 230; Smyth, *Secrets*, p. 42; RSHA/ Death Ciano; SCI Detachment Weimar, L.E. de Neufville to CO, SCI, Germany, The RSHA and Edda Ciano in Switzerland, Source: Interrogation of Frau Hildegard Burckhardt Beetz, 16 June 1945, NARA, RG 263, Entry ZZ-18, Box 9, File: Beetz, Hildegard, Vol. 1, 2 of 2 (Hereafter: RSHA/Switzerland); Beetz/SD Executive/Agent; Charlesworth and Salter reference a 29 July 1945 telegram in which Dulles calls Beetz 'our agent', intimating that she was such during the war already. Charlesworth/Salter, 'Ensuring', p. 576, note 89. The recently declassified CIA files give no indication of such an early – formal – association between Beetz and American intelligence.

35. RSHA/Death Ciano; Moseley, *Shadow*, pp. 218–22; Smyth, *Secrets*, p. 44.

36. RSHA/Death Ciano.

37. Moseley, *Shadow*, p. 205. Much of Moseley's account here is based in a 1990s piece in the Italian gossip paper *Gente*. It appears that Beetz spoke to *Gente* in exchange for keeping her post-war identities and concrete whereabouts secret. See also: Ciano, *Truth*, p. 205.

38. Beetz/SD Executive/Agent. This is one of the few instances when her US interrogators noted their doubts about her statements.

39. RSHA/Switzerland; Appendix D.

40. RSHA/ Switzerland; Beetz to E. Ciano, no date [English translation), NARA, RG 263, ZZ-16, Box 5, Beetz, Hildegard, vol. 1.

41. RSHA/Switzerland.

42. RSHA/Switzerland. Mussolini also used Pancino as an intermediary to send money to his daughter.

43. RSHA/Switzerland; Moseley, *Shadow*, p. 246.

44. Appendix D.
45. RSHA/Switzerland.
46. RSHA/Switzerland. On Beetz's successes in delivering the substantial part of the documents to her office, see: Smyth, *Secrets*, pp. 54–6.
47. Other plans as to how to get rid of Ribbentrop took centre stage. K. Paehler (2008/2009) 'Creating an Alternative Foreign Office: A Reassessment of Office VI of the Reich Main Security Office', *Journal of Intelligence History*, vol. 8, no. 2, 27–42.

6

Regulating Marriage: Gender, the Public Service, the Second World War, and Reconstruction in Britain and Canada

Helen Glew

From the point of view of many officials in charge of the Civil Service in Britain and Canada, there was no doubt that the marriage bar – which prevented married women from holding permanent jobs and which was lifted in both countries for much of the war – would be re-imposed at the cessation of hostilities. Both nations had imposed such bars on female public service employees, with varying degrees of severity, throughout the 1920s and 1930s and in some cases had only reluctantly lifted these restrictions once it was clear that the exigencies of war would demand it. Discussions began towards the end of the war about the timing and precise practicalities of presumed re-implementation. However, it became clear relatively quickly that the future of this policy would be considerably more complicated in Britain especially. In particular it was the circumstances of reconstruction, rather than the war, which dictated changes in Britain, and in both countries the desire to re-implement the marriage bar in the Civil Service and other sections of public employment was based on the supposition that wartime changes had been temporary, merely expedient, and ultimately superficial to the real pattern of society.

Thus, the war, married women's contributions to war work, and the insights gained by employers and employees during this time were almost entirely absent from discussions about the future of the marriage bar and a resumption of the status quo ante was assumed. This chapter therefore focuses particularly on the later years of the war and the early part of the post-war period. It analyses the discussions amongst public service officials and the ways in which perceptions about married women were framed, drawing also on staff association responses, debates in Parliament, and, for Britain, evidence from Mass Observation (MO).

The marriage bar had been a dominant part of women's interwar work culture in public service employment, many types of white-collar employment, and a number of blue-collar occupations in Britain, Canada, and elsewhere. It presumed heterosexuality and normalized gendered expectations of women. It reinforced, and was reinforced by, a wider culture in both nations that expected married women to be provided for by breadwinner husbands and therefore to be out of the workforce.[1] In addition, there were restrictions in Britain on married women's rights to claim unemployment benefits in the depression of the 1930s, which made clear the presumed status of married women in relation to the workplace.[2] Thus, the marriage bar and the idea that married women should not work were pervasive and all women who entered paid work and embarked on what they considered a career did so knowing that they would, effectively, have to choose between their work and marriage in all occupations where a marriage bar existed and even in those where more informal expectations abounded.

A number of women's groups contested the existence of the bar in public service employment (and in other spheres of employment more generally) in both Canada and Britain. Other organizations, including some women's organizations and trades unions, were more ambivalent, arguing that in a hierarchy of workers' needs, men (who were always assumed in these scenarios to be breadwinners for whole families) and single women supporting themselves should be given preference for jobs.[3] The ambivalence about the marriage bar amongst pressure groups on both sides of the Atlantic was surely a minor contributory factor in its persistence in the interwar years. There were some small changes such as in the British Civil Service after 1934, when the exemption from the marriage bar clause became easier to operate for certain roles, and an important victory in 1935 when the marriage bar was abolished for women teachers working for the London County Council (LCC), the UK's largest local authority.[4] For the most part, however, the marriage bar remained dominant in women's working and life experiences in the interwar years. Despite this, it is not necessarily evident that the marriage bar encapsulated the views of the public in Britain by the end of the period. Gallup polls in 1938 and 1939 asked male and female interviewees about the marriage bar. The question for 1938, categorized under the heading 'Equality for Women', asked 'Do you think a woman should be barred from any form of employment simply because she is married?', elicited a 'no' from 69 per cent of respondents. More specific questions were asked in 1939 under the heading 'Working Married Women', one asking whether respondents 'favoured' teachers and professional women workers resigning on marriage, to which 48 per cent responded 'yes' and 46 per cent 'no' (the remaining 6 per cent answered that they had no opinion). The second question asked whether women doing unskilled work should resign on marriage and the answers this time were slightly clearer: 56 per cent said yes and 39 per cent said no (with 5 per cent professing no opinion).[5] Thus, the poll results show ambivalence or indecision towards married women's paid work rather than opposition, and also suggest that the public could identify the issue as one of equal rights if they were prompted to do so. The fact that the questions were asked in the first place also suggests the topicality of the issue at the end of the 1930s.

In 1930s' Canada, the mood was rather different. The depression of the 1930s took longer to lift than in Britain and so marriage bar restrictions were reinforced throughout the 1930s at federal, provincial, and city levels. In Toronto, a marriage bar was strictly enforced which prevented anyone holding a city job whose spouse had any form of employment at all. Although the regulation was worded in a gender-neutral way, it is clear from discussions amongst city staff, and indeed in instances of implementation, that it was expected that the husband would be in paid work and the wife would not. Reported cases of infractions were investigated. There were also, in Canada as a whole, fewer signs of contestation of marriage bars in the 1930s and, as Margaret Hobbs has shown, the National Council of Women of Canada and the Federation of Business and Professional Women were not always outspoken or unqualified in their opposition to the marriage bar.[6]

The outbreak of war and married women's employment

When war broke out, the context and rhetoric surrounding women's work changed quite significantly. Single women were urged to undertake work for the war effort, and married women in both Britain and Canada were encouraged to volunteer. At the same time, the message was also couched in terms of married women joining the workforce 'for the duration' and temporarily taking on either 'women's' or 'men's' jobs in a labour market which was still, even in the professions and white-collar office jobs, segmented by gender.[7] Thus, in public service employment, some women took on conventionally female white-collar roles, such as typing, shorthand, and clerical work, whereas the need for extra or replacement labour in wartime bureaucracy and administration meant that women also took on work hitherto generally carried out by men or in which smaller numbers of women were usually employed.

At the same time as the emphasis on work 'for the duration', there were painstaking debates in Britain within the Women's Consultative Committee (set up by the Ministry of Labour to provide guidance on women's war work), various other sections of the Ministry of Labour and in Parliament about whether to conscript married women or even whether they should be mobilized for war work. Such discussions reveal the extent to which public figures were concerned to protect the gendered norm of the married housewife who was not perceived as being in employment or needing to work.[8] The work of Ruth Roach Pierson also highlights the ambivalences in the debate about the use of married women's labour in Canada.[9] These debates occurred alongside a broader discourse, particularly in Britain, which took in fashion, makeup, and other aspects of daily life, about women remaining feminine and the home front remaining a constant from the interwar years to which troops abroad would want to return.[10] The thrust of this wartime discourse was an articulation of women's traditional roles, and wartime changes were seen as an aberration.

Therefore, while the dominant message was for women to join the war effort, the government as an employer was keen, in both Canada and Britain, to underline that this was not going to constitute a sea change in married women's employment rights. In 1940, the National Association of Women Civil Servants (NAWCS) – long-time staunch feminist campaigners in the British Civil Service – wrote to the Treasury, who effectively controlled the Civil Service, asking for a service-wide lifting of the marriage bar. Although temporary employment of married women was well underway at this point to support the war effort, and the NAWCS' long-time opposition to the marriage bar was well known, their point was directly related to the working conditions for married women. The salary for temporary staff was lower than that for permanent staff and so women who married during the war, but were retained because of their expertise, now had less favourable working conditions whilst rendering important service to the nation.[11] In the LCC there were particular fears about the ramifications of a wartime lifting of the marriage bar, despite the fact that the Council had lifted the bar in the mid-1930s for its women teachers. The bar was lifted gradually throughout 1940 in individual departments, particularly those connected with public health and welfare which needed senior staff, and often specifically female staff. By March 1941 a blanket decision was introduced removing the marriage bar for all grades into which women were normally appointed.[12] This decision took some considerable time to agree to, however, seemingly because of fears about what would happen when the war was over.[13] In Canada, the federal government suspended the marriage bar and from the middle of the war was encouraging women civil servants, now married, to return to their erstwhile roles.[14] As the vestiges of the depression disappeared and the need for labour continued, city legislators in Toronto, for example, finally dropped the draconian ruling preventing spouses of city employees from working at all in 1942, though it was made clear that this was to facilitate war work only.[15] The discrepancies between the state-as-government and the state-as-employer were, then, not insignificant here. On the one hand the government needed to encourage as much female labour as possible, especially in Britain, but on the other hand its own departments were often reluctant to change employment regulations for their own female employees for fear of setting a precedent.

Envisioning the end of the war: debates about the future of married women as government employees

Amongst all of the reconstruction debates, there was much discussion about whether married women would want to continue in employment after the war. These discussions were sometimes based on social survey data, though more often on particular interpretations of this data or on suppositions or generalizations about what married women were assumed to want. As Denise Riley's work suggests, conclusions drawn from the surveys in Britain were less than clearcut.[16] In Canada, as Jennifer A. Stephen has shown, the government Committee on the Postwar Problems of Women argued that it was illiberal and unfair to exclude women from the workforce but at the same time placed a stronger emphasis on recognizing women's – and, by implication, married women's – situation and contributions in the home.[17] There was, as emphasized by both Stephen and Ruth Roach Pierson, much debate about the need to encourage women into either the home or specifically women's work so that preference could be given to ex-servicemen for government vacancies and training.[18] Thus, in Canada, there was a real impetus among public employers to re-enact restrictions on married women's employment, which was backed up by mid-war legislation guaranteeing returning veterans, often defined as male, their previous jobs.[19] In October 1945, the President of the Canadian Telegraph Association declared that married women who had been employed during the war had six months to leave and that a similar ruling would apply to all single women who subsequently married.[20] The instruction, however, was couched in terms of the need to ensure that there was adequate replacement staff, which fits with Veronica Beechey's characterization of married women as a reserve army of labour.[21] In December 1945, it was agreed that married women should be dispensed with before men and single women when reductions of staffing were made.[22] Any dismissal of married women on grounds other than the need to reduce the workforce on the Canadian railways was contested by car-men in the union in 1946 who argued that men and women should have equal rights regardless of marital status.[23] However, implicit in this was the fact that they still saw married women as the first group to be released when worker layoffs became necessary.

In the Canadian federal Civil Service, dismissals of married women – or 'releases' as they tended to be termed, perhaps to try to add a positive spin – had begun in 1944, creating particular anxiety amongst women who did not have sufficient other income. In 1945, a federal service circular asked departments to identify which married women could be dismissed in order to accommodate veterans who qualified for employment in government service.[24] The National Council of Women of Canada sent a letter arguing against the re-application of the marriage bar and utilized the rhetoric of war experience directly, asserting that 'the contribution of Canadian women during this war has been of outstanding and inestimable value to our country and should preclude the return of pre-war discriminatory policies'.[25] For the Council, the war was a moment which signalled a break with the past. However, by 1947, it was ruled that married women not reliant on their own incomes to support their families would be the fifth group of individuals whose services would be dispensed with, after 'persons whose services are not fully satisfactory'; 'persons ... ready to accept retirement'; part-time, casual employees; and those already above the normal retirement age.[26] It is not clear, however, how women's dependency on their income from their jobs was determined. Although this began as an 'order of dismissal' there was also by this time a re-imposed marriage bar affecting new recruits and single women already on the staff, which operated until 1955. However, exceptions were made: for work considered wholly women's, such as typing and shorthand, there was no marriage bar restriction because of the need to maintain the workforce at requisite levels.[27] Thus, marital status was used as a means to determine women's right to state employment, but this could be overridden during labour shortages.

The case study of Vancouver also signals the ambiguity and diversity of positions surrounding the marriage bar in the post-war years. The Vancouver School Board had received legal advice in 1944 to the effect that requiring women teachers to resign when they married amounted to discrimination, and so it allowed women who married whilst in employment to continue and re-employed married women on temporary contracts initially.[28] Although this change may have had benefits for staffing levels and staff wages during the war, it seems likely that the legal advice regarding the discriminatory nature of the marriage bar would have held regardless of the war. This, then, was a change to the marriage bar brought about for reasons other than the war, in contrast to many of the adjustments made in this period. Vancouver's social work department, on the other hand, continued its pre-war insistence on married women being employed on temporary contracts only for a number of years to come.[29]

The question of whether to re-impose the marriage bar in the post-war British civil service was first seriously discussed in 1943. The discussion was initiated by Miss (later Dame) Evelyn Sharp, a high-ranking woman civil servant, though it is clear that Sharp was raising it in the normal course of her duties – or at the request of a superior – rather than it being something she raised as a question of principle on behalf of fellow women civil servants. Interestingly, the memorandum circulated to departments asked for views on the marriage bar but the options listed for consideration were whether the bar should be re-imposed or whether it should be modified; there was no prompting that it might be done away with altogether and indeed the spur to the whole question seems to have been to revisit a discussion from the 1930s regarding whether it would be possible to exempt the higher grades of the service from the marriage bar while retaining it for the women who did the more routine work.[30] Thus, the intention seems to have been to consider how the marriage bar could be made more effective from the employer's point of view so as to allow more high-ranking women with years of training to remain in the service after they married. The replies to the 1943 memorandum were many and various. A number of officials were of the opinion that no more modifications to the bar could be made without bending it to breaking point; it either had to remain as it had been, or be abolished altogether.[31] For the most part, the experience of increased married women's work during the war was ignored or treated as anomalous in the replies, suggesting it was considered something not to be taken into consideration when re-evaluating the marriage bar as a whole. One notable exception to this was in a memorandum by Archibald Carter, who was at the Department of Customs and Excise. In this memorandum, which was distinct from the official response of his department, he recognized that contemplating the end of the marriage bar represented a reassessment of 'social habits'. He argued that

> During the war married women (though not, of course, those actually looking after young children) have been required, even if they did not wish to leave their responsibilities in their homes, to work for the State. It seems to me that it would be an extraordinarily difficult feat of political reasoning to justify an attitude that, once the war emergency had passed, involved saying to married women – "You

shan't now work directly for the State even if you want to". It is true that war necessitates many measures that are intrinsically undesirable; but having accepted, indeed compelled, married women's services during the war, it seems to be untenable to take away from them the right of free choice to adopt Government Service as a career after the war.[32]

For Carter, then, the war constituted a potential watershed. His recognition that government rhetoric would be undergoing a highly visible shift was significant, but even Carter, in his otherwise fairly liberal-minded memorandum, left room for the possibility that single men and women might prove the better recruits because married women would be supposedly distracted by domestic affairs. A running theme throughout the other replies was that marriage was a full-time career for a woman but not for a man and thus, traditional assumptions about gender prevailed.[33] Carter was the only respondent to think critically about this assumption – even if he ultimately upheld women as the primary housekeepers and carers for children – and his views as a whole were interesting because he thought about the issue of married women's paid work much more broadly than just considering the immediate context and previous conventions of the Civil Service. As Evelyn Sharp noticed when she reflected on the responses some time later, Carter's liberal views were surprising.[34] There is little we can know about his marriage given the lack of surviving sources but it is perhaps worth noting that in 1923 Carter had married Gertrude Painter, a novelist and playwright who continued to publish under her own name throughout their marriage. His life with a woman who pursued a career of her own may have had an impact on his perspective.[35]

Whilst most heads of Civil Service departments and other officials pondered futures with a potentially renewed or adapted marriage bar, it was clear at the same time that the public mood might be changing. In January 1944, MO asked its directive respondents 'What are your feelings about the possibility of married women going out to work after the war?'. The wording of the question made it clear that it was a reconstruction question but it was given 'priority B' status so not all 268 correspondents for that month answered it. Although a minority of respondents had staunch views against married women's paid work, many emphasized the right of married women to make their own decision, often with the caveat that if the wife was also a mother then childcare and child-rearing should be the priority above paid work.[36]

The abolition of the marriage bar for women teachers in 1944 clearly also gave Civil Service officials pause for thought.[37] The end to the marriage bar in teaching was accepted in Parliament by the Minister of Education in March 1944 after a debate which noted the severe shortage of teachers (especially in view of the intended provisions of the Education Bill currently before Parliament), the benefits married women teachers were perceived to provide to classroom experiences and, to a lesser degree, the issue of fairness.[38] Although this does not appear to have been articulated fully in Civil Service circles, the abolition of the bar in teaching but its continuance in the Civil Service would have meant that the state as an employer would have been supporting contradictory policies for two large groups of female employees.

By early 1945 the Civil Service marriage bar was being discussed in Parliament. Sir John Anderson, Chancellor of the Exchequer, told Thelma Cazalet-Keir MP in January that the intention was to re-implement the marriage bar.[39] At the same time the National Whitley Council, the employer–employee negotiation machinery in the Civil Service, was tasked with appointing a subcommittee to discuss the question further. One side of this committee was composed of heads of Civil Service departments or their representatives and the other by representatives from the numerous staff associations and unions throughout the service. The marriage bar was an issue on which the group of staff associations had not been able to reach consensus in the interwar years; the women-only associations, which were largely not represented on the National Whitley Council, were staunchly against the marriage bar, but other associations, with majority male memberships, had been either in support of the dismissal of married women or had an executive whose views were ambiguous at best.[40]

However, by November 1945, one high-ranking civil servant told another that 'the whole question of the marriage bar rests on a pretty fine balance' and it is clear that there was a wider diversity of opinion amongst high-ranking Civil Service officials now than at any point in previous decades, when they had tended to be in favour of the marriage bar.[41] It is also clear that perceptions of public opinion swinging towards married women working held weight.[42] However, the Committee was unable to make a recommendation, in part because the staff associations were still divided on the question of the marriage bar, despite a noticeable shift amongst some staff associations since the previous decade or so in favour of abolition.[43]

Although there was some mention of married women's wartime work in the Civil Service in the course of the committee's deliberations, suggestions that such efforts be taken into account were dismissed as irrelevant and sentimental by Civil Service officials, accompanied by the underlying assumption that dispelling such sentiment would thereby lead to an 'objective' and 'correct' decision.[44] Notably, the war was mentioned in the report substantively only to argue that it had probably not provided a real reflection of married women's abilities: war conditions meant that shopping and other domestic duties were more complex than they would be in peacetime; women had sometimes needed leave at short notice; and they had not necessarily received thorough training because of the pressures of war.[45] This was, at least, some recognition of the extra burdens women had faced in wartime. It was also noted that a woman in peacetime who chose to continue her career after marriage would have found a means to balance her work with domestic commitments,[46] a point which does not seem to have been considered in previous peacetime discussions of the marriage bar.

On receipt of the Whitley Committee's report, Hugh Dalton, Chancellor of the Exchequer, originally intended to remove the marriage bar but he changed his mind. The reason for this reversal seems to have been that he was not sure how well any 'safeguard' against potential inefficiency on the part of married women could be expected to work.[47] In the end, the final removal of the bar in October 1946 came from the instructions of the Cabinet, where it was argued that it would appear inconsistent if the government was urging industry to keep married women in order to deal with the labour shortage but at the same time ruled that the Civil Service should keep its marriage bar.[48] The decision, then, was determined first by the government's need to appear consistent to industry and then, more widely, by continuing labour needs in the years after the war. The actual experiences of, and services offered by, women in wartime – or indeed the potential of what they could offer in peacetime – had very little, if anything, to do with the decision, just as in Canada. The fact that the war was more or less disregarded in the debates, and officials reverted to arguments used over the longer twentieth century, shows that it was viewed as an aberration with little of value to inform policymakers.

The LCC seems to have been motivated differently – despite its mid-war fears – when it decided in 1945 to remove the marriage bar from the remaining staff to which it had applied in 1939. It would have been aware that Civil Service discussions were taking place but the Council issued its decision a year or so earlier. Eric Salmon, the Clerk of the Council, argued in a memo that 'the question seems to me to require consideration from a rather broader angle' and asserted that the marriage bar forced women to resign 'with loss to the Council as well as to themselves, or [to] deny themselves of what is, for most people, a normal way of life'.[49] Picking up on rhetoric that was similar to that used by interwar feminist groups, Salmon argued that if a woman had proved herself capable of Council work, then the Council had no right to deprive her of a job.[50] Salmon was known for his progressive views on equal pay for women, too, and although it is difficult to argue that these views, which were ratified by Council decision, were the result of generational shifts or even experience of the war, it is clear that the influence of specific personalities was also important in determining the future of the marriage bar in certain instances.[51] Salmon and Archibald Carter had similar views, but Salmon was in a role in which he had a far greater influence over decisions and Council procedures.

The abolition of the marriage bar in the British Civil Service and the LCC, as well as in teaching, encouraged the abolition of the marriage bar – where it still existed – in other elements of public employment. The contrast between the situations in Britain and Canada in this respect was highlighted in the late 1940s when a woman working for the Canadian National Railways (CNR) in London was allowed to continue working after marriage, even though she was technically subject to the CNR marriage bar. However, she was also valuable to the company because of her experience and the marriage bar was lamented – as it often was in other similar instances – as an unfortunate impediment. Her case was argued, through a series of letters, partly on the grounds that it was now common practice in Britain, her place of residence, for women to stay on at work after marriage if they so wished.[52]

Conclusion: Marriage bar debates, the Second World War, and gender

The debates discussed in this chapter constitute another example of the ways in which traditional gender roles and attitudes to married women in the workplace were underscored by the war. The conventional perceptions of women's roles with regard to motherhood and running a household remained so fundamental that they formed a central, implicit point in discussions of the marriage bar. The end of the war provided an opportunity to ask a question about the future of the public service marriage bar. In Canada, discussions were essentially framed in terms of the practicalities of removing excess labour from the workforce; in Britain the question became about whether the pre-war marriage bar could be modified to enable easier retention of professional-grade women who wished to work. Abolition in Britain was not the original intention of Civil Service officials or of two successive Chancellors and the removal of the bar was largely in spite of, and not because of, the collective mood and opinions of Civil Service officials. The needs of the labour market, and the political difficulties of appearing to contradict these, permitted married women's presence in the public service. In Canada, the long-standing labour hierarchy, which held that married women were not ordinarily part of the workforce, prevailed with the need to recalibrate the workforce and provide jobs for returning servicemen. Thus, the policies in each nation were rather different in the 1940s and into the 1950s. However, despite this contrast, there was far less of a gap in attitudes to the working wife both within the workplace and in wider society in both nations.[53]

Recommended reading

Glew, H. (2016) *Gender, Rhetoric and Regulation: Women's Work in the Civil Service and the London County Council, 1900–55* (Manchester: Manchester University Press).

Hobbs, M. (1996) 'Equality and Difference: Feminism and the Defence of Women Workers during the Great Depression' in A. Prentice, P. Bourne, G. C. Brandt, B. Light, W. Mitchinson, and N. Black (eds) *Canadian Women: A Reader* (Toronto: Harcourt Brace & Co.).

Roach Pierson, R. (1986) *'They're Still Women After All': The Second World War and Canadian Womanhood* (Toronto: McClelland & Stewart).

Rose, S. O. (2003) *Which People's War? National Identity and Citizenship in Britain, 1939–1945* (Oxford: Oxford University Press).

Stephen, J. A. (2007) *Pick One Intelligent Girl: Employability, Domesticity and Gendering Canada's Welfare State, 1939–1947* (Toronto: University of Toronto Press).

Summerfield, P. (1984) *Women Workers in the Second World War* (London: Croom Helm).

Notes

1. For discussions of the marriage bar in interwar employment see H. Glew (2016) *Gender, Rhetoric and Regulation: Women's Work in the Civil Service and London County Council, 1900–55* (Manchester: Manchester University Press), pp. 178–235; A. Oram (1996), *Women Teachers and Feminist Politics* (Manchester: Manchester University Press); M. Hobbs (1996), 'Equality and Difference: Feminism and the Defence of Women Workers during the Great Depression' in A. Prentice, P. Bourne, G. C. Brandt, B. Light, W. Mitchinson, and N. Black (eds) *Canadian Women: A Reader* (Toronto: Harcourt Brace & Co.); V. Strong-Boag (1993) *The New Day Recalled: Lives of Girls and Women in English Canada, 1919–1939*, 2nd edition (Mississauga: Copp Clark Pitman), p. 45; N. Morgan (1988) *The Equality Game: Women in the Federal Public Service, 1908–1987* (Ottawa: Canadian Advisory Council on the Status of Women), pp. 7–8.

2. For a discussion of a comparable discourse in Canada see R. Roach Pierson (1990) 'Gender and the Unemployment Insurance Debates in Canada, 1934–1940', *Labour/Le Travail*, 25, 77–103 and N. Christie (2000) *Engendering the State: Family, Work and Welfare in Canada*, (Toronto: Toronto University Press), esp. pp. 196–199

3. Hobbs (1996); P. M. Graves (1994), *Labour Women*, (Cambridge: Cambridge University Press), pp.189–191; Strong-Boag (1993), p. 45.

4. Glew, *Gender, Rhetoric and Regulation*, pp.178–215; Oram, *Women Teachers and Feminist Politics*, pp. 170–1.

5. G. Gallup (ed.) (1976), *The Gallup International Opinion Polls, 1937–1964*, p. 12; p. 18.

6. Hobbs (1996), p. 215; pp. 220–4.

7. For a discussion of this in Canada see, in particular, R. Roach Pierson (1986) *'They're Still Women after All': The Second World War and Canadian Womanhood* (Toronto: McClelland & Stewart), pp. 22–48, and for Britain, see, among others, P. Summerfield (1984) *Women Workers in the Second World War* (London: Croom Helm); S.O. Rose (2003) *Which People's War? National Identity and Citizenship in Britain, 1939–1945* (Oxford: Oxford University Press).

8. See, for example, *Hansard*, National Service Bill, HC Deb 9 December 1941 vol. 376, col.1434; Cols.1451–2; Summerfield (1984), pp. 29–51; pp. 61–2. H. Smith (1984) 'The Womanpower Problem', *The Historical Journal*, vol. 27, no. 4, pp. 933–4.

9. Roach Pierson, *'They're Still Women after All'*, pp. 22–61.

10. C. Gledhill and G. Swanson (eds) (1996) *Nationalising Femininity* (Manchester: Manchester University Press); Rose (2003), *Which People's War?*, pp. 133–5.

11. The National Archives (TNA), T162/822, 3754/03, letter from Mary Morris, Acting General Secretary of the NAWCS to the Treasury, 16 July 1940 and reply, 2 November 1940. For a discussion of the NAWCS's opposition to the marriage bar, see Glew, *Gender, Rhetoric and Regulation*, pp. 178–215.

12. London Metropolitan Archives (LMA), LCC CL/ESTAB/1/3, record of Civil Defence and General Purposes Committee, 3 September 1939.

13. See, in particular, LMA, LCC/CL/ESTAB/1/3, memorandum to the Clerk of the Council, 22 January 1941.

14. Roach Pierson, *'They're Still Women after All'*, p. 29. For a discussion of married women's re-employment in the federal Civil Service in the press, see *Ottawa Citizen*, 15 July 1942, p. 12.

15. City of Toronto Archives, Fonds 200, Series 1234 File 297, 'Employees, Employment of wives, 1930–52', Extract from Report No.10 of the Board of Control, 4 May 1942.

16. D. Riley (1981) '"The Free Mothers": Pronatalism and Working Women in Industry at the End of the Last War in Britain', *History Workshop Journal*, vol. 11 (Spring), pp. 58–118, here pp. 79–86.

17. J. A. Stephen (2007) *Pick One Intelligent Girl: Employability, Domesticity and Gendering Canada's Welfare State, 1939–1947* (Toronto: University of Toronto Press), p. 105.

18. Stephen, *Pick One Intelligent Girl*, p. 174, 177; Roach Pierson, *'They're Still Women after All'*, pp. 76–94.

19. Roach Pierson, *'They're Still Women after All'*, p. 82.

20. Library and Archives Canada, (LAC); RG 30 13105, 4805-X2 Employment of Married Women, Memorandum Covering the Employment of Married Women. 'Commercial Telegraphers' Agreement, [October 1945].

21. LAC, RG 30 13105, 4805-X2 Employment of Married Women, letter dated 4 October 1945 from R C Vaughan, President of the Canadian National Railways.

22. LAC, RG 30 13105, 4805-X2 Employment of Married Women, 'Synopsis of Correspondence in connection with the employment or non-employment of married female employees' [n.d.].

23. RG 30 13105, 4805-X2 Employment of Married Women, Employment of Married Women, Memorandum Covering the Employment of Married Women. 'Commercial Telegraphers' Agreement'.

24. LAC, Civil Service Commission, RG 32 vol 379, circular 1945-13.

25. LAC, RG 32 vol 376, file 25-4, letter to Mr C. H. Bland, Chairman of the Civil Service Commission, Ottawa, from Mrs G. D. Finlayson, Corresponding Secretary of the National Council of Women of Canada, 5 December 1945.

26. LAC, Civil Service Commission RG 32 vol 379, circular 1947-7.

27. K. Archibald (1970) *Sex and the Public Service* (Ottawa: Queen's Printer), p. 17; Morgan (1988) *The Equality Game*, pp. 7–8.

28. City of Vancouver Archives [CoV Archives], RG 8 Series D-6, vol. 16, file 18, 59-A-1, folder 18, 'Report to the Personnel Committee re Status of Married Women employed as temporary teachers', 7 February 1955, p. 1.

29. CoV Archives, S20, Social Services Department, Box 82-A-6 folder 4.

30. TNA, T162/822, circular from Miss E. A. Sharp of the Treasury to Establishment Officers, 16 August 1943. For more on the interwar debates about removing the marriage bar for the higher grades but not the lower grades, see Glew, *Gender, Rhetoric and Regulation*, pp. 196–7.

31. T162/822, letter from Ministry of War Transport, 19 August 1943; letter from the Ministry of Health, 30 August 1943; letter to Miss Sharp from W. E. Rhydderch at HM Customs and Excise, 30 August 1943.

32. T162/822, letter from Archibald Carter, 30 August 1943.

33. T162/822, responses from various departments.

34. T162/822, memorandum from Evelyn Sharp to Wilson Smith, 17 February 1945.

35. For a biography of Archibald Carter see 'Obituary', *The Times*, 12 November 1958, p. 13. For a brief biography of Gertrude Painter/Lady Gertrude Maud Carter, see the entry for her papers on the Archives Wales website: http://www.archiveswales.org.uk/anw/get_collection.php?inst_id=1&coll_id=781&expand, date accessed 25 August 2015.

36. *Mass Observation Online*, directive for January 1944, Adam Matthew Digital Publications, accessed August 2015.

37. T162/822, letter from A. Overton to Treasury [?], 8 July [1944]; Minutes of National Whitley Committee on the Marriage Bar, 19 November 1945.

38. *Hansard*, CLAUSE 23.—(Appointment and dismissal of teachers in county schools and in auxiliary schools), HC Deb 10 March 1944, vol 397 cc2368-95.

39. *Hansard*, Civil Service (Women Recruits) HC Deb 16 January 1945 vol 407 c54W.

40. Glew, *Gender, Rhetoric and Regulation*, pp. 178–215.

41. T162/822, 3754/03/02, excerpt from letter from Dorothy C. L. Hackett to E. J. Mares at the Ministry of Production, 3 November 1945.

42. T162/822, 3754/03/02, circular from Miss E. A. Sharp of the Treasury to Establishment Officers, 16 August 1943; letter from J. R. C. Helmore [?] at the Establishment Department of the Board of Trade, 28 September 1943; memorandum of all-party deputation on the removal of the marriage bar, 9 March 1945.

43. *Marriage Bar in the Civil Service*, Report of the Civil Service National Whitley Council Committee, (London: HMSO, 1946), paras. 32–8; para. 48.

44. *Marriage Bar in the Civil Service,* para. 26.

45. *Marriage Bar in the Civil Service,* paras. 23–4.

46. *Marriage Bar in the Civil Service,* para. 24.

47. T162/822, memo between E. E. Bridges and Hugh Dalton, 14 April [1946]; 'Note for Mr John Freeman's Adjournment – 25th July', 23 July 1946; memorandum by Hugh Dalton, 17 August 1946.

48. TNA, CAB 128/6/18, Cabinet Conclusions, 9 September 1946, pp.16–17. See also Smith (1984) p. 943.

49. LMA, LCC/CL/ESTAB/1/4, Employment of Married Women, memorandum by Sir Eric Salmon, 5 July 1945.

50. LCC/CL/ESTAB/1/4, memorandum by Sir Eric Salmon, 5 July 1945.

51. For a discussion of Salmon's views on equal pay, see Glew, *Gender, Rhetoric and Regulation,* p. 151.

52. LAC, Canadian Telegraphs and Railways, RG 30 13105 4805-X2 Employment of Married Women, letter from Jas A. Thom to Mr Alistair Fraser, Vice President, Montreal, QC, 16 October 1950.

53. This chapter is drawn from a larger project by the author on married women's right to work in Britain and Canada, c.1870–1960.

Part 3
The Meeting of Military and Civilian Identities

7

'The saddest symptom of our time': Bigamy cases in Vienna after the Second World War

Helen Steele

In 1948 the newspaper *Wiener Montag* published an article on bigamy, declaring it 'the saddest symptom of our time'. Reporting on the near-weekly appearance of such cases in court, bigamy was described as a 'tragedy of the postwar period'. The article continued to quote a lawyer who declared, 'For the "normal" bigamy case, destruction of marriage by the war is almost always the reason.'[1] This chapter will investigate how the legacy of the Second World War can be identified in cases of bigamy heard in Vienna's Civil Court. The focus is how the legacy was used to excuse behaviour and how gendered expectations for men and women were challenged during this era. If the war was to blame for destroying marriages, what set of factors meant acts of bigamy occurred, rather than divorce? Bigamy cases often took years to come to light and the subsequent trials and appeals lasted many more, meaning that the conventional periodization for studies of the Second World War and the post-war period in Austria would unnecessarily truncate discussion. This chapter will examine the legacy of war marriages but also the experiences of waiting, missing, and an absence that, for many, did not end.

The research for this chapter focuses on cases of bigamy where men were the accused, but the evidence allows consideration of the expectations and pressures of relationships and status for both men and women in post-war Austrian society. The cases were all heard at the *Landesgericht für Strafsachen* and relate to the charge §206 of the criminal law (*Strafgesetz*): '... to commit the crime of double marriage of a married person who undertakes a marriage with another person.'[2] This is the model which all of the cases fit, despite the circumstances being highly varied. The cases began in 1946 and all span several years at least – from initial arrest to witness testimonies, transcripts of the main proceedings, (the *Hauptverhandlungsprotokoll*) and verdicts (*Urteil*). A number of cases did not come to trial, but the evidence contained in the files is still important, exposing the procedures and limitations of the legal system.[3] The system therefore, reflects the developments, circumstances, and opinions of the post-war years. The reported sentences were generally between six months to one year of a severe prison sentence or the accused was convicted to a conditional sentence.[4] In the files examined, the maximum punishment was five years' imprisonment.

Bigamy cases have received little attention in discussions of post-war marriage relations. Secondary literature concerning relationships in this era has previously focused on women's involvement with Allied soldiers or men's struggle as veterans to adapt to post-war life. In one of the few discussions of bigamy in post-war Germany, Richard Bessel comments on the 'particularly attractive propositions for fraudsters: clergy and nobility'.[5] The tendency to focus on the fantastical was also a contemporary habit. Austrian newspapers were full of reports of men posing as nobility, as doctors, and as detectives, all usually deliberate 'marriage swindlers' with an exploitative and commercial aim. 'Baron Sprockhoff' turned out to have fabricated his identity,[6] while another swindler found his victims by placing an advert as follows: 'Returnee, poor, no family, seeks suitable woman.'[7] In this case, there were three women involved and the swindler was sentenced to two years in prison. His advert deliberately played on the sympathies of women and it should be noted that a common theme in the swindler's story is both an emphasis on the susceptibility and vulnerability of women, desperate for attention, and also on the exploitation of the sympathy towards veterans. The bigamy cases examined for this chapter do not cover such sensational stories. Although a tendency to the fantastical can be seen in some, reinvention did not need to be so elaborate. The professional swindlers made the best news stories, but one Austrian lawyer commented in 1948 that many more cases of bigamy occurred through misunderstanding or exploitation of the upheaval in the post-war period.[8] This opinion is supported by the evidence found in the case files.

The first spate of newspaper reports on bigamy cases came in 1949–1950 as statistics for convictions were revealed. Bigamy cases were held up in the press as examples of the unique madness of the times, demonstrating 'the turmoil and confusion caused by the last war'.[9] There was an inherent weariness at the continued consequences of the war, still causing 'family dramas and personal conflicts' well into the early 1950s.[10] Chris Grover and Keith Soothill see a wider agenda for the reporting of such stories in the press beyond simply the criminal offence of bigamy or the 'titillation' of the story. They argue that 'by focusing upon wider socio-economic issues, the press reporting of bigamy can be placed within discursive frameworks constructing the "problems" of "family breakdown"'.[11] Grover and Soothill are referring to legal cases of bigamy heard in British courts during the early 1990s, but their analysis seems pertinent when applied to post-war Austria, where the subsequent reporting of cases in the press can be seen within a framework of contemporary discussion about the legacy of the war, morals, and the family.

The dominant discourse of the late 1940s was concerned first with the effect of the Second World War on morals, and, second, on how to reconstruct the family – the family being regarded as the key indicator of a post-war return to 'normality'. This was seen as the last bastion of morality and a marker in terms of recovery, and the reconstruction of the family was promoted as a private and public goal of the Austrian people.[12] Maria Mesner and Johanna Gehmacher identify the role played by tradition and both political and economic factors in the reinstatement of the family ideal and the return to peacetime gender norms. The societal ideal of the family was seen as a convergence of very different influences from Catholic, social democratic, and German national ideas, albeit expressed in different ways.[13] The family was – or was intended to be – the dominant life form, a model of hegemony, and a counterpoint to the shattered, the estranged, and the depraved. Opinions on this topic were embodied in the parliamentary discussions of a reform of the marriage law which took place during the post-war decade, as well as reports in contemporary newspapers which allowed all sides to articulate what values should be embodied by a successful marriage and family.[14] Before the *Anschluss* in 1938, Austrian marriage and family law had been based on the Civil Code (1811) which followed a hierarchical gender model and placed the man as head of the family and household.[15] After 1938 the German marriage law brought the secular 'civil marriage' which made it easier to get divorced and to remarry. In the post-war period, bigamy cases were held up as examples of a perceived wider decline in morals, showing an explicit disregard for participating in the reconstruction of the family. Yet, paradoxically, bigamists demonstrated a commitment to the institution of marriage, what Beverley Schwartzberg has termed a 'high regard for and value of marriage'.[16] Men and women (re)married despite the law not allowing them to do so. They were honouring the institution of marriage, rather than intending to damage it. Therefore discussion of bigamy cases in contemporary reports does occupy a peculiar space: those responsible were not condemned in the same way as the couples of all ages who were turning their back on the convention and cohabiting instead.[17]

Gendered expectations

The bigamy cases examined for this chapter allow us to consider the expectations and preconceptions of gender roles in the post-war era.

Heimkehrer

All of the bigamy cases discussed below involved former soldiers as the perpetrators. The expected narrative of the post-war period was that these men would return home, the German term *Heimkehrer* meaning 'homecomer' or 'repatriate'. That they were returning defeated meant that feelings of worthlessness were endemic amongst the returnees who were trying not to see their whole military service as a waste of time.[18] Individual feats of heroism and personal courage were not necessarily able to be accommodated under Allied victory and occupation. There may have been no admission of guilt but this contributed to the gulf between military experience and life as a civilian. Mesner and Gehmacher acknowledge a sense of humiliation and a feeling of indignity experienced by the returnees.[19] In the absence of a heroic welcome, what space was there in the Second Republic for the veterans?[20]

The expectation under Austrian marriage law was that husbands and fathers would resume their role as head of the household. But the men were returning from the war, damaged by it, and confused, injured, or defined by the experience. Siegfried Mattl and Karl Stuhlpfarrer describe how many of the returnees had lost their identity and were 'searching for themselves as "men"'.[21] They had to reconcile their 'official' identity with their previous social position and this was not easy. 'Out of the security of military discipline and coercive power, the returnees found themselves in a daily life of chaos and spontaneity.'[22] They were also trying to negotiate a reinstatement of their authority over their female partners and relatives and their children. It is argued by Mattl and Stuhlpfarrer that this search took place in a sphere of powerlessness and impotency. This reorientation was taking place under the weight of an idealized notion of return, fuelled by what Hornung describes as 'sentimentalised newspaper reports relaying "Welcome Home" scenarios'.[23] The experience of reintegration could be made more difficult by the shortages of food and living conditions, but also numerous social and psychological factors: pressure and expectations within families, nerves destroyed by combat experience, and anxiety over financial matters.[24] However, the bigamists did not even try to reclaim their space or position; they created a new space instead. The expectation that the man would return to his household and to a clearly defined gender role of provider is discredited and undermined by many of the testimonies given in bigamy cases. They avoided the 'reorganization' of the existing relationship because they started again. Karl K. had lost contact with his wife after being posted from Königsberg to Italy in November 1944.[25] He told the court: 'I heard no more from my wife and assumed that she would be transported by ship to Denmark.' He made enquiries to the authorities in Königsberg after the war but this did not result in any contact. After April 1946, Karl K. gave up: 'Since I received no message from my wife, I assumed that she was no longer alive.' Four months later, he remarried, recording his status at the time of marriage as 'single'. If he believed his wife was dead, it is curious that he did not present himself as 'widowed'. Frau K. revealed she had 'a little baby daughter, 13 months old' and that she had tried to track down her husband. She wrote: 'I searched for you five times through the Red Cross. This terrible war has brought so much grief.' There is a noticeable contrast between Karl K.'s efforts to find his wife and her own. This case demonstrates the difficulties of finding people in the immediate post-war period, even through official channels. There were surely numerous cases similar to this where leads or old addresses returned no information and whereabouts became unknown. This was especially the case if people were not registered with any authorities. How long could or should a search continue? The actions of Karl's wife conform to the ideal of the 'waiting woman' which will be discussed below. This pattern of the wife waiting in limbo and the man moving on recurs in many of these cases. Karl K. was sentenced to six months' imprisonment, covering the convictions for both bigamy and falsification of documents – in the latter case, his wage book with the name of his new wife. Karl K.'s defence rested on his belief that his first wife was dead. This was not accepted by the court, who declared: 'The claim of the accused that he only heard from his wife for the first time again *after* his second marriage is inconsequential if one considers that he had received no official message of the death of his first wife.'[26]

The significance that an official declaration of death could have in bigamy trials is also demonstrated by the case of Franz R.[27] His conviction for bigamy rested solely on the whereabouts of his first wife, Marie O. Her death would have negated the bigamy charge, but any trace of her still living meant Franz R. remained guilty. The case file included telegrams between Austrian and German police reporting attempts to find Marie O. Parish records were consulted and former neighbours interviewed. Marie O. was finally located in a resettlement convoy (*Umsiedlertransport*) which had left Vienna for Germany in February 1946. This was enough evidence to convict Franz R. and sentence him to six months' detention.[28] Despite Franz R. having two children with Marie O., his concern was only for his second wife, Elisabeth S. He declared: 'I confess my guilt. I only did it out of love for my current wife.'[29] Once again, defaming the first wife seemed to be a key part of the defence. Franz R. raised questions about Marie O's character and declared, 'I could not live with her at all … we did not live together, that is how bad our marriage had become.'[30]

Both Franz R. and Karl K. left first wives with children. There is no discernible difference in the bigamy cases between the ease with which bigamists left a wife, or a wife and children, and children are seldom mentioned in the defence statement. As shown above the confirmation of a first wife being alive was enough to convict a bigamist. However, the appearance of the bigamist could also have a profound effect on the fortunes of the first family, with regard to income generated by a military pension or aid received for dependants of the missing. While some cases of bigamy were due to people remarrying under the assumption they had been widowed, genuine cases of people believed dead (*Totgeglaubte*) were rare, yet it was frequently used as a defence in the courts. Such cases were being heard while the difficulties of official declarations of death were discussed in the newspapers and being processed by the city administration. The former soldiers who had not yet returned home were part of a much wider landscape of lost and forgotten people. This included those missing since the war years: civilians involved in air raids, those interrogated by the Gestapo, and some who had spent the war in hiding due to fear of persecution. Contemporary newspapers appealed to such people to make contact to confirm their existence to avoid a 'declaration of death' being made against them.[31] At the end of 1946 it was estimated that 17,000 such declarations had been claimed at the *Landesgericht für Zivilrechtssachen* (Regional Court for Civil Law) in Vienna.[32] While the authorities had hoped to impose an end point for registering queries, this was compromised by the delayed return of the prisoners of war. This uncertainty made the decision very difficult given that once someone was declared dead, they no longer existed according to the law. Significantly for cases of bigamy, remarriage after a false official declaration of death contravened specific rules of the marriage law.[33]

The 'waiting woman'

Elizabeth Heineman discusses the 'fluidity' of marital status in this era and how the close links to personal identity could lead to new difficulties for the woman.[34] The status of the first wife, determined by the court to be alive, now shifted both financially and in terms of categorization (widow, waiting woman, wife). The 'waiting woman' is one of two key images of women in the post-war era.[35] Both images are linked to the reconstruction of physical life (the women of the rubble) and of emotional life. Both provided lenses through which women's experiences were discussed, and an expectation against which women were measured, particularly regarding 'appropriate' behaviour. One case, reported widely in the Austrian newspapers, concerned Johann V. who was declared officially missing when the war ended but reappeared in 1952.[36] Visiting the cemetery in Vienna with his new wife, Johann V. found his first wife tending his mother's grave. The detail of the first wife tending her mother-in-law's grave was repeatedly used in the news reports as a reflection of her good character and demonstrated the devotion she still had to her husband. She was still waiting for him, seven years on, and epitomized the 'eternally waiting' woman so far into the post-war decade.

Conceptualizing the woman as Penelope to the returning Odysseus was the most common post-war discourse for married couples and one explored fully by Ela Hornung's study of a single married couple in post-war Austria.[37] Mesner and Gehmacher vividly describe the 'mass of waiting women' at the train stations in Vienna, waiting for their men returning from war or from prisoner of war camps, or desperately searching for colleagues who might have news of the missing. This is an active application of the concept, but the more passive version was within the walls of the home. Women were expected to wait, patiently, and be there if and when their husband returned. Hornung found that: 'In psychological and medical discourse during the postwar years the ideal of the loyal, patiently waiting, passive, motherly and caring woman was propagated; such women would make the men healthy again.'[38] But this ideal relied on the men returning at some point, and the absence coming to an end. In many cases men were absent for longer periods after 1945 than during the war, usually due to imprisonment in prisoner of war camps. While the Western Allies returned all prisoners of war to Austria by 1948, the question of the missing was drawn out by the staggered release of lists of prisoners by Russian authorities. The waiting and absence had become the norm for women and can be construed as continuity between the two eras.[39]

There is a discernible gulf in the court files of bigamy cases between the expectation that women would simply wait for their husband and the reality of the vulnerable limbo in which they found themselves. Heinrich A. remarried after he believed his first wife to have been killed by an air attack in Brandenberg.[40] He received information in September 1945 that she was still alive. In her letters to her mother-in-law, used as evidence in court, Heinrich's first wife conveyed a desire for resolution after years of waiting for his return. She wrote: 'I cannot continue living with this uncertainty. If he will not come to us then I'll have to say (to her daughter) Papa doesn't want us, he will leave us alone and never come back to us.'[41] This was written in April 1946, and she still had had no direct contact with her husband. She knew he was alive, but she was still waiting. Such testimonies reveal the strain and grief caused by waiting. Waiting was usually done with the expectation that the situation would be resolved; it depended on hope and was based on confronting the void that stretched ahead with memories of the past. This echoes narratives used by women writing letters to their husbands at the front.[42] For the original wives of bigamists, the waiting proved to be futile and under false circumstances. The conclusion to the waiting should have been a return or an official declaration of death. Rather than returning to their pre-war life the bigamists had instead started a new life and a new family, avoiding the necessity of rebuilding and reconstructing. While it is clear from studies such as Hornung's sources that the reality of the eventual return often fell short of expectations on both sides, nevertheless some form of 'return', even if just purely physical, was usually experienced.[43]

Mattl and Stulhpfarrer argue that a 'collective phenomenon of 'suspicion'' pervaded social life after 1945.[44] Their discussion focuses on sexual uncertainty and accusations of unfaithfulness, coupled with the loss of identity that the returnees felt. The ideal of women waiting in the home, ready for her husband to return, did not match the reality in the case of Karl L.[45] He married his first wife at the start of 1943 before returning to his conscripted post in the Wehrmacht. He returned home unexpectedly during 1944. In his defence statement he said: 'I arrived in Vienna at 5pm and my wife was not at home. When she still had not returned at midnight I had the growing suspicion that she was not adhering to marital fidelity.'[46] Karl had used his time waiting to ask questions of her neighbours and heard from them that she was frequenting pubs with a foreign man. By 1944 there were just under 300,000 foreign workers in the wider Vienna region from over eleven different countries, two thirds of whom were male.[47] Many were volunteers from neighbouring allied countries, as well as those from recently occupied lands. While contact between the local population and foreign workers was regulated, much depended on the nationality of the labourer and the status of their country. The imagined misbehaviour of Karl L.'s wife with this 'foreign man' makes up a substantial part of his defence statement for committing bigamy. His wife's implied behaviour fits the common fear during the war and the post-war years that women would not wait or remain faithful. By suggesting that his wife was with a 'foreigner', Karl L's defence fitted into contemporary debates about women throwing themselves at the Allied soldiers occupying the country. However, it also echoed earlier fears that such relationships 'struck at the core of National Socialist racial proscriptions'.[48] The Nazi ideal was for women to fulfil their role as mothers, committed to the development of a 'pure' German family, at the very least symbolizing the *Volk* and the nation in their behaviour. Women were expected to uphold the virtue of the home front, while the soldiers fought on the military front. Behaviour which contradicted orders and expectations could easily unsettle this balance, particularly if the woman was married and was suspected of adultery. As Vandana Joshi argues: 'The much-propagated figure of the unfaithful and debauched soldier's wife was forever present like a ghost at the front haunting the soldiers.'[49]

When considering the preconceptions regarding gender roles in this period, the 'waiting woman' is key to our understanding of the statuses available to women. It can be seen to act as a barometer in the press for discussion of what constituted acceptable behaviour for such women. In the bigamy cases it was an understood norm that the bigamist had disregarded, denying their Penelope the resolution and ending for which they had been waiting.

One newspaper article on a female bigamist, the case of Herta P., aids our understanding of the options available to the 'waiting women', particularly on the issue of how long one should wait.[50] Herta P. married in 1942 and shortly afterwards her husband, a soldier, was declared missing at Stalingrad. He did not return after the war ended, but nor was he confirmed as dead. By 1948 she married again, declining to mention her first marriage. In 1953 it was reported that she had turned herself in to the police when she realized the consequences of her actions. With no confirmation of her first husband being dead, she was guilty of bigamy. Her case falls into the 'tragic' post-war situation described by Mattl whereby 'women who, after years of waiting hoping for news from their missing men, gave up hope and started a new relationship'.[51]

The legacy of the war

The post-war years had seen a steady increase in divorce rates, with 1948 as the peak year for Vienna and Austria. A third of all cases were attributed to marriages conducted after 1945, but the impact of the war remained the most common reason cited in the tendency for divorce for couples married before 1945.[52] Attributing blame to the war can be seen in almost all of the defences in the bigamy cases examined for this chapter. In this respect, the defendants' arguments in the bigamy cases were in line with contemporary debates about the fallibility of war marriages, and possibly directly influenced by them. For example, the *Arbeiter Zeitung* named 'nerves weakened through difficult experiences, long separation, a third person' as all playing a role in destroying marriages.[53] At least three court cases concerned second marriages taking place between 1939 and 1945. In three cases both marriages of the bigamists took place within the period of the war.[54] Some marriages conducted during the Second World War were often characteristically impromptu, perhaps based on only a few weeks of having known someone or conducted during a brief period of leave from the barracks. These marriages barely had time to get started before conscription or postings made long separations inevitable. Often no actual 'home' had been set up and the couple had next to no experience of living with each other and establishing a domestic routine. From the cases examined it is hard to say if this was a strong pattern or, when making comparisons to cases with pre-1939 first marriages, that only such 'young' marriages were vulnerable to bigamy. However, it is important to recognize these specific cases as having perhaps more pressure placed on them. A new dynamic was added to the 'family' which had not even been established properly, particularly if it was revealed that children had been born during the father's absence. For some bigamists the 'magical war romance' was not destroyed by the harsh reality of the post-war years because they had already moved on to a second marriage.

The court testimonies of the bigamists cite issues of distance, confusion, and suspicion as a defence. These factors are all equally applicable to the breakdown of wartime marriages, but these cases reveal a justification for the actions of the bigamist or an excuse, based on the legacy of the war. The confusion of the post-war administration, and the fluidity and speed with which borders and nationalities changed for some people meant that in some defences the line between feigned and actual ignorance of the law was possibly a fine one. Josef C. claimed that he could not be prosecuted for his second marriage, which took place during his posting in Berlin, because he was 'abroad' at the time. Since both of his marriages were conducted while Austria was part of Germany (1943 and early 1945 respectively), this defence did not stand.[55] Heinrich A. argued that all marriages between Austrians and Germans during the war were no longer valid, therefore he was not guilty of bigamy. This, too, was not accepted as a convincing defence.[56] The change in borders did mean that some bigamists escaped prosecution. There were at least two cases of bigamy involving foreign workers based in Vienna which came to a dead end when the defendants evaded prosecution by returning to their home country in refugee transports.[57] However, although the chaos of the war aided the ability to commit bigamy, it was possibly also the downfall of many as camps and refugee transports returned people to where they belonged. It was important for veterans to retain or reclaim their rights as an Austrian citizen. Returnees had to register at their arrival station to be properly processed and then to be eligible for medical care. They were tested to see if they were eligible for further financial support.[58] The eventual return of these men is one of the main reasons that cases of bigamy were uncovered: the bigamist returned to Vienna and his chance or deliberate encounters revealed the situation.

The case of Rudolf S. demonstrated how the circumstances of the war and difficulties in communication could be appropriated. At first glance the returnee Rudolf S. had suffered a devastating loss.[59] Two telegrams reached him in March 1945 to announce the death of his parents, his wife Kamilla, and his child after an air raid in Vienna. Rudolf S. duly changed his status to 'widowed' in his wage book (*Soldbuch*) and in the discharge papers he received from the American prisoner of war camp. He married Elsbeth S. in September 1945. Only a few days later, Rudolf S. returned to Vienna and discovered his family and wife were actually alive and well. The prosecution in the bigamy case dismissed the telegrams as 'fairy tales' and accused Rudolf S. of deliberately fabricating a story and marrying under false pretences. He initially assured the court that he had had no reason to want to leave his wife and her death was the only reason he had remarried. However, he later admitted that there had been some difficulties in his relationship: 'I had lived well with my wife up until my last holiday ... the later period of my first marriage left a great deal to be desired.'[60] Kamilla concurred with the statement that his last period of leave was a turning point in their marriage. She said: 'Since his last holiday the defendant (Rudolf S.) no longer wrote to me ... we were already estranged.' Kamilla was bombed out on 13 February 1945 and this was followed a few weeks later by the death of her youngest child.[61] She told the court: 'After the second time of being bombed out no-one looked after me.' But she did not blame the war for contributing to the difficulties between her and her husband: 'After my second pregnancy quarrels began ... we did not have our own flat ... there were disagreements between us, he did not care for the children but only for sport.'[62]

However, Rudolf *did* blame the events of the war and argued in his defence that it prevented contact with his relatives and wife in Vienna and, through confusion and circumstance, led to a misunderstanding.[63] Kamilla had twice been bombed out and temporarily buried under rubble, therefore the court declared it was 'at least possible that the defendant was actually notified of the death of his wife through a department or official of the NSDAP in the mistaken opinion that Kamilla S. and her family had died in an air attack'.[64] The jury were also reminded that the postal connection during the months of February and March was impeded by repeated air attacks. The war was used to both support and contradict Rudolf's argument, but evidence is also presented from personal conflicts and both husband and wife apportion some blame. Difficulties in communication could have caused him to believe he had been widowed and the same could have allowed him to fabricate a story and avoid verifying it. Rudolf S. was finally acquitted of bigamy owing to sufficient doubt that he had deliberately falsified his documents.[65]

The testimonies of the Viennese bigamists reveal the apparent ease with which one could forget the past and move into new lives. The dislocation from their civilian life had often begun with a physical relocation. Whether enlisting or being conscripted, many men found themselves at a distance from their home. Some may not have found themselves that far away initially, but often simply not being in the same city presented an opportunity to distance themselves from family commitments and begin a new life. However, the key space for reinvention and distance came during 1945 when the chaotic conditions 'created opportunities for forging papers and establishing new identities'.[66] The war enabled some men to alter their identity as a husband and father, and present themselves as single or widowed and able to marry. New identities were constructed in prisoner of war camps; amendments were made in the wage books of married men to present themselves to the authorities as 'single' or 'widowed'; and documents that existed could be falsified, or may not have existed at all. Bessel concludes that: 'These opportunities might have been deliberate, or they might have been based on tragic misunderstanding.'[67]

'War-related dislocation' can be seen as a common motif of bigamy cases that came to light in the post-war era.[68] While the dislocation was normally linked to a change of place, it is worth mentioning one example, where the bigamist's defence rested on a change in mental health. Karl U. did not try to feign ignorance, he stated at his trial: 'It isn't clear to me why I married for the second time. I blame it all on my frame of mind.'[69] This frame of mind, Karl U. argued, had been impacted by his experience serving in the Wehrmacht and his time in an American prisoner of war camp. The testimonies from both wives supported this defence. His first wife described how his nerves were 'completely shot' when he returned home wounded during the war and that she felt he was 'emotionally disturbed'. His second wife described him as 'mentally abnormal'. The evidence file for this case included a 29-page report from a doctor for nervous diseases on the 'Mental Health of Karl U'. The court took into account his 'depression and fear' but still found him fully responsible for his actions and gave him a three-month sentence and a two-year probation.[70]

Conclusion

A discussion of bigamy is a vital component of the narratives of the post-war era in Austria, and in particular, to analyses of the institution of marriage and the legacy of the war. It is contradictory, in that bigamy could fit within the discourse on the loss of morals and the destruction of the family that the newspapers bewailed, but then the very act also showed an acknowledgement of the value of and the need for marriage. The idea that there was some form of 'return to normality' in the later occupation years is disrupted by this thread of activity running parallel in the courts. The defences given by the bigamists and examined in this chapter all return to the impact of the war: the idea that extraordinary times had resulted in extraordinary actions. Appeals for clemency were able to rest on the 'special circumstances of 1945' and the frequently invoked 'events of the war and the confusion'. Naming bigamy as the 'saddest symptom' of this era encapsulates a deep-seated dismay and unhappy acceptance that the legacy of the Second World War continued to disrupt Austrian lives and was the root cause of many problems in society throughout the post-war decade.

Recommended Reading

Bandhauer-Schöffmann, I. and E. Hornung (1990) 'Trümmerfrauen- ein kurzes Heldinnenleben' in A. Graf (ed.), *Zur Politik des Weiblichen: Frauenmacht und – ohnmacht. Beiträge zur Innenwelt und Außenwelt* (Vienna: Verlag für Gesellschaftskritik), pp. 93–120.

Freund, F. and B. Perz (2000) 'Zwangsarbeit von zivilen AusländerInnen, Kriegsgefangenen, KZ-Häftlingen und ungarischen Juden in Österreich' in E. Tálos, E. Hanisch, W. Neugebauer, and R. Sieder (eds), *NS Herrschaft in Österreich. Ein Handbuch* (Vienna: öbv & htp) pp. 644 –95.

Gehmacher, J. and M. Mesner (2007) *Land der Söhne. Geschlechterverhaltnisse in der Zweiten Republik* (Innsbruck: Studien Verlag).

Heineman, E. D. (1999) *What Difference Does a Husband Make? Women and Marital Status in Nazi and Postwar Germany* (Berkeley: University of California Press).

Hinteregger, M. (2001) 'The Austrian Matrimonial Law – A Patchwork Pattern of History', *European Journal of Law Reform*, vol. 3, pp. 203–19.

Kundrus, B. (2005) 'Forbidden Company: Romantic Relationships between Germans and Foreigners, 1939 –1945' in D. Herzog (ed.), *Sexuality and German Fascism* (New York and Oxford: Berghahn Books), pp. 201–22.

Mattl, S. (1985) 'Frauen in Österreich nach 1945' in R. G. Ardelt, W. J. A. Huber, and A. Staudinger (eds) *Unterdrückung und Emanzipation: Festschrift für Erika Weinzierl* (Vienna: Geyer), pp. 101–26.

Notes

1. 'Zerreißung der ehelichen Gemeinschaften durch den Krieg ist fast immer die Ursache', *Wiener Montag*, 18 October 1948.
2. Item 17, 7790/46, 2.3.4.A11/ WStLA.
3. Three different types of marriage dissolution were available: nullity, annulment, and divorce. Three impediments existed for marriage: close relationship, adoption, and

bigamy (Para. 8). A marriage could only be dissolved by death or court decree. See: I. Seidl-Hohenveldern (1950) 'Austrian Decisions on Private International Law, 1945–1950', *The International Law Quarterly*, vol. 3, no. 4, pp. 487–502. The original files of the court proceedings are held at the Wiener Stadt und Landesarchiv (WStLA).

4. *Arbeiter Zeitung*, 4 January 1950.
5. R. Bessel (2009) *Germany 1945: From War to Peace* (London: Simon & Schuster), pp. 272–3.
6. *Wiener Zeitung*, 4 May 1950.
7. *Wiener Zeitung*, 25 April 1951.
8. *Wiener Montag*, 18 October 1948.
9. 'Totgeglaubter Mann am Friedhof gefunden', *Der Abend*, 5 November 1952.
10. 'Totgeglaubter Mann', *Der Abend*, 5 November 1952.
11. C. Grover and K. Soothill (1999) 'Bigamy: Neither Love nor Marriage, but a Threat to the Nation?', *The Sociological Review*, vol. 47, no. 2, pp. 332–4, 340.
12. J. Gehmacher and M. Mesner (2007) *Land der Söhne. Geschlechterverhaltnisse in der Zweiten Republik* (Innsbruck: Studien Verlag), p. 56.
13. Gehmacher and Mesner, p. 57.
14. Gehmacher and Mesner, pp. 60–1.
15. S. Mattl and K. Stuhlpfarrer (1988) 'Abwehr und Inszenierung im Labryinth der Zweiten Republik' in E. Talos et.al. *NS-Herrschaft in Österreich 1938–1945* (Vienna: Verlag für Gesellschaftskritik), pp. 601–24.
16. B. Schwartzberg (2004) '"Lots of Them Did That": Desertion, Bigamy, and Marital Fluidity in Late-Nineteenth-Century America', *Journal of Social History*, vol. 37, no. 3, pp. 573–600, 574.
17. *Osterreichische Volksstimme*, 17 January 1950.
18. Mattl and Stuhlpfarrer, 'Abwehr und Inszenierung', p. 906.
19. Gehmacher and Mesner, p. 30.
20. Mattl and Stuhlpfarrer, p. 906.
21. Mattl and Stuhlpfarrer, p. 908.
22. Schuetz quoted in Mattl and Stuhlpfarrer, p. 70.
23. E. Hornung (2005) *Warten und Heimkehren: Eine Ehe während und nach dem zweiten Weltkrieg* (Vienna: Turia + Kant), p. 108.
24. Gehmacher and Mesner, *Land der Söhne*, p. 56; 3710/49, 2.3.4.A11/WStLA.
25. 10099/46, 2.3.4.A11/WStLA.
26. Item 7, 10099/46, 2.3.4.A11/WStLA.
27. 9166/46, 2.3.4.A11/WStLA.
28. Item 16, 9166/46, 2.3.4.A11/WStLA.
29. Item 6, 9166/46, 2.3.4.A11/WStLA.
30. Item 6, 9166/46, 2.3.4.A11/WStLA.
31. *Wiener Zeitung*, 25 September 1949.
32. 'Das Problem Todeserklaerungen', *Wiener Tageszeitung*, 28 December 1946.
33. §43 and §44 of the Ehegesetz. See: M. Hinteregger (2001) 'The Austrian Matrimonial Law – A Patchwork Pattern of History', *European Journal of Law Reform*, vol 3, pp. 203–19.
34. E. D. Heineman (1999) *What Difference Does a Husband Make? Women and Marital Status in Nazi and Postwar Germany* (Berkeley: University of California Press), p. 209.
35. The other is '*Trümmerfrauen*', women of the rubble. See Gehmacher and Mesner, *Land der Söhne*, p. 27; I. Bandhauer-Schöffmann and E. Hornung (1990) 'Trümmerfrauen- ein kurzes Heldinnenleben' in A. Graf (ed.) *Zur Politik des Weiblichen: Frauenmacht und –ohnmacht. Beiträge zur Innenwelt und Außenwelt* (Vienna: Verlag für Gesellschaftskritik), pp. 93–120.

36. Totgeglaubter Mann', *Der Abend,* 5 November 1952.
37. Hornung, 'Trümmerfrauen- ein kurzes Heldinnenleben', p. 11.
38. Hornung, p. 11.
39. H. Steele (2011) '"Schreiben oder schweigen?": Feldpost and Frauenalltag in Vienna, 1943–1945' in V. Didczuneit, J. Ebert, and T. Jander (eds) *Schreiben im Krieg, Schreiben vom Krieg. Feldpost im Zeitalter der Weltkriege* (Essen: Klartext Verlag), pp. 272–82.
40. 78/46, 2.3.4.A11/WStLA.
41. 78/46, 2.3.4.A11/WStLA.
42. Steele, 'Schreiben oder schweigen?', p. 281.
43. Hornung, 'Trümmerfrauen- ein kurzes Heldinnenleben', p. 187.
44. Mattl and Stuhlpfarrer, 'Abwehr und Inszenierung', p. 907.
45. 8048/46, 2.3.4.A11/WStLA.
46. 8048/46, 2.3.4.A11/WStLA.
47. F. Freund and B. Perz (2000) 'Zwangsarbeit von zivilen AusländerInnen, Kriegsgefangenen, KZ-Häftlingen und ungarischen Juden in Österreich' in E. Tálos, E. Hanisch, W. Neugebauer, and R. Sieder (eds), *NS Herrschaft in Österreich. Ein Handbuch* (Vienna: öbv & htp), p. 660. Concentration camp inmates are not included in the statistics compiled by Freund and Perz.
48. B. Kundrus (2005) 'Forbidden Company: Romantic Relationships between Germans and Foreigners, 1939–1945', in D. Herzog (ed.), *Sexuality and German Fascism* (New York and Oxford: Berghahn Books), p. 202.
49. V. Joshi (2003) *Gender and Power in the Third Reich: Female Denouncers and the Gestapo, 1933–45* (Basingstoke: Palgrave Macmillan), p. 151.
50. *Österreichische Volksstimme,* 13 February 1953.
51. S. Mattl (1985) 'Frauen in Österreich nach 1945' in R. G. Ardelt, W. J. A. Huber, and A. Staufinger (eds), *Unterdrückung und Emanzipation: Festschrift für Erika Weinzierl* (Vienna: Geyer), pp. 101–26. Female bigamists warrant their own study and preliminary work with court registers suggests there are some cases.
52. 4491/46, 2.3.4.A11/WStLA.
53. *Arbeiter Zeitung,* 24 November 1949.
54. 7790/46; 8048/46; 3710/49 2.3.4.A11/WStLA.
55. 7790/46, 2.3.4.A11/WStLA.
56. 78/46, 2.3.4.A11/WStLA.
57. 4491/46 and 2806/46, 2.3.4.A11/WStLA.
58. Hornung, 'Trümmerfrauen- ein kurzes Heldinnenleben', p. 120.
59. 2718/46, 2.3.4.A11/WStLA.
60. Anklageschrift, 2718/46, 2.3.4.A11/WStLA.
61. Anklageschrift, 2718/46, 2.3.4.A11/WStLA.
62. 2718/46, 2.3.4.A11/WStLA.
63. Item 10, 2718/46, 2.3.4.A11/WStLA.
64. Item 10, 2718/46, 2.3.4.A11/WStLA.
65. Item 10, 2718/46, 2.3.4.A11/WStLA.
66. Bessel, *Germany 1945,* p. 272.
67. Bessel, p. 272.
68. Bessel, p. 272.
69. 3710/49, 2.3.4.A11/WStLA.
70. 3710/49, 2.3.4.A11/WStLA.

8

'Being a Real Man': Masculinities in Soviet Russia during and after the Great Patriotic War

Robert Dale

The war on the Eastern Front between June 1941 and May 1945, known in the Soviet Union as the Great Patriotic War, was amongst the most violent, murderous, and destructive episodes of the Second World War. The war, and the manner in which it was waged, tore the material and social fabric of Soviet society apart. The extraordinary economic and human costs borne by the Soviet Union are well documented. In the immediate wake of war, vast swathes of Soviet territory were laid waste; 1,700 towns, 70,000 villages, and housing for approximately 25 million people were totally destroyed. Worse still was the demographic catastrophe created by the death of 27 million Soviet citizens.[1] Approximately 75 per cent of these deaths were amongst men, something which created a post-war gender imbalance. In 1946, for example, there were 10 million fewer men aged twenty to forty-four than in 1940.[2] The Armageddon on the Eastern Front, and its aftermath, touched every aspect of Soviet life. Inevitably, the demands of waging modern industrialized warfare, the total mobilization of society, combined with the war's disastrous demographic impact had a profound impact on the construction of gender identities and relations in wartime and post-war Soviet society.

Historiographical context

In the past twenty years historians of Soviet Russia have made impressive progress in studying the far-reaching social, economic, and cultural effects of the Great Patriotic War. Those who focus on the frontline war have moved far beyond traditional histories of battlefield tactics and strategy, towards a more nuanced social history of life in the Red Army, combat motivation, and Soviet soldiers' inner worlds.[3] Building upon path-breaking social histories of the home front and post-war reconstruction, scholars have produced important studies of the war's impact on cities, public culture, and key social groups, including workers, evacuees, veterans, children, and youth.[4] Historians have also begun to narrow their sights on wartime gender identities and the recalibration of gender relations in the wake of war. The first scholars to explore these issues often found the women who served in the Red Army in their analytical cross hairs. Between 800,000 and 1 million Soviet women served in the wartime Red Army. They served on the frontlines as combat soldiers, in tank and artillery crews, as pilots and snipers, and as doctors, nurses, radio operators, translators, cooks, and laundresses. Women, despite their relatively small numbers, and the limits placed upon their involvement in combat, played a symbolically important role in the partisan movement. The extent of female military participation, therefore, was unprecedented, outstripping the mobilization of women of any other nation.[5] Unsurprisingly, then, the obstacles faced by women on or behind the lines, during and after the war, have dominated discussion about wartime gender identities.

More recently, historians have begun to explore how the Great Patriotic War shaped Soviet masculinity. Although the presence of so many women on or near the front lines was remarkable, the overwhelming majority of Soviet soldiers were men. This reality, combined with a growing interest in masculinities amongst historians of Russia and the Soviet Union more generally, has placed the war's impact upon men firmly on the agenda. Much of this scholarship concentrates upon how war shaped the archetypes available to men, and the shifts in the idealized representation of masculinity in the press, popular journals, visual culture, and literature. Karen Petrone, for example, has explored the evolution of an identifiably Soviet model soldier-hero.[6] Catherine Merridale has written about the role soldiers' sense of their own maleness played in forming wartime identities. Gender, however, was just one of many bases for creating individual and collective identities. 'In almost every case', as Merridale argues, 'gender was less important than rank, age, training or nationality'.[7]

The full effect of war upon Soviet masculinities was not felt until after 1945. The gender identities forged in the hypermasculine front-line Red Army now had to be recalibrated to meet new circumstances. In a society where men were now a minority, and a generation of children were growing up without fathers, expectations on men and their behaviour suddenly shifted in ways which some men found impossible to adjust to. Historians are only now beginning to explore how men, the party-state, and wider society sought to come to terms with the war's effects on masculinity. Several scholars have considered how the gender identities of the 2.75 million disabled veterans spat out by the war, were affected by dismembered and disfigured bodies, loss of sight and hearing, and chronic illnesses.[8] Ethan Pollock has explored how the Russian bathhouse (*bania*), a traditional setting for homo-social bonding, served as a space in which post-war masculinities were renegotiated.[9] Most recently, Claire McCallum has charted the fundamental shifts in the representation of idealized manhood in post-war Soviet visual culture, particularly the depiction of men as fathers in domestic space.[10]

This chapter speaks to this developing research field by exploring the dissonance and disparity between official constructions of appropriate masculine behaviour and what 'being a real man' meant in practice. It argues that war's effects on masculinity were complicated and multivalent. The war and its aftermath did not produce a single simple form of masculinity, but rather an array of competing forms of masculinity that illustrate the messy reality of a society experiencing enormous upheaval. Official exemplars of masculinity were necessary precisely because masculine responses to war proved so varied. Although the archetypes and representations of masculinity promoted during and after the war reveal a great deal about official thinking and the social and cultural pressures created by war, they are potentially misleading. While there are numerous examples of men internalizing the rhetoric of bravery, stoicism, and self-sacrifice, the reality of total warfare was that it produced masculine behaviours that fell short of exemplary 'heroes'. At the front, moments of brutality, drunkenness, and cowardice co-existed, as did moments of compassion, tenderness, and kindness. Although what follows explores Soviet masculinities both during and after the Great Patriotic War, the focus is on the immediate post-war period, when a new set of gender expectations were placed on veterans' shoulders. The war's effects on masculinity should not be reduced to martial experiences. Indeed, the long-term effects of war on masculinity only began to be felt once the guns had stopped firing and soldiers had returned home.

Soviet masculinities at war

Idealized masculinity

The prevailing image of Soviet wartime masculinity, which dominates both popular and academic discourses, was that of 'the pure, strong, noble and unimpeachable heterosexual male' fostered by wartime propaganda and the post-war myth-making of the official war cult.[11] This ubiquitous gender-specific image of Soviet heroism was propagated in films, war memorials, photographs, and paintings. The ideal-type soldier was consistently presented as a young, strong, and vigorously healthy ethnic Russian, whose masculine features and well-defined muscles symbolized collective valour and national victory. These visual statements of exemplary masculinity had their literary equivalents in the reports of battlefield exploits in *Pravda* as well as in the positive heroes of Soviet fiction. For example, Alexander Tvardovsky's extraordinarily popular epic poem *Vasily Terkin* offered models of both patriotism and masculinity. Terkin's attraction stemmed from his strength, stoicism, good humour, selflessness, and positive outlook, as befitted a simple peasant lad, which appealed to the Red Army's vision of itself.[12] As the patriotic cult of the Great Patriotic War solidified after 1945, this official presentation of masculinity became almost inescapable.

During the war Soviet soldiers were expected to demonstrate a wide range of qualities and values, frequently gendered as masculine, including heroism, valour, courage, aggression, strength, self-sacrifice, discipline, loyalty, and endurance. The ideal Soviet soldier, like all combatants, was expected to kill and be killed in the name of national salvation. An important role in promoting this vision of heroic-military masculinity to soldiers, as a means of improving combat performance, was played by the Red Army's Main Political Administration. Details of heroic exploits were often circulated in leaflets and unit newspapers, as a model for soldiers to emulate. *Krasnaia zvezda* (Red Star), the army's popular national newspaper, frequently published lists of decorated soldiers and pen portraits of the most outstanding warriors.[13] Heroes such as the legendary Alexander Matrosov, famed for blocking a German pill-box with his body, were widely celebrated.[14] Few soldiers could hope to emulate or achieve the fame of these cult heroes, not least because propaganda officers often, 'disregarded the truth and freely manipulated the names, circumstances, dates, and other details of the deeds in order to create a script for the rest of the army and future conscripts to follow'.[15] Heroism was frequently mythologized, with only the most suitable and instructive examples hitting the headlines. Nevertheless, these idealized forms of masculinity often shaped younger soldiers' sense of themselves, especially for the so-called front-line generation, who had little life experience beyond war.[16]

It is, however, problematic to suggest that 1941–1945 marked a decisive point of departure in the construction of Soviet masculinities. The idealized masculine qualities propagated during the war drew upon deeply rooted traditions of masculine Russian heroism and valour (*muzhestvo*). This is not to say that these heroic archetypes were fixed in aspic. As Petrone has demonstrated, notions of courage, heroism, and military masculinity, while a common factor in the language of all wars, shifted substantially in the first four decades of the twentieth century. Under Stalin more nuanced, fallible heroes gave way to 'mythic hyper masculinity', but individual acts of heroism were also rooted in collective camaraderie. Heroes were distinguished, in part, by brave support of their comrades.[17] Nevertheless, there were strong continuities between the heroic discourses of the Great Patriotic War and tsarist and civil-war masculinities. The army had long been the key institution in Russian society for moral training and cultivating masculine values. Masculinity was increasingly nationalized, with masculine attributes becoming national qualities, shaped by the state rather than families or local communities. 'The army', as Joshua Sanborn argues, 'was the most competent teacher of "proper" masculine virtues like selflessness and discipline, thus took on the burden of training Russians to be citizens'.[18] Well before 1941 the Soviet state linked masculine qualities with citizenship. 'Men who sought membership in the political community soon learned that membership and mobility entailed becoming hard, courageous, and strong.'[19] Expressions of military masculinity and appeals to heroism were central to the political discourse in Soviet socialism's highly mobilized society. Even attempts to foster murderous hatred of the enemy, a defining feature of Soviet wartime masculinity, had much in common with the rhetoric of the 1930s. As Ilya Ehrenburg famously exhorted men in *Pravda* in 1942, 'If you haven't killed a German in the course of a day, then your day has been wasted … If you have killed one German, kill another.'[20] These campaigns cast soldiers as battlefield Stakhanovites, killing proficiently and prodigiously instead of over-fulfilling industrial production. Even this hyperviolent form of masculinity, then, was informed by wider trends in Stalinism.

Primary groups

Official constructions of masculinity were not, however, the only acceptable wartime forms of behaviour. The typical Soviet soldier was neither a faceless unthinking brute who lacked the emotional and moral makeup of soldiers in the West, nor the one-dimensional stereotype celebrated in Soviet propaganda. They had complicated inner worlds and exhibited a wide range of behaviours that were often at odds with official gender identities. This was particularly apparent in the dynamics of the small groups of friends, known as primary groups, which played such an important role in maintaining individual and collective morale at the front. Loyalty to one's immediate comrades, especially the desire to not let them down, helped bind military units together and played an important part in keeping the Red Army fighting in difficult situations.[21] Primary groups, although significant in explaining combat effectiveness, were also important for forging a particular wartime form of homo-sociability. As one soldier wrote to the fiancée of his deceased friend: 'Frontline life brings people together very quickly. It is enough to be with someone for a day or two, and you already know all his qualities, all his feelings, as if you had known him for a year in civilian life. There is no stronger friendship than frontline …'[22] In this social context 'being a real man' did not rest on gung-ho exploits or ruthlessly efficient killing, but on loyalty to one's comrades. A good man, so far as soldiers made conscious evaluations, was a comrade who could hold his drink, a tune when the mood needed lightening, and his tongue in front of informers, and would generously share his tobacco, rations, and news from home. These close bonds of trust and masculine comradeship provided essential support in extreme circumstances. The lack of women on the front lines meant that these small groups often found themselves supporting and caring for each other in ways which might be gendered feminine. 'Although they would have not acknowledged it', as Merridale puts it, 'men assumed many traditional female roles in relation to each other – cooking, cleaning, consoling the frightened or bereaved, even dressing wounds and checking on each other's boils'.[23] In the midst of mass death, and perhaps because of it, men found it necessary to carve out space for moments of tenderness. This impulse frequently found expression in the adoption of unaccompanied children, the so-called 'sons of the regiment'. The presence of children amidst the violence and destruction reminded men of their families, and offered them a hint of normality and an emotional outlet.[24] For many it must have been, 'a relief to take care of someone after months of military harshness and routine'.[25] Indeed, as the Red Army began to liberate Soviet territory their fatherly support found expression in a number of posters, most notably Vladimir Ladiagin's 1945 poster, *I waited for you Soldier-Liberator!* (Figure 8.1). Soldiers who exhibited these behaviours were not, however, feminized. The pose and expression of Ladiagin's soldier could hardly have been more masculine. These were normal parts of men's everyday war experience – aspects of the war to which the patriotic military-masculinity gave little expression.

Figure 8.1 Vladimir Ladiagin, *I waited for you Soldier-Liberator! We will liberate all Soviet people from Fascist Captivity* (1945).
Reproduced courtesy of Akg-images / Sputnik.

Darker realities

Beyond the idealized versions of masculinity and the nostalgic memories of the front-line brotherhood, however, lay darker and less acceptable forms of masculinity. Soldiers' behaviour frequently fell short of official and popular archetypes. There was little room for expression of many aspects of men's war experiences in the official presentation of muscular heroes, or even soldiers' own wartime memories. Although frequently denied or unacknowledged, soldiers felt fear, broke down under combat, or deserted.

On 12 April 1943 Vasily Zaistev, the celebrated sniper made famous in the West by the 2001 film *Enemy at the Gates*, was interviewed by a representative of the Commission on the History of the Great Patriotic War. In his account of the Battle of Stalingrad, Zaistev talked about not knowing fatigue, and being motivated by the determination to 'slaughter even more Germans'. Yet the atrocities he had witnessed and the deadly pressures of being a sniper had taken their toll: 'I was wounded three times in Stalingrad. Now I have a nervous disorder and I'm shaking all the time. I find myself thinking about it a lot, and these memories have a strong effect.'[26] Although men frequently scripted their accounts of battle according to official tropes, Soviet soldiers' accounts of the battlefield frequently expressed similar emotions to those of American, British, and German soldiers.[27] 'Although wartime and post-war Soviet propaganda was fond of the terms *fearless* and *valiant* when describing Soviet soldiers in combat, few men denied being afraid.'[28] At its most extreme, fear, combined with the sustained hardships of the front, caused men to break down completely. Although trauma and mental illness were taboo in the hypermasculine world of the Soviet military, psychiatric casualties never entirely disappeared from official history or memory. Psychiatrists treated a wide variety of mental disorders, ranging from major physical brain damage to psychological breakdown. Soldiers' remarkably diverse symptoms ranged from concussion, lack of sleep, exhaustion, and chronic pain through to convulsions, paralysis, and mutism, and were frequently lumped together under the term *kontuziia* (concussion). Soldiers often interpreted these terms as a 'weasel word used to cover up cowardice and lack of will'.[29] Similarly some psychiatrists saw these labels, 'as a slur on the patriotism of the soldiers who fell ill'.[30] In a political and social context where patriotism was a key masculine virtue, traumatized soldiers ran the risk of having their credentials as 'real men' questioned.

In many cases Soviet men's courage and heroism were found wanting. Despite the constant appeals to patriotism and the harsh penalties against it, desertion was a consistent problem for the Red Army. Desertion rates were particularly high amidst the confusion and panic of the early months of the German invasion, but were by no means halted by later improvements in Soviet military performance. Between 1941 and 1945 the Soviet military recorded 2,846,000 instances of men and women deserting or draft dodging.[31] 'Desertions on this scale', as Merridale writes, 'were evidence that tyranny alone could not make heroes out of frightened men'.[32] Indeed, there was a potential connection between desertion and psychological trauma. Confused and exhausted soldiers were particularly likely to be labelled as traitors or cowards, and executed for desertion.[33]

Primary groups should not be romanticized. Tightly bonded groups of male soldiers, frequently behaved in undesirable ways which transgressed the boundaries of acceptable male behaviour. Misogyny was rife in the Red Army. Women might be frozen out of the group, or subjected to name-calling and insults.[34] More seriously, women could encounter violence and abuse from men in uniform. Sexual exploitation and the objectification of women by partisan units, for example, were common. Bands of drunken male partisans frequently robbed or behaved violently towards civilian populations.[35] As Slepyan writes, 'The treatment of women was part of a powerful masculinized partisan identity that marginalized and objectified women while elevating male status.'[36] The brutality of Soviet soldiers towards women, however, is best demonstrated by the mass rape of German women. The horrors to which hundreds of thousands of women and young girls were subjected at the hands of the marauding Red Army make for grim reading.[37] These were not crimes committed by isolated sex-starved soldiers, but by groups of violent men acting in concert. While primary groups had positive effects in sustaining soldiers during war, they had the capacity to descend into angry mobs, subjecting civilian women to horrific acts of sexual and non-sexual violence. These collective atrocities served to both humiliate the enemy and reinforce damaged masculine identities. Shared emotional bonds and a sense of collective anonymity between soldiers combined to intensify the violence.[38]

Soviet masculinities in the wake of war

Disorderly demobilization

Such collective acts of violence did not end in May 1945 with Germany's unconditional surrender. As Filip Slaveski argues, 'The violence carried out by the troops endured long after the war because the whole army, officers and men, was simply incapable of shifting from war to peace.'[39] In the days and weeks following the war's end *Krasnaia zvezda* attempted to create the impression that the Red Army was returning to normal peacetime rhythms. Soldiers garrisoned in Vienna, Budapest, and Berlin were reported and photographed visiting theatres, galleries, and museums, playing football or volleyball, or spending their evenings singing nostalgic songs of home.[40] In reality, however, cultured and sporting pastimes had not replaced drunkenness, looting, and violence. Not until 1947 or 1948 did the threat of rape subside from German women's daily lives.[41] Far from dissipating violence, demobilization aggravated indiscipline. By demobilizing the oldest age cohorts first, the Red Army lost its oldest, most experienced, and best educated soldiers, the men who wielded the authority to impose, maintain, and restore order.[42] Indeed, demobilization transports regularly descended into drink-fuelled mob violence, which on occasion verged on pitched battles with local security forces.[43] Soldiers serving on Soviet territory sometimes visited outrageous acts of violence on the communities which months before they had been fighting to protect. Well before the war's end, reports from the Leningrad region documented soldiers destroying buildings, stealing food, and property, expropriating horses and carts and even blowing up fish-ponds with grenades.[44] Reports of soldiers robbing trade points, shops and apartments, and behaving indecently in cinemas, clubs, and cafés continued after 1945.[45] On 27 October 1946, for example, fifteen soldiers went on the rampage in Keksgolm. Already drunk when they arrived, they proceeded to assault several customers in a café, demanded bread from a shop, and then stood in the town square firing their guns in the air.[46] In the immediate aftermath of the war, incidents replicating this pattern of disruptive, violent masculinity were commonplace.[47]

Exemplary masculinity in the workplace

The masculinities fostered at the front did not dissolve after the conflict. It took time for men to learn to live with peace. The war's effects on gender identities often took years to work through. While men were trying to adjust to the war's impact on their lives, the Soviet party-state began to offer Soviet men new models of masculinity. This created new pressures and demands that proved just as difficult for men to meet. One of the new markers of a 'real man' was performance in the workplace and dedication to post-war reconstruction. Veterans' post-war duty was clear. They were to return to work as quickly as possible, and devote themselves to production with the same diligence and determination demonstrated at the front. A series of posters produced by the graphic artist Viktor Koretsky exhorted men to devote themselves to civilian labour as if it was an extension of battle. Their titles echoed popular slogans: *As in battle – as in labour* (1910), *We were victorious in battle – We will be victorious in labour* (1947), and *Be in the forefront everywhere* (1947). Civilian labour was to be approached with the same heroism and stoicism as combat. Infantry were transformed into miners; tank drivers into combine-harvester drivers. Commanders of guns were to become commanders of production.[48] Young men tempered at the front were supposed to become exemplary civilian workers.

In a society where work was a key component in shaping socialist citizens, and where the exploits of Stakhanovite labour heroes were publicly celebrated, this was hardly surprising. Yet there were critical differences in the expectations placed upon post-war men. They could not rest on their laurels; victory should not go to their heads. As a pocketbook for ex-servicemen reminded its readers: 'You are obliged, as your duty before the motherland, to always and everywhere uphold the highest honour and virtue of the Red Army, and on returning to the motherland to be an example of modesty, discipline, orderliness and procedure.'[49] The mark of a 'real man' was not simply his war record, but how he behaved after the war. As the hero of Semen Babaevsky's novel *Cavalier of the Gold Star*, a prototype for the new post-war masculinities, is reminded:

> You'll have to renew your military glory every day in your work, so it will not be tarnished and appear corroded with conceit. They say that the decorations on a soldier's chest are the mirror of his soul. That's probably quite right. But in that mirror people see only our past and our present; the future must find its reflection in our deeds.[50]

There were plenty of examples of men who internalized these values, and strove to become archetypal workers. Factory newspapers proudly boasted of veterans achieving impressive feats of Stakhanovism. As one former soldier employed at Leningrad's Elektrosila plant concluded an article: 'Everybody asks me: well *frontovik*, how are you doing? How are you adapting to civilian life after the war? Well I answer it's like this – you've got to roll up your sleeves and work, and work.'[51]

Yet many men found it difficult to demobilize wartime masculinities, and adapt to the demands of civilian life. This was not primarily a question of brutalization. Although disorderly and violent behaviour was not uncommon, most men proved remarkably successful at compartmentalizing the violent impulses cultivated during the war. But, not all wartime masculine qualities could easily be recalibrated. Bravery, decisiveness, independence, and risk-taking were invaluable on the battlefield, but often dysfunctional in civilian life.[52] As Merridale writes, *frontoviki* were fine for winning wars, but Stalinism required, 'people with the souls of bureaucrats'.[53] War and its modes of association bred a new type of assertive masculine identity that was often at odds with officially promoted masculinities. As Weiner has argued, the front produced, 'an assertive Soviet individual who held tight to his (and it was mostly his and not her) new right, earned in blood, to define his identity and status based on wartime exploits'.[54] On occasion the official satirical journal *Krokodil* gently poked fun at demobilized soldiers unable to resist the reflex to salute officers, or break the habit of speaking in military jargon.[55] These cartoons, however, trivialized the nuisance that 'assertive Ivan' presented. Ex-soldiers banging their fists on desks, behaving as if they were still in the army, and demanding special treatment rarely endeared themselves to the rest of society. Relationships between veterans returning to or beginning higher education and a younger generation of students were particularly tense, but difficulties were common across society.[56]

Wounded masculinities

While the party-state, and indeed many men, presented the war's effects on masculinities in positive terms, war exacted a terrible toll on men's minds and bodies, severely wounding Soviet masculinity. Modern industrial war had an almost limitless capacity to dismember and disfigure combatants. Between 1941 and 1945 there were over 22.3 million instances of hospitalization, including 14.7 million cases of injury and 7.6 million cases of illness.[57] Few soldiers escaped the war without experiencing some damage to their bodies. Even if they were not officially classified as disabled, the conflict took its toll on their health. Lingering aches and pains, dental problems caused by malnutrition, hearing loss, mental and physical exhaustion, and premature ageing were all part of the price paid for victory. In a society which celebrated supple young bodies through regular physical culture parades, it is easy to see why many men thought of themselves as damaged goods.[58]

Wartime and post-war novels were full of physically and mentally damaged men, whose 'troubled male personalities' had to be nursed back to health.[59] Responding to the experiences of men whose identities were shaped by the horrors of war, Soviet literature began to readjust its representations of men accordingly. Fiction produced a host of disabled male characters who through their devotion to rebuilding the nation succeeded in overcoming their physical disabilities.[60] The most famous of these were the heroes of Boris Polevoi's 1946 novel *The Tale of a Real Man* and Pytor Pavlenko's Stalin prize winning 1947 novel *Happiness*. Both characters were exemplary individuals lauded for making valuable contributions to Soviet society despite their physical disabilities. Indeed, Pavlenko's hero Colonel Voropaev became something of a cult hero, creating 'a movement of Voropaevism – a sui generis post-Patriotic War wounded veterans' Stakhanovism'.[61] These disabled literary heroes owed a debt to the pre-war cult of Pavel Korchagin, a blind and paralysed civil war veteran who is the central protagonist of Nikolai Ostrovsky's semi-autobiographical novel *How the Steel Was Tempered*.[62] The official narratives of rehabilitation and the rebuilding of fragile masculinities, as Maria Cristina Galmarini has demonstrated, were often embraced by disabled men as models for their autobiographies and self-identities.[63] Although disabled veterans' everyday lives were often characterized by impoverishment, neglect, and deep-seated resentments, many nevertheless refused to see their masculinity as irrevocably damaged. While wounded and damaged masculinities were a social and cultural reality in late Stalinist Russia, few men wished to identify themselves as victims or damaged goods. In a society where the death of so many men left a gaping void, persuading the war-disabled that they could still be 'real men' and have a place in society, especially in the face of their increasing marginalization, was vitally important to national reconstruction efforts.

The other key post-war space in which 'real men' demonstrated their masculine credentials was the family. Since Soviet socialism made little distinction between the public and private, it was entirely natural that the regime sought to encourage desirable male behaviour within men's personal and familial relationships. Many men, however, found it difficult to adjust to family and domestic routine so soon after the hypermasculinity of the Red Army. Soviet public culture tended to treat the family as a space in which men could be nursed back to full physical and psychological health, a space in which fragile masculinities could be restored.[64] Women's magazines such as *Rabotnitsa* (Female worker) and *Krest'ianka* (Female collective farmer) frequently carried short stories in which the female protagonists sacrificed themselves to care for their disabled husbands.[65] Spouses and families could greatly assist men's post-war transitions in helping to find work and housing, and by offering psychological support and a sense of belonging.[66] The July 1945 cover of *Rabotnitsa* offered a clear ideological statement of families standing behind returning soldiers. A uniformed officer, his chest covered in medals, sits in parkland painting the landscape, while his smartly dressed wife and son stand at his shoulder providing their support and attention (Figure 8.2). Yet, in many cases, men no longer had families to return to. At best they had been evacuated eastward and were not yet able to return home. At worst their families were dead. All too often the family was not a therapeutic space, but another battleground in which the nature of post-war masculinity was thrashed out.

Post-war families: sources of solace and anxiety

The Great Patriotic War destroyed and dismembered millions of families, and created a deep gender imbalance that reshaped post-war society and took decades to resolve. Indeed, the gender imbalance was so acute that it had a significant bearing on the Soviet Union's ability to begin to fill the demographic void. The shortage of men was felt most acutely in the countryside. In 1940 the ratio of women to men on collective farms was approximately 1.1 to 1; by 1946 it had risen to 2.7 to 1.[67] In the 18–49 age group there were just 28 men for every 100 women in rural areas.[68] In some villages there were hardly any able-bodied men left. In 1947 the American John Strohm visited a collective farm in the Stalingrad region which had sent all of its 146 men to the Red Army. Only fifteen returned to the farm, and ten of these were amputees.[69]

Figure 8.2   The Cover of *Rabotnitsa*, No. 7 (July, 1945).

Demobilization did little to improve this situation. In 1959, fifteen years after the war's end, there were still 2.8 million more rural women aged 20–49 than men.[70] Even in urban areas, which drew men in from surrounding regions in search of industrial employment, the gender imbalance persisted. For every 1,000 women living in Russian cities in 1959 there were just 814 men.[71] Whereas destroyed buildings, factories, and infrastructure could be gradually replaced, the loss of so many young men in a key reproductive age group could never be made good.

   This demographic crisis was felt across late Stalinist society, but particularly acutely in the family. A whole generation of children grew up without fathers, and a generation of young women lived their lives without a partner. The social implications of this demographic crisis upon Soviet life formed the backdrop to the forms of masculinity encouraged in the wake of war. The necessity of increasing the birth rate and producing stable families dictated new representations of masculinity. After the war official constructions of masculinity were increasingly linked to paternity. Soviet men were expected to make a contribution to post-war recovery not just in the rural and urban reconstruction, or the workplace, but also within the home. Being a 'real man' also meant being a family man. It was no coincidence that one of the most common images of demobilization was of families reunited, children running to greet their fathers, or men proudly holding their children aloft. As McCallum has brilliantly demonstrated, the post-war period represented a fundamental shift in the presentation of both fatherhood and masculinity in Stalinist visual culture. Presenting the demobilized soldier as first and foremost a father had profound consequences for the construction of Soviet masculinity.[72] Men were now expected to be active participants in family life, spending time with their children and investing in their upbringing. Family life and parenting were no longer to be left exclusively to women; it was a man's duty to have children and assist in raising the next generation.

Negotiating the transition from wartime martial masculinities towards a domestic and familial masculinity in such a short period of time was a challenge. Visual culture tended to present men's homecoming as a happily-ever-after story.[73] Yet the war generated many tragic stories. One such was Sergei Bondarchuk's 1959 film *Sud'ba cheloveka* (Fate of a Man), based on a 1946 short story by Mikhail Sholokhov. 'Bondarchuk's film is a psychological study of an individual who, while being exceptionally strong, courageous, and having the qualities of a true hero, is nonetheless broken by a war so horrendous that it cripples the minds and souls of the strongest.'[74] Although the hero adopts a war orphan, as damaged by war as himself, this relationship fails to heal either of them.[75] A similar scenario plays out in Marlen Khutsiev's 1958 film *Dva Fedora* (Two Fyodors). On his return home Fyodor the hero, a demobilized veteran, adopts an orphan, also called Fyodor, and takes him home. Throughout the film both Fyodors care for each other, but when the adult Fyodor falls in love and marries, the bond between them suffers. Although a new family is gradually created for the boy, surrogate fatherhood is a challenge, and family life far from plain sailing.[76]

Although there were hundreds of thousands of happy reunions after the war, it was inevitable that many relationships, marriages, and families would not survive years of separation and dislocation. 'Even the couples who managed to rebuild their lives together', as Merridale writes, 'were aware of a gap, of a blank space that no amount of talking could enliven'.[77] Husbands and wives separated by war, and under great psychological pressure, often grew apart and found solace elsewhere. The short stories that filled the pages of women's magazines often acknowledged infidelities. These fictional wives often forgave husbands their infidelities or sacrificed their own affairs to care for them.[78] In reality, however, many relationships broke down in the face of separation and infidelity. One veteran demobilized in Leningrad in November 1946 returned to find that his wife had been having an affair and had no desire to rebuild the marriage. He took the news badly, and after months of turmoil hanged himself.[79] Such tragic cases were exceptional, but this example illustrates that family life was often a source of anxiety.

Children were no more likely to provide a source of comfort. In August 1945, for example, Fyodor Gromov was demobilized and reunited with his 20-year-old daughter Liubov. She had been evacuated with a training school from Leningrad in 1942, after the death of her mother, but had assumed an itinerant lifestyle moving between towns and cities, supporting herself by theft. Family life did not turn out as Gromov might have wished. After several months living with her father and working at a tram depot, Liubov drifted back to her chaotic lifestyle, and was eventually charged for committing two burglaries.[80] Gromov was sadly no longer able to keep his daughter out of trouble. Rebuilding relationships with young children, who barely remembered their fathers before the war, was especially difficult. *The Return*, a short story written by Andrei Platonov and published by *Novyi Mir* in 1946, captured the difficulties of re-establishing traditional family hierarchies in the wake of war. The story tells the tragic tale of Alexei Ivanov's return to his wife and two children, a family which had changed beyond recognition. The plot revolves around this family's failed reunification. Unused to domestic life, Alexei becomes deeply concerned by his inability to understand his much altered wife and children. In particular, he finds the changes in his 12-year-old son, who in his absence had become the man of the house, shocking and difficult to comprehend. Given the difficulties of repairing his family relations he decides to leave for a woman he had known in the army, demobilized at the same time, and equally as disorientated.[81] Although Alexei is ultimately unable to leave, countless men in a similar position did abandon their families. Platonov's depiction of post-war families proved too realistic for Soviet literary authorities and was viciously attacked. The sense of estrangement described in the story, however, would have been all too familiar to many veterans. Former soldiers who felt that their families could not possibly understand them or their war experiences often faced the most difficult transitions. In contrast, marriages between male and female soldiers, couples with a shared war experience, often proved the happiest and most durable.[82]

The assertive masculinities and demographic pressures created by the war, combined with the consequences of official policy, undercut the official representation of Soviet men as loyal husbands and devoted fathers. The years of mass demobilization (1945–1947) prompted a wave of marriages and a spike in births as couples were reunited and young men and women formed new relationships. Yet there were simply not enough men to go around. Even in 1959 marriage rates amongst women aged 25–29 and 30–34 were 54.9 and 48.3 per cent respectively.[83] While the gender imbalance made it extremely difficult for many women to become wives and mothers, many men found that it presented them with opportunities. The 1944 Family Law was intended to boost birth rates and support mothers and the family, but in practice it generated great tension between genders. Nikita Khrushchev, who drafted the legislation, believed, 'that accelerated population growth would be possible only if men were given incentive to impregnate women other than their wives, and if unmarried and widowed women were given sufficient support to raise out-of-wedlock children'.[84] The policy presented a male-centred perspective on the family that ran counter to the images in the press of men at the centre of families. Despite the creation of new categories of hero mothers and rewards for them, the 1944 law acted largely to the benefit of men. Biological fathers were no longer required to bear legal or financial responsibilities for children born out of wedlock. Indeed, their names were not even recorded on birth certificates.[85] Unsurprisingly, many men exploited the opportunities legislative changes presented for continuing old and pursuing new extramarital affairs.

In a society where men were in such short supply, and the opportunities for starting new relationships so abundant, the pressures to remain in marriages or to help bring up the children were very different. Indeed, there were thousands of post-war cases of Communist Party members being expelled or reprimanded for irregularities in their family lives, such as affairs, drunkenness, and failure to pay child support.[86] Although divorce was made harder after 1944, and the number of registered divorces fell, men were nevertheless at the forefront of applications for divorce.[87]

Conclusion

The Second World War and the immediate post-war period had a substantial impact on the construction of both official masculinities and Soviet men's self-perceptions. Far from generating a monolithic form of masculinity and universally applied models of masculine behaviour, the war and its lasting aftermath had complicated and often contradictory effects on men's gender identities. Beyond the anodyne myths of heroic masculinity, and the nostalgic memories of young men bravely fighting for the honour of the front-line brotherhood, lay a range of less acceptable and more disruptive masculine behaviours, but which nevertheless had a profound effect on society. Soviet men internalized the official models of masculinity, but also proved capable of subverting these and acting in very different ways depending on social context. Although the war had profound implications for experienced gender identities, the shifts prompted by the war took years to play out. Patriotic martial masculinities drew upon long-standing models of heroic male behaviour. However, the post-war shifts in masculinity, in terms of both idealized norms and the reality of men's behaviour, ultimately proved to be more significant.

Recommended reading

Krylova, A. (2001) '"Healers of Wounded Souls": The Crisis of Private Life in Soviet Literature, 1944–1946', *The Journal of Modern History*, vol. 73, no. 2, pp. 307–31.

Linz, S. J. (ed.) (1985) *The Impact of World War II on the Soviet Union* (Totawa, NJ: Rowman and Allen Held).

McCallum, C. E. (2015) 'Scorched by the Fire of War: Masculinity, War Wounds and Disability in Soviet Visual Culture, 1941–65', *Slavonic and East European Review*, vol. 93, no. 2, pp. 251–85.

McCallum, C. E. (2015) 'The Return: Postwar Masculinity and the Domestic Space in Stalinist Visual Culture, 1945–53', *Russian Review*, vol. 74, no. 1, pp. 117–43.

Merridale, C. (2012) 'Masculinity at War: Did Gender Matter in the Soviet Army?' *Journal of War and Culture Studies*, vol. 5, no. 3, pp. 307–20.

Merridale, C. (2006) *Ivan's War: The Red Army 1939–1945* (London: Faber and Faber).

Nakachi, M. (2010), 'Gender, Marriage and Reproduction in the Postwar Soviet Union', in G. Alexopoulos, J. Hessler, and K. Tomoff (eds), *Writing the Stalin Era: Sheila Fitzpatrick and Soviet Historiography* (Basingstoke: Palgrave Macmillan).

Nakachi M. (2006) 'Population, Politics and Reproduction: Late Stalinism and its Legacy', in Juliane Fürst (ed.), *Late Stalinist Russia: Society between Reconstruction and Reinvention* (London: Routledge).

Petrone, K. (2002) 'Masculinity and Heroism in Imperial and Soviet Military-Patriotic Cultures', in B. Evans Clements, R. Friedman and D. Healey (eds), *Russian Masculinities in History and Culture* (Basingstoke: Palgrave Macmillan), pp. 172–93.

Pollock, E. (2010) '"Real Men Go to the Bania": Postwar Soviet Masculinities and the Bathhouse', *Kritika: Explorations in Russian and Eurasian History*, vol. 11, no. 1, pp. 47–76.

Reese, R. R. (2011) *Why Stalin's Soldiers Fought: The Red Army's Military Effectiveness in World War II* (Lawrence: University Press of Kansas).

Notes

1. On the war's impact, see S. J. Linz (ed.) (1985) *The Impact of World War II on the Soviet Union* (Totawa, NJ: Rowman and Allan Held); S. Lovell (2010) *The Shadow of War: Russia and the USSR, 1941 to the Present* (Oxford: Wiley-Blackwell); E. Zubkova (2000) *Poslevoennoe sovetskoe obshchestvo: politika i povsednevnost' 1945–1953* (Moscow: ROSSPEN).

2. E. Zubkova (1998) *Russia After the War: Hopes, Illusions and Disappointments, 1945–1957*, ed. and trans. by H. Ragsdale (Armonk, NY: M. E. Sharpe) p. 20.

3. C. Merridale (2006) *Ivan's War: The Red Army 1939–1945* (London: Faber and Faber); R. R. Reese (2011) *Why Stalin's Soldiers Fought: The Red Army's Military Effectiveness in World War II* (Lawrence: University Press of Kansas).

4. D. Filtzer (2002) *Soviet Workers and Late Stalinism: Labour and the Restoration of the Stalinist System After World War II* (Cambridge: Cambridge University Press); R. Manley (2009) *To the Tashkent Station: Evacuation and Survival in the Soviet Union at War* (Ithaca, NY: Cornell University Press); M. Edele (2008) *Soviet Veterans of the Second World War: A Popular Movement in an Authoritarian Society, 1941–1991* (Oxford: Oxford University Press); O. Kucherenko (2011) *Little Soldiers: How Soviet Children Went to War 1941–1945* (Oxford: Oxford University Press); J. Fürst (2010) *Stalin's Last Generation: Soviet Post-War Youth and the Emergence of Mature Socialism* (Oxford: Oxford University Press).

5. A. Krylova (2010) *Soviet Women in Combat: A History of Violence on the Eastern Front* (Cambridge: Cambridge University Press); R. D. Markwick and E. Charon Cardona (2012) *Soviet Women on the Frontline in the Second World War* (Basingstoke: Palgrave Macmillan); R. Pennington (2007) *Wings, Woman and War: Soviet Airwomen in World War II Combat* (Lawrence: University Press of Kansas).

6. K. Petrone (2002) 'Masculinity and Heroism in Imperial and Soviet Military-Patriotic Cultures', in B. Evans Clements, R. Friedman, and D. Healey (eds), *Russian Masculinities in History and Culture* (Basingstoke: Palgrave Macmillan), pp. 172–93.

7. C. Merridale (2012) 'Masculinity at War. Did Gender Matter in the Soviet Army?', *Journal of War and Culture Studies*, vol. 5, no. 3, pp. 307–20, here p. 310.

8. B. Fieseler (2006) 'The Bitter Legacy of the "Great Patriotic War": Red Army Disabled Soldiers under Late Stalinism', in J. Fürst (ed.), *Late Stalinist Russia: Society between Reconstruction and Reinvention* (London: Routledge), pp. 46–61; B. Fieseler (2013) 'Soviet-style Welfare: the Disabled Soldiers of the "Great Patriotic War"', in M. Rasell and E. Iarskaia-Smirnova (eds), *Disability in Eastern Europe and the Former Soviet Union: History, Policy and Everyday Life* (London: Routledge), pp. 18–41; F. L. Bernstein (2013) 'Prosthetic promise and Potemkin limbs in late-Stalinist Russia', in Rasell and Iarskaia-Smirnova (eds), *Disability in Eastern Europe and the Former Soviet Union*, pp. 42–66; F. L. Bernstein (2014) 'Rehabilitation Staged: How Soviet Doctors "Cured" Disability in the Second

World War', in S. Burch and M. Rembis (eds) *Disability Histories* (Urbana, Chicago, and Springfield: University of Illinois Press), pp. 218–36; C. E. McCallum (2015) 'Scorched by the Fire of War: Masculinity, War Wounds and Disability in Soviet Visual Culture, 1941–65', *Slavonic and East European Review*, vol. 93, no. 2, pp. 251–85.

9. E. Pollock (2010) '"Real Men Go to the Bania" Postwar Soviet Masculinities and the Bathhouse', *Kritika: Explorations in Russian and Eurasian History*, vol. 11, no. 1, pp. 47–76.

10. C. E. McCallum (2015) 'The Return: Postwar Masculinity and the Domestic Space in Stalinist Visual Culture, 1945–53', *Russian Review*, vol. 74, no. 1, pp. 117–43.

11. Merridale, 'Masculinity at War', p. 308.

12. G. Hosking (2006) *Rulers and Victims: The Russians in the Soviet Union* (Cambridge, MA: Belknap Press of Harvard University Press), pp. 209–10; Merridale, *Ivan's War*, p. 5; R. Braithwaite (2006), *Moscow 1941: A City and its People at War* (London: Profile), p. 139.

13. J. Hellbeck (2015) *Stalingrad: The City That Defeated the Third Reich*, trans. by C. Tauchen and D. Bonfiglio (New York: Public Affairs), pp. 47–50.

14. R. Sartorti (1995) 'On the Making of Heroes, Heroines, and Saints', in R. Stites (ed.), *Culture and Entertainment in Wartime Russia* (Bloomington and Indianapolis: Indiana University Press), pp. 176–93, here pp. 181–2.

15. Reese, *Why Stalin's Soldiers Fought*, p. 191.

16. E. Seniavskaia (1995) *Frontovoe Pokolenie 1941–1945: Istoriko-psikhologicheskoe issledovanie* (Moscow: IRI-RAN).

17. Petrone, 'Masculinity and Heroism', p. 185.

18. J. A. Sanborn (2003) *Drafting the Russian Nation: Military Conscription, Total War and Mass Politics, 1905–1925* (DeKalb: Northern Illinois University Press), p. 144.

19. Sanborn, *Drafting the Russian Nation*, p. 163.

20. Quoted in Hosking, *Rulers and Victims*, p. 194.

21. On the role of primary groups in the Red Army, see Reese, *Why Stalin's Soldiers Fought*, pp. 216–27.

22. Seniavskaia, *Frontovoe Pokolenie 1941–1945*, pp. 85–6.

23. Merridale, 'Masculinity at War', p. 312.

24. Kucherenko, *Little Soldiers*, pp. 151–92, here p. 179; Merridale, *Ivan's War*, pp. 214–16, 273.

25. Merridale, *Ivan's War*, p. 216.

26. Hellbeck, *Stalingrad*, p. 371.

27. Reese, *Why Stalin's Soldiers Fought*, p. 155.

28. Reese, *Why Stalin's Soldiers Fought*, p. 156.

29. B. Zajichek (2009) 'Scientific Psychiatry in Stalin's Soviet Union: The Politics of Modern Medicine and the Struggle to Define "Pavlovian" Psychiatry, 1939–1953', PhD Dissertation, University of Chicago, p. 128.

30. Zajichek, 'Scientific Psychiatry in Stalin's Soviet Union', p. 132.

31. Reese, *Why Stalin's Soldiers Fought*, p. 174.

32. Merridale, *Ivan's War*, p. 232.

33. Reese, *Why Stalin's Soldiers Fought*, p. 234; Merridale, *Ivan's War*, p. 232.

34. Krylova, *Soviet Women in Combat*, pp. 183–8.

35. Marwick and Charon Cardona, *Soviet Women on the Frontline*, pp. 138–40.

36. K. Slepyan (2006) *Stalin's Guerrillas: Soviet Partisans in World War II* (Lawrence: University of Kansas Press), p. 196.

37. N. Naimark (1995) *The Russians in Germany: A History of the Soviet Zone of Occupation, 1945–1949* (Cambridge, MA: Belnap Press of Harvard University

Press,), pp. 69–140; A. Grossmann (1995) 'A Question of Silence: The Rape of German Women by Occupation Soldiers', *October*, vol. 72, pp. 43–63; Merridale, *Ivan's War*, pp. 266–79.

38. Merridale, *Ivan's War*, pp. 267, 275.
39. F. Slaveski (2013) *The Soviet Occupation of Germany: Hunger, Mass Violence, and the Struggle for Peace, 1945–1947* (Cambridge: Cambridge University Press), p. 28.
40. 'Pervye dni posle voiny', *Krasnaia zvezda*, 17 May 1945, p. 3; 'Sovetskie garnizony v zarubezhnykh stolytsakh', *Krasnaia zvezda*, 23 May 1945, p. 1; 'krasnoarmeiskaia pesnia za rubezhom', *Krasnaia zvezda*, p. 3.
41. Naimark, *The Russians in Germany*, p. 79.
42. Slaveski, *The Soviet Occupation of Germany*, pp. 35–6.
43. Edele, *Soviet Veterans of the Second World War*, pp. 26–7.
44. TsGA-SPb/f.7179/op.11/d.1266/l.1 and TsGA-SPb/f.7179/op.53/d.90/l.19 in A. Z. Dzeniskevich (ed.) (2007), *Iz raionov oblasti soobshchaiut…: Svobodnye ot okkypatsii raiony Leningradskoi oblasti v gody Velikoi Otechestvennoi voiny: 1941–1945. Sbornik dokumentov.* (St. Petersburg: Dmitrii Bulanin), pp. 367–8 and p. 456.
45. TsGA-SPb/f.7179/op.53/d.132/ll.278–80.
46. TsGA-SPb/f.7179/op.53/d.132/l.259.
47. For examples see TsGA-SPb/f.7179/op.53/d.132/l.151; TsGA-SPb/f.7179/op.53/d.132/ l.164; TsGA-SPb/f.7179/op.53/d.167/l.21.
48. 'Snova na rodnom zavod', *Trud*, 23 February 1946, p. 2.
49. *Demobilizovannomy voiny Krasnoi Armii* (Tbilisi: Izdanie politicheskogo upravleniia Tbivo, 1946), pp. 17–18.
50. Quoted in Weiner, *Making Sense of War*, p. 316.
51. 'Zasuchit' rukava, da rabotat', rabotat'', *Elektrosila*, 12 November 1945, p. 1.
52. E. Seniavskaia (1999) *Psikhologiia voina v XX veke: istoricheskii opyt Rossii* (Moscow: ROSSPEN), p. 187.
53. Merridale, *Ivan's War*, p. 306.
54. A. Weiner (2000) 'Saving Private Ivan: From What, Why, and How?', *Kritika: Explorations in Russian and Eurasian History*, vol. 1, no. 2, pp. 305–36, here p. 317.
55. 'Sluchai s demobilizovannym', *Krokodil*, 20 December 1945, p. 8;'Na privychnom yzyke', *Krokodil*, 10 August 1945, p. 3.
56. Fürst, *Stalin's Last Generation*, pp. 60–1.
57. G. F. Kirosheev (ed.) (1997) *Soviet Casualties and Combat Losses in the Twentieth Century* (London: Greenhill Books), pp. 97–8.
58. S. Grant (2013) *Physical Culture and Sport in Soviet Society: Propaganda, Acculturation and Transformation in the 1920s and 1930s* (London: Routledge).
59. A. Krylova (2001) '"Healers of Wounded Souls": The Crisis of Private Life in Soviet Literature, 1944–1946', *The Journal of Modern History*, vol. 73, no. 2, pp. 307–31, here p. 310.
60. Krylova, '"Healers of Wounded Souls"', pp. 315–16.
61. V. Dunham (1989) 'Images of the Disabled, Especially the War Wounded, in Soviet Literature', in W. O. McCagg and L. Siegelbaum (eds), *The Disabled in the Soviet Union: Past and Present, Theory and Practice* (Pittsburgh, PA: University of Pittsburgh Press), pp. 151–64, here pp. 152–3.
62. Krylova, '"Healers of Wounded Souls"', p. 316.
63. M. C. Galmarini (2014) 'Turning Defects to Advantages: The Discourse of Labour in the Autobiographies of Soviet Blinded Second World War Veterans', *European History Quarterly*, vol. 44, no. 4, pp. 651–77.
64. Krylova, '"Healers of Wounded Souls"'.
65. L. Attwood (1999) *Creating the New Soviet Woman: Women's Magazines as Engineers of Female Identity, 1922–53* (Basingstoke: Macmillan), pp. 155–8.

66. Edele, *Soviet Veterans,* pp. 55–8.

67. Zubkova, *Russia After the War,* p. 21.

68. M. Nakachi (2006) 'Population, Politics and Reproduction: Late Stalinism and its Legacy', in Fürst, *Late Stalinist Russia,* pp. 23–45, here p. 23.

69. J. L. Strohm (1948) *"Just Tell the Truth" The Uncensored Story of How the Common People Live Behind the Iron Curtain* (New York, London: Charles Scribner's and Sons), p. 27.

70. O. M. Verbitskaia (2009) *Rossiiskaia sel'skaia sem'ia v 1897–1959 gg.* (Moscow – Tula: Grif i K), p. 207.

71. N. A. Aralovets (2009) *Gorodskaia sem'ia v Rossii 1927–1959 gg.* (Tula: Grif i K), p. 137.

72. McCallum, 'The Return', p. 127.

73. McCallum, 'The Return', p. 142.

74. E. Baraban (2007) '"The Fate of a Man" by Sergei Bondarchuk and the Soviet Cinema of Trauma', *The Slavonic and East European Journal,* vol. 5, no. 3, pp. 514–34, here p. 519.

75. Baraban, '"The Fate of a Man"', p. 530.

76. J. Woll (2000) *Real Images: Soviet Cinema and the Thaw* (London and New York: I. B. Tauris), pp. 92–3; B. Beumers (2009), *A History of Russian Cinema* (Oxford: Berg), p. 123.

77. Merridale, *Ivan's War,* p. 317.

78. Attwood, *Creating the New Soviet Woman,* pp. 155–6.

79. TsGA-SPb/f.7384/op.36/d.276/ll.30–4.

80. LOGAV/f.R-4380/op.1/d.1211/ll.4–6.

81. A. Platonov (1999) *The Return and Other Stories,* trans. by R. and E. Chandler and A. Livingstone (London: Harvill Press), pp. 173–203.

82. Merridale, 'Masculinity at war', p. 315.

83. G. Iankovskaia (2010) '"Shel soldat s fronta" Poslevoennye realii i gendernye obrazy sovetskikh illiustrirovannykh zhurnalov', in B. Fieseler and N. Muan (eds), *Pobediteli i pobezhdennye. Ot voiny k miry: SSSR, Frantsiia, Velikobritaniia, Germaniia, SShA (1941–1950)* (Moscow: ROSSPEN), pp. 284–96.

84. M. Nakachi (2010) 'Gender, Marriage and Reproduction in the Postwar Soviet Union', in G. Alexopoulos, J. Hessler, and K. Tomoff (eds), *Writing the Stalin Era: Sheila Fitzpatrick and Soviet Historiography* (Basingstoke: Palgrave Macmillan), pp. 101–16, here pp. 101–2.

85. Nakachi, 'Gender, Marriage and Reproduction', p. 106.

86. E. D. Cohn (2009) 'Sex and the Married Communist: Family Trouble, Marital Infidelity, and Party Discipline in the Postwar USSR, 1945–64', *Russian Review,* vol. 68, no. 3, pp. 429–50; S. Fitzpatrick (2005), *Tear off the masks! Identity and Imposture in Twentieth-Century Russia* (Princeton: Princeton University Press), pp. 240–61.

87. On divorce, see D. A. Field (1998) 'Irreconcilable Differences: Divorce and Conceptions of Private Life in the Khrushchev Era', *Russian Review,* vol. 57, no. 4, pp. 599–613.

9

Pacific Partners: Gendered Memories of the US Marines in Melbourne, 1943

Kate Darian-Smith

Reminiscing fifty years later about his extended leave in wartime Melbourne during 1943, a veteran of the 1st Marine Division, United States Marine Corps reflected that:

> In Australia we were on our own. Not depending on parents. We had our own money and we were free to make our own choices to a certain degree. For most of us, it was a time to sow our wild oats. There were plenty of young ladies who were willing to help us. Wine, women and song became the norm for a period. Then that wore off. For most of us, we looked and found lasting relationships. It really was a growing up process.[1]

Coming-of-age narratives such as this remain the dominant trope within a sweeping array of literary and cinematic representations of the personal and collective experiences of soldiers during World War II. This is not surprising, given the youth of the majority of combatants and war's extraordinary and transformative impact from the battlefields to the home front. As writer and ex-Marine Leon Uris has aptly commented: 'World War II is the biggest thing that ever happened to anybody that fought in it. For most people—let's say 95 per cent—it was the biggest thing that happened in their life, and it happened when they were very young.'[2]

This chapter examines one episode in the shared Australian and American histories of the Pacific War, and how this has been remembered across time. In January 1943, battle-weary and in poor health following the gruelling Guadalcanal campaign in the Solomon Islands, 15,000 men of the 1st Marine Division were shipped to Melbourne, and smaller Victorian towns, for a lengthy recuperation leave of eight months. Greeted with warm hospitality by Australian civilians, these young American men found, in their own words, a 'home away from home'. Many formed firm friendships with Australian families, and some entered into romantic attachments, including formal engagements and marriage, with young Australian women.

Following World War II, the lives of most former Marines revolved around establishing their careers and forming and supporting their families in towns and cities across the United States. However, as the men retired, their recollections of Australia often came to assume a particular importance and were shared, including for the first time, with families and friends. Old age offered both the time and the inclination to reflect on the successes and disappointments of the men's life course, a process whereby the remembrance of youthful experiences may be emotionally beneficial for individuals.[3] As ex-Marines reviewed their lives, memories of wartime Melbourne could provide a positive contrast to those recollections of fighting against the Japanese and the associated traumas, both immediate and longer-term, of gruelling combat – which for the 1st Marine Division included fighting at Guadalcanal, Cape Gloucester, Peleliu, Okinawa, and Iwo Jima.

'The remembered war is sometimes very different to the fought war. The details of pleasant wartime experiences can be recalled long after the rotten smell, the sour taste and the menacing sounds of battle are forgotten', the 1st Marine Division's official historian George McMillan observed in 1949.[4] In those immediate post-war years, the 1st Marine Division Association was formed, growing out of a small reunion held in Boston. It eventually comprised forty chapters throughout the United States, and one in Melbourne whose members were Marines who had settled in Australia, usually because their wives were Australian. The fluctuating financial and political fortunes of the Association can be traced through its official publication, the *Old Breed News.* Membership slumped following the Vietnam War. By the 1990s, numbers had swelled and many ex-Marines who had seen service in the Pacific War became active participants, especially following the 50th anniversary of the Battle of Guadalcanal.[5] The Association and related gatherings fostered memories of Melbourne, and emphasized the centrality of the link with Australia to the 1st Division's core identity. This remains significant, with the 1st Marine's official battle-hymn, the Australian folksong 'Waltzing Matilda', still played on ceremonial occasions.

In the early 1990s, Australian historian Rachel Jenzen made contact with around 150 ex-Marines, all members of the veterans' Association, who had been stationed in Melbourne during 1943. Her research resulted in a unique and comprehensive archive of letters, memorabilia, and around fifty oral histories which I have drawn upon for this chapter. In the 1980s, I had undertaken a complementary group of oral histories with Australian women about their lives in Melbourne during World War II.[6] Many of the narratives running through these Australian memoirs highlight how World War II disrupted and unsettled traditional gendered expectations and behaviours, most notably, if not exclusively, for young women. Indeed, the majority of those women I interviewed recounted their wartime experiences through tropes of romance and adventure, recalling their sexualized younger selves and their emotional attachments to Australian and American servicemen, and the meanings of those relationships in the past and the present.[7] National and community responses to women's transgression of pre-war behaviours, whether in the public sphere of the work-force or in the private realm, were shaped, to a degree, by the cross-cultural interactions between the two Allied nations on the Australian home front. Both collections of oral histories also illustrate the gender-specific nature of memory, and the significance of evolving personal and collective understandings of femininity and masculinity during World War II to the structure and form of life narratives.[8]

Today, seven decades after the Japanese surrender to the Allied forces on 15 August 1945, the vast majority of men and women who experienced that war as young adults have died. The passage of time has meant that the oral interviews Jenzen and I recorded in the 1980s and 1990s are now historically contextualized by the moment of their collection. The rising wave of popular interest around the world in the experiences and reverberations of civilians and soldiers during World War II suggests – paradoxically – that as the war is no longer present within lived memory, the forms of its commemorative representations have become increasingly prominent in national understandings of its cultural and political impact. In 1995, for instance, the Australian government's official programme to mark the 50th anniversary of victory in the Pacific contributed to a national memory about the Pacific War by focusing attention on this event and its impact on individuals, families, and the nation. From 2014, the centenary of World War I has been commemorated internationally. This has been most vigorously undertaken in Australia, where a relatively large government budget has produced an avalanche of publicly funded activities to memorialize Australia's role in both world wars.[9]

This chapter examines the Australian sojourn of the 1st Division Marines during 1943 in its historical context, and how it is situated within the larger World War II accounts of the Australian–American alliance and its influences on social, and gendered, changes on the home front. It then explores the ways in which, in the 1990s, as ageing ex-Marines reviewed their wartime experiences, they gave prominence to the affirming time they spent in Melbourne with Australian families and girlfriends. More than twenty years later, television and public history representations of Australian and American interactions during the Pacific War have contributed to the ways that new 'memories' of the US Marines in Melbourne are transmitted across generations and positioned in cultural and political contexts.

Australia and the United States: Pacific partners

In the wake of the Japanese bombing of the American naval base at Pearl Harbor, Hawaii on 7 December 1941, and the entry of the United States into World War II, a new military theatre opened in the Asia-Pacific region. Australia had been at war since September 1939, with its military forces fighting in Europe and the Middle East. As the crisis in the Pacific unfolded, the newly elected Labor Prime Minister John Curtin recalled the Second Australian Imperial Force back home, and issued his famous New Year message to the nation on 27 December 1941: 'I make it quite clear that Australia looks to America, free of any pangs as to our traditional links or kinship with the United

Kingdom.'[10] While ties with Britain were by no means broken, Australia was heavily reliant on the military power of the United States in the Pacific theatre.

In early 1942, the Japanese advanced through the Malay Peninsula, capturing the 'impregnable' British naval base at Singapore on 15 February 1942 and taking 85,000 Allied soldiers, including an entire Australian division, as prisoners of war. When Darwin was bombed on 19 February, it appeared a Japanese invasion of Australia was imminent and civilian morale plummeted. The nation was swiftly transformed for total war, with comprehensive government controls over labour, production, and consumption. The Manpower Directorate oversaw all employment, industry was regulated, and a system of rationing was introduced based on the British model of exchanging coupons for tea, sugar, meat, and clothing. Luxuries such as chocolates, cigarettes, and alcohol were unavailable or in short supply. Other wartime restrictions over every aspect of daily life, from travel to leisure, meant that the Australian population was placed under greater regulation than any time prior or since.

By early 1942, the appearance of Australian cities was transformed by the introduction of air raid precaution (ARP) measures, again taken from British precedents. A nightly 'blackout' was enforced in Melbourne and other industrial cities, and trenches and air raid shelters built in public parks, school grounds, and in private homes. Sandbags were piled up in the city streets to contain damage if bombing occurred. Thousands of civilians volunteered as ARP wardens and organized drills. A scorched earth policy was discussed, including a potential plan to abandon the top half of the continent in the event of a Japanese invasion.[11]

One of the largest challenges facing the government was the control of labour. Australian had entered the war on the back of the high unemployment and distress of the Depression. Unlike Britain and the United States, Australian women had not moved in significant numbers into the industrial workforce during World War I and their contribution was generally restricted to voluntary activities for the Red Cross and similar organizations. When war broke out in 1939, the government set up a Women's Voluntary Register, but initially it concentrated on male employment. With war in the Pacific, however, exports to Britain and US Lend-Lease contracts meant that manufacturing grew at an unprecedented rate, with severe labour shortages in industry and agriculture.

In response, the government turned more actively to the recruitment of women into munitions, food processing, and textiles plants, as well as into the women's auxiliary military services, the Women's Land Army, and clerical and professional employment. Such war work was publicly aligned with a new and respectable form of feminine patriotism, and there was much acclaim for women who released men to fight and took on pre-war 'male' jobs (though seldom receiving equal pay) for 'the duration'. By 1944, women's participation in paid employment peaked at around 25 per cent of the total workforce, a figure that included a greater number of women who were married, and had children, than in pre-war years.[12] There were other changes: more middle-class women were in paid employment, and the earning capacity of working-class women was increased through wartime bonuses and overtime.

The expansion of employment opportunities for Australian women during World War II was highly visible, and signalled broader shifts in gendered behaviours and the social constructions of femininity. Women's memories of wartime, as seen in my oral interviews, include stories of youthful independence, including the flouting of pre-war and parental expectations but also the emotional and financial difficulties experienced by those whose husbands were away on military service. By the time of the Pacific War, the contradictions between the traditional roles of women as wives, mothers, and home-makers, and their new significance as workers was widely discussed in newspapers, on radio, and in popular magazines such as the *Australian Women's Weekly*. Australian novels set on the home front, such as the best-selling *Come in Spinner* by Dymphna Cusack and Florence James, also offered a critique of social dislocation of war and the resulting divisions between civilians and the military, the Australians and Americans, and – most deeply – between men and women.[13] Novels, autobiographies, and much contemporary commentary have focused on women's changed opportunities and behaviours as an immediate consequence of war. However, wartime representations of women also reflected continuity with the increasingly overt representations of female sexuality and consumerism that came to dominate popular culture and advertising during the 1920s and 1930s.[14]

The arrival of the US forces in Australia emphasized gender as much as national differences. As the supply base for Allied operations in the South West Pacific during World War II, almost 1 million US service personnel passed through Australian ports, cities, and towns en route to military engagement in the region. Their presence was numerically highest during 1942 and 1943, declining rapidly in the last two years of war. For many American service personnel, Australia was a fleeting and transitory destination. Others spent weeks or months stationed throughout the continent, especially in the remote north, including the Queensland towns of Townsville and Rockhampton, and state capital Brisbane.[15] Melbourne, as the industrial hub of the south, served as the initial headquarters of the South West Pacific Area, under the supreme command of US General Douglas MacArthur. When MacArthur arrived in Melbourne on 17 March 1942, after a dramatic flight from the Philippines, a cheering crowd of thousands greeted him as a saviour. By June, there were 30,000 American troops stationed in Melbourne, primarily in military camps in the city's open parklands.

The Australian people were relieved and excited at the American presence and eager to meet the GIs. Comparisons were made between the two national groups, with the Americans issued with *A Pocket Guide to Australia* to explain its slang, customs, and history.[16] In turn, Australians were fascinated with the accents and uniforms of the GIs, and amazed at their social ease with women, including providing regular gifts of chocolates or flowers. There were regular commentaries in the Australian press about the contrasting models of masculine behaviour displayed between Australian and American men, and this also features in the oral and written memories of both sexes and nationalities. The US Hospitality Bureau organized social events, inviting civilian women to serve as 'Victory Girls' at dances. American military policy was to promote a 'healthy' heterosexuality among its troops during World War II, as a measure not only to quell homosexuality, but also to boost the morale of soldiers. However, Melbourne's inadequate entertainment facilities and overcrowding meant that every night throngs of American soldiers and Australian civilians wandered the city streets, or gathered at hotels and amusement parks in beach-side St Kilda. This prompted local church leaders and the police to express concern about the perceived moral breakdown of Australian women, and what they saw as the questionable behaviour of American servicemen.

Nightly curfews, and legislation enabling the forcible detainment of women suspected of having a sexually transmitted disease, were introduced to control female sexual promiscuity. In June 1942, the murders of three women in inner Melbourne, with their bodies found in a state of undress, created a sensation. The Americans were held responsible by the Australian population even before US Private Eddie Leonski confessed to the crimes. Leonski was swiftly court-martialled and hanged, as the American military sought to repair the reputational damage. In addition, increasing tensions between US and Australian troops contributed to anxiety about what was seen as a darker and perverse side of American masculinity. When MacArthur relocated his headquarters to Brisbane in July 1942, soon followed by his troops, there was considerable relief in Melbourne.[17]

Consequently, in January 1943, the 1st Division Marines' presence in Melbourne, and the towns of Ballarat and Mount Martha, was stage-managed as a public relations exercise. The notion of 'Pacific Partners' with a shared history and values was emphasized by the American and Australian military authorities, and extended into the organization of hospitality services within local communities. In addition, the Marines were presented to the Australian population not only as the heroes of Guadalcanal, where the Americans had seen victory, but as an elite volunteer military force. The ethos of the Marine Corps had an extraordinary impact on its members' sense of self and understandings of masculinity, both as serving soldiers and as veterans. The emphasis on selective recruitment processes, rigorous training, and the expectation of extreme mental and physical toughness conditioned the Marines to perceive themselves as 'a breed apart' from the other armed forces and to see themselves as especially 'macho'. Such beliefs exerted a lasting psychological hold, to the extent that veterans make a point of stating 'there is no such thing as an ex-Marine'.

The men of the 1st Marine Division had enlisted in the Corps because of its reputation for adventure. They mostly came from agricultural and blue-collar backgrounds, with an average age of under twenty years.[18] Bob Barton was typical. He dropped out of school to volunteer for the Corps immediately after the Japanese bombing of Pearl Harbor. Before he left for boot camp at Parris Island, South Carolina, Bob had not travelled further than seven miles from his home. Bob described arriving in Melbourne on 12 January 1943 after four and a half months on Guadalcanal as 'really wonderful, almost beyond explanation'.[19] Like his fellow Marines, he was very ill. Veteran Norris Cole recalled: 'The Division suffered 100% casualties, with the dead, wounded, and those sick from malaria, dengue fever, jungle rot, malnutrition and combat fatigue ... we were a pretty sickly bunch.'[20] The men most severely affected were hospitalized, although bouts of malaria were recurrent. As they recovered, the Americans came to view Melbourne as a kind of paradise, representing the antithesis of war. In the 1990s, they were still grateful for the way Melbournians 'adopted a group of malaria ridden teenagers who were a long way from home'.[21] Irving 'Red' Schlesinger expressed his overwhelming sense of gratitude: 'I cannot put into proper perspective the manner in which those fine Australian people treated we fellows, who had just come out of combat with the enemy and were in dire need of love and affection. Honestly, it was love at first sight.'[22]

Over the next eight months, the 1st Marine Division was accommodated in the covered spectator stands of the Melbourne Cricket Ground, although many officers were placed in private apartments. When 'on liberty' and eager to forget about the war, the men were keen to explore Melbourne; for some, it was the biggest city they had ever seen. The Australian and US military authorities were keen to minimize any friction between the Marines and Australian civilians, and public demonstrations of goodwill were held. On 22 February 1943, the Marines staged a public parade through central Melbourne in celebration of George Washington's birthday, and local people were encouraged to cheer them on. Relations between Australian servicemen on leave and the Marines were sometimes tense, especially when alcohol was involved; a large brawl that erupted in the city one night became popularly known as the 'Battle of Melbourne'. In March 1943, a timely public relations function with food and copious amounts of beer was held at the Melbourne Cricket Ground to promote ongoing goodwill between the Allied military partnership. Banners strung up reading 'Hi'Ya Digger' welcomed Australian soldiers into the American camp.

As they recovered their health, many Marines struck up close friendships with local families. The unique length of their eight months' recuperation leave meant these relationships were often very close (see Figure 9.1). Mrs Doris MacKenzie of East St Kilda 'adopted' Marine private Jack Callaghan, and sent long letters of reassurance to his mother in Oklahoma:

> My dear Mrs. Callaghan – You no doubt will be surprised to hear from me but I am writing to let you know where your son "Jack" is. I have had him staying with me and my family and I might tell you my dear that he is having a good rest and is looking wonderfully well. They have been here about 2 months. We have grown so fond of "Jack", and he is one of the family. He says we remind him so much of home. I try to cook him things that he used to get at home. He is a great kid. I have only one son and he is in uniform too. He is a great pal of Jack's … They go everywhere together…

> [Jack] has a bit of a cold. His cold seems to affect him when he gets into bed at night. I had to mix some honey and lemon. The other night I had not been in bed very long when he started to cough so I got up and made him the mixture and he slept the rest of the night…

> I had a nice fruit cake for Jack's birthday with 18 candles on it and we all drank his health with a large bottle of "Sparkling Hock". He asked me to send the card off his cake for you to keep for him … I do hope that I have put you at ease about Jack.[23]

Figure 9.1   US Marines and Melbourne friends, 1943.
Courtesy of Rachel Jenzen (Private Collection).

Marine Mitchell C. Grover found a substitute family in the Martins, and remembered: 'Mum and Pop fixed a table and provided me freely with food-stuffs that I just gorged myself on ... the main courses, salads, breads all prepared by that Most Admired "Mum"... almost daily from then throughout my stay.'[24] Grover continued to correspond with this family for decades, maintaining contact with his Australian 'sisters', and naming his first son in honour of his Australian 'father'.[25]

Alongside their memories of Australian families, are narratives about the romantic friendships developed between the 1st Division Marines and Australian women. Fifty years later many veterans spoke in great detail about their sexual experiences, often within a wider life narrative of the transition from boyhood to adulthood and the development of a new emotional maturity. For instance, in a typical example, one Marine remembered:

> Much happened to me there [in Melbourne] such as first love, and the 'rite of passage' from boy to man through the gentle and understanding guidance of a lonely war widow, the first experience of helping someone else find themselves in the topsy-turvy world of that time, the appreciation of art, poetry and classical music.

Another recalled the intensity of his first sexual experiences:

> [She] was the first girl I ever saw in the nude. (Does she think I could have forgotten? No way, the events are as vivid as yesterday). It was driven, intense, epic. It

gave life meaning in the utmost sense. When she would get off the train at the Flinders Street [Railway] Station and join the group of girls walking across the Yarra [River] to [work], she would fill them in on our past night's activities. I had not told a single person, and didn't until some 4 years ago... She was just that free-spirited... It was life at its erotic best, it was paradise. There was nothing before that was worth remembering and nothing after has been its equal.[26]

Other memories of wartime romance were about longer-term relationships, and have been retold many times, especially when they resulted in marriage. Around 12,000 to 15,000 Australian women migrated to the United States at the end of World War II to join the men they had met during the war, and this included several hundred women who had partnered with the 1st Division Marines.[27] Among them was Melbourne girl Dawne McLeod-Sharpe. She later recalled in an interview, in a narrative of excited expectation, that before the arrival of the 1st Division Marines in 1943:

Melbourne was an empty city. The only men you saw were little boys or very old men, or men who had a special pin on their lapel to tell you that they were not physically fit to serve... Women drove the trains, women delivered the mail, women did everything, which made it very difficult when the war was over of course and they couldn't do those jobs. And it really was a very sad city because our men were over in places like Tobruk and the news was very, very bad... When [the Marines] came the whole city came alive again.[28]

In a written memoir, based on her wartime journal and narrated as a love story, Dawne described meeting by chance on a suburban train the 'handsomest boy I had ever seen in my life', Marine Corporal Fred Balester. They began courting and Dawne remembered:

Early in our relationship I realized I was in love. Not quiet love. I knew what passionate love was now. It blinded me. Fred never used the word love ... after all, what future did we have? I was seventeen, he was nineteen. How could we even be sure of a life together?... So I made the most of every moment and never worried about the outcome.[29]

Fred returned to battle, and Dawne resolved to forget him. Then Fred sent a letter, and they began corresponding regularly. In 1945 Fred proposed, and a year later Dawne embarked on the lengthy sea voyage on the SS *Monterey* to the United States with other war brides. She travelled on to meet Fred at the coalmining town of Wilkes-Barre, Pennsylvania. After three years apart, the couple married within a week and honeymooned at Niagara Falls. They were to have five children, and a happy marriage that ended when Fred died in 2009 (see Figure 9.2).

In contrast to the shared reminiscences of the Balesters, some ex-Marines harboured memories of loss and regret, and a yearning in old age to confront the past. In later life, there were attempts to reunite with former Melbourne girlfriends, and to address past misunderstandings. Marine Bob Barton was stationed at the Melbourne Cricket Ground during 1943, but spent much time

Figure 9.2   Melbourne war bride Dawne McLeod-Sharpe and husband Fred Balester pictured on their wedding day in Wilkes-Barre, Pennsylvania in 1946 and in the mid-1980s. *Courtesy of Rachel Jenzen (Private Collection).*

with his girlfriend Shirley and her family. They became engaged just before he left for the military front. He remembered:

> When I got hit in the face and lost my front teeth from Jap[anese] mortar sc[h]rapnel on Peleliu I just stopped writing....Since I was disfigured and she was such a beautiful girl [I guessed] she would no longer be interested in me. She wrote a couple of more times and when I didn't answer she figured I had broke[n] our engagement off. About one and a half years later when my face had healed and I had my false teeth, I regained my confidence and wrote to her. Her family replied to my letter, told me I had screwed-up her life enough, that she was engaged to a fellow and for me to please leave her alone. I did!![30]

After the war, Barton returned to the United States and enjoyed a long marriage, but fifty years later he sent a letter to a Melbourne newspaper inquiring about his former fiancée, a 'beautiful girl' from Footscray. Titled 'Desperately Seeking Shirl', the article was accompanied by photos of a glamorous Shirley in a bathing costume and broad-brimmed hat and Bob in his Marine Corps uniform. Barton was quoted: 'I am a happily married man and my only intentions are to correspond as I have been curious as to her whereabouts and welfare for many years.'[31] It was subsequently revealed that Shirley had died of illness in 1948, aged just twenty-eight. In 1994, Barton wrote in a letter to Jenzen that he 'was really disappointed that Shirley's parents did not inform me of her illness (even though she was married)', as he had been particularly close to them during his months in Melbourne.[32]

As these brief excerpts from the oral and written memories of ex-Marines reveal, their interlude in Australia during World War II were to gain a new significance as decades passed. The immediate priority for the men upon return to the United States was to secure employment. As one veteran explained: 'Moving on with life in college on the GI Bill, getting a job and raising a family, I mostly suppressed the bad memories of the war, although it is impossible to do this totally ... it seemed that people knew a little about Okinawa but nothing at all about Peleliu — what had happened there was obviously not of any great concern in central North Carolina.'[33] And in the 1st Marine Division's official history, published in 1949, a poem written by 'two Australian Red Cross girls' presents the Marines' months in Melbourne as lots of fun but already relegated to the past, and while sexual and emotional intimacy occurred it was of little ongoing consequence: 'Thanks for the memory/ Of troops who'd been in strife/ Kids who enjoyed life/ Of love affairs/ And foolish cares/ And photos of your wife./ How lovely it was.'[34]

Thanks for the memories

From the last decades of the twentieth century, an increasing prominence has been given to public and popular representations of Allied experiences during the Pacific War in both Australia and the United States. These have included an escalating number of commemorative events, memorials, museum exhibitions, and popular and academic publications in the lead-up to the 70th anniversary of the end of that conflict. From an Australian perspective, the Asia-Pacific military theatre has been central to national understandings of the impact of World War II: the fall of Singapore; the experiences of Australian prisoners of war; the bravery of Australian soldiers in the Pacific Islands and New Guinea; and Australia's changing cultural, security, and trade ties with the United States as a consequence of the wartime military alliance.[35]

In contrast, the public discourse in the United States about World War II has focused on the European campaigns, and such incidents as the D-Day landings of American troops on the beaches of Normandy. Aside from the Japanese attack on Pearl Harbor and the US atomic bombings in Japan – events which respectively brought the United States into the war and led to Japanese surrender – the Pacific theatre has long constituted America's 'forgotten war'. There has been, however, a popular 'rediscovery' of America's Pacific War, which can be understood within the wider political context of the United States reasserting its contemporary influence in Asia and the Pacific. The production of mainstream Hollywood films such as those directed by Terence Malick and Clint Eastwood has been instrumental in taking a fresh look at a faraway war, and in doing so narrating a story of nation as well as individual heroism and manhood.[36]

The history of the 1st Marine Division experiences in battle and on recuperation leave in Melbourne has also been retold in the HBO ten-part mini-series *The Pacific*. At a cost of over $200 million, *The Pacific* was the most expensive mini-series ever produced by a network, and much of the action was filmed in Australia. *The Pacific* is based primarily on two memoirs of US Marines: *With the Old Breed: At Peleliu and Okinawa* (1981) by Eugene Sledge and *Helmet for My Pillow* (1957) by Robert Leckie.[37] Following HBO's highly successful mini-series, *Band of Brothers* (2001), which traced the fortune of American soldiers in Europe, *The Pacific* told the story of the war 'that took place on the opposite side of the globe and seemed to have less of a hold on the imagination of most Americans'.[38] The third episode was set in Melbourne, with plot lines that included romance, and sexual intimacy, between the Marines and Australian women. It also highlighted how war had disrupted gendered expectations on the Australian home front, just as the series was a reflection on war and American masculinity.

The Pacific was screened in Australia in 2010, and as in the United States the critical response was generally positive. At the same time, a social history exhibition opened at the City Gallery in the Melbourne Town Hall provocatively titled *Over-Paid, Over-Sexed and Over Here? The U.S. Marines in Wartime Melbourne, 1943*.[39] The exhibition, which I curated with Rachel Jenzen, included the display of a Marine uniform and various 'props' (cigarette and food packages, magazines, and other memorabilia) that had been donated by the HBO art department and used in *The Pacific*. But it drew primarily upon historical materials, including oral and written materials from Jenzen's archive, in its interpretation of the impact and legacies of the 1st Marine Division's time in the city.

The exhibition drew a record crowd to the gallery over three months, including a small number of elderly men and women who had been teenagers or children during World War II and wanted to share and reflect upon their own memories.[40] A more significant segment of the audience were those whose parents, particularly their mothers, had friendships in wartime Melbourne with US soldiers and in some cases with Marines. Many were eager to share these transgenerational memories with the curators, or to leave comments in a visitors' book that was set up for this purpose. Among this group were a small number of adults who were the children of American servicemen, including at least one who was a Marine. This was not surprising, as recent research in New Zealand and the Pacific has highlighted how sexual intimacies between American servicemen and local women resulted in thousands of part-American children. The vast majority were illegitimate, and marriage between Pacific Island indigenous women and American servicemen was forbidden under US federal immigration and state anti-miscegenation legislation.[41]

None of these Australian individuals who were the children of US servicemen and attended the Melbourne exhibition had known their fathers, and with one exception they had been adopted or placed in care at birth. Their stories were both powerful and sad, highlighting how the silences and hopes of the past can be carried for decades. 'I really enjoyed the exhibition', wrote one woman who had only discovered in the 1990s that her father was an American serviceman. 'It helped me understand what those boys went through. I can feel closer to my dad, and *now have some memories of what he may have been like* [emphasis added]…'[42] As comments such as this show, the shaping of memories across generations, and outside the realms of lived experience, is complex and evolving and linked to individual circumstance and wider social and national forms of history-making and commemoration.

Conclusion

World War II was experienced by those who fought and lived through it as civilians in highly gendered ways. Indeed, the disruption to the roles of men and women was recognized in Australia at the time in relation to women's widening employment and social opportunities, as patriotism legitimized more active and public forms of femininity. While the arrival of the US military forces elicited official comments on the similarities between the histories and peoples of the two nations, it also placed a spotlight on the differing behaviours of Australian and American men, especially when it came to their interactions with women. Decades later, as the men of the 1st Marine Division looked back on their wartime youth, their memories of recuperation leave in Melbourne, and the relationships they formed with Australian families and girlfriends, were often the one affirming episode they had of the Pacific War. For young Melbourne women, the presence of the Marines in 1943 has been remembered as one wartime episode amid broader narratives of opening opportunities and relationships with Australian and American men – though of course this is a very different memory for those who were US war brides. Now, with few of that generation still alive, and as the 'lessons' of World War II are transmitted to subsequent generations through television dramas or in social history exhibitions, it is the personal stories of war – like those of the 1st Marine Division – that remain at the core of such remembrance work.

Recommended reading

Barker, A. J. and L. Jackson (1996) *Fleeting Attraction: A Social History of American Servicemen in Western Australia During the Second World War* (Nedlands: University of Western Australia Press).

Bennett, J. A., J. Leckie, and A. Wanhalla (2015) 'Mothers' darlings: Secrets and Silences in the Wake of the Pacific War', in C. Twomey and E. Koh (eds), *The Pacific War: Aftermaths, Remembrance and Culture* (Abingdon: Routledge), pp. 214–32.

Bornat, J. (2011) 'Remembering in Later Life: Generating Individual and Social Change', in D. Richie (ed.) *The Oxford Handbook of Oral History* (New York: Oxford University Press) pp. 202–18.

Cusack, D. and F. James (1951) *Come in Spinner* (Melbourne: Heinemann).

Darian-Smith, K. (2005) 'Remembrance, Romance and Nation: Women's Memories of Wartime Australia', in S. Leydesdorff, L. Passerini, and P. Thompson (eds), *Gender and Memory*, (New Brunswick, NJ: Transaction Publishers; first published Oxford: Oxford University Press, 1996), pp. 151–64.

Darian-Smith, K. (2009) *On the Home Front: Melbourne in Wartime 1939–1945*, 2nd edn (Melbourne, Melbourne University Press).

Lake, M. (1995) 'Female Desires: The Meaning of World War II', in J. Damousi and M. Lake (eds), *Gender and War: Australians at War in the Twentieth Century* (Melbourne: Cambridge University Press), pp. 60–80.

Potts, E. D. and A. Potts (1985) *Yanks Down Under 1941–45: The American Impact on Australia* (Melbourne: Oxford University Press).

Notes

1. J. Burgess, questionnaire sent to R. Jenzen, 6 September 1994.

2. Interview with L. Uris, cited in W. D. Jones Jr. (1998) *Gyrene: The World War II United States Marine* (Shippensburg, PA: White Mane Books), p. xxxi. Leon Uris (1924–2003) is an internationally known author; his autobiographical novel *Battle Cry*, published in 1953, described the experiences of his own Marine unit during World War II, when Uris was based at Guadalcanal and elsewhere in the Pacific. Uris also wrote the screenplay for the film of the same name, *Battle Cry* (1955) directed by R. Walsh, Warner Bros.

3. See, for instance, J. Bornat (2011) 'Remembering in Later Life: Generating Individual and Social Change' in D. Richie (ed.) *The Oxford Handbook of Oral History* (New York: Oxford University Press), pp. 202–18.

4. G. McMillan (1949) *The Old Breed: A History of The First Marine Division in World War II* (Washington, DC: Infantry Journal Press), p. 148.

5. For discussion of 1st Marine Division Association, see R. Jenzen (2001) *A Band of Brothers: United States Marines Remember World War II in the South-West Pacific, 1942–1945* (Master of Arts Dissertation, Department of History, University of Melbourne); K. Darian Smith and R. Jenzen (2009) 'Memories from America: Australian War Brides and US Marines Remember Australia and the Pacific during the Second World War', in M. Crotty (ed.), *When the Soldiers Return: Conference Proceedings* (Brisbane: University of Queensland), pp. 12–25.

6. I am grateful to R. Jenzen for generously granting permission to draw upon her archive for this article, and for her collegiality as a fellow scholar. Both archival collections are held privately, although some materials are available on the *Over-Paid, Over-Sexed and Over Here? The U.S. Marines in Wartime Melbourne 1943* website at: http://history.unimelb.edu.au/overhere/indexmain.html.
   See Jenzen (2001); K. Darian-Smith (2009) *On the Home Front: Melbourne in Wartime 1939–1945*, 2nd edn (Melbourne, Melbourne University Press).

7. K. Darian-Smith (2005) 'Remembrance, Romance and Nation: Women's Memories of Wartime Australia', in S. Leydesdorff, L. Passerini, and P. Thompson (eds), *Gender and Memory*, (New Brunswick, NJ: Transaction Publishers; first published Oxford: Oxford University Press, 1996), pp. 151–64; K. Darian-Smith (1997) 'War Stories: Remembering the Australian Home Front during the Second World War', in K. Darian-Smith and P. Hamilton (eds), *Memory and History in Twentieth Century Australia* (Melbourne: Oxford University Press), pp. 137–57; K. Darian-Smith (1995) 'Remembering Romance: Memory, Gender and the Second World War', in J. Damousi and M. Lake (eds), *Gender and War: Australians at War in the Twentieth Century* (Melbourne: Cambridge University Press), pp. 117–32.

8. A significant literature on gender, memory, oral history, and life narratives includes S. Leydesdorff, L. Passerini, and P. Thompson (eds) *Gender and Memory*, (New Brunswick, NJ: Transaction Publishers; first published Oxford University Press, 1996); S. H. Armitage (2011) 'The Stages of Women's Oral History', in D. Richie (ed.), *The Oxford Handbook of Oral History* (New York: Oxford University Press), pp. 169–86.

9. Australian federal and state governments have invested over $550 million (AUD) in World War I centenary activities, a much higher figure than other nations. For the 1995 World War II commemoration, see L. Reed (2004) *Bigger than Gallipoli? War, History and Memory in Australia* (Perth: University of West Australian Press).

10. *Herald* (Melbourne), 27 December 1941, p. 10.

11. For Australia at war see M. McKernan, (1983) *All In! Australia During the Second World War* (Nelson, Melbourne); K. Darian-Smith, K. (2013) 'World War 2 and Post-

war Reconstruction, 1939–49', in S. Macintyre and A. Bashford (eds), *Cambridge History of Australia, Volume 2* (Cambridge: Cambridge University Press), pp. 88–111.

12. Darian-Smith, *On the Home Front*.

13. D. Cusack and F. James (1951) *Come in Spinner* (Melbourne: Heinemann).

14. M. Lake (1995) 'Female Desires: The Meaning of World War II', in J. Damousi and M. Lake (eds), *Gender and War: Australians at War in the Twentieth Century* (Melbourne: Cambridge University Press), pp. 60–80.

15. The most detailed account of the US presence in Australia is E. D. Potts and A. Potts (1985) *Yanks Down Under 1941–45: The American Impact on Australia* (Melbourne: Oxford University Press). See also J. H. Moore (1981) *Over-Sexed, Over-Paid and Over Here: Americans in Australia 1941–1945* (St Lucia: University of Queensland Press); R. Campbell (1989) *Heroes and Lovers: A Question of National Identity* (Sydney: Allen and Unwin); and K. Darian-Smith (2013) 'The Home Front and the American Presence in 1942', in P. J. Dean (ed.), *Australia 1942: In the Shadow of War* (Cambridge, Cambridge University Press), pp. 70–88. Regional studies include A. J. Barker and L. Jackson (1996) *Fleeting Attraction: A Social History of American Servicemen in Western Australia During the Second World War* (Nedlands: University of Western Australia Press) and K. Saunders (1993) *War on the Home Front: State Intervention in Queensland 1938–1948* (St Lucia: University of Queensland Press).

16. United States Army (1943) *Pocket Guide to Australia* (Washington, DC: Government Printing Office). Journalist and author George Johnston wrote a more popular book explaining the Australian character to Americans. See G. Johnston (1944) *Pacific Partner* (New York: World Book Company).

17. Darian-Smith, *On the Home Front*, pp. 176–233.

18. G. McMillan (1949) *The Old Breed: A History of The First Marine Division in World War II* (Washington, DC: Infantry Journal Press), p. 15.

19. B. Barton, letter to R. Jenzen, 11 July 1995.

20. N. Cole, unpublished personal memoir. Date of composition unknown. Copy sent to R. Jenzen. [Received 7 November 1992.]

21. J. Biggins, letter to R. Jenzen, 5 November 1992.

22. I. Schlesinger, letter to R. Jenzen, 22 June 1992.

23. Mrs. D. MacKenzie, letter to Mrs. Callaghan, 16 March 1943; Mrs. D. MacKenzie, letter to Mrs. Callaghan, 5 July 1943; Mrs. D. MacKenzie, letter to Mrs. Callaghan, 28 September 1943. Copies of letters held by R. Jenzen. Unfortunately, there are no copies of Mrs. Callaghan's response.

24. M. C. Grover, letter to R. Jenzen, 28 July 1992.

25. Interview with P. Ellis by R. Jenzen, 16 July 1992.

26. See http://www.history.unimelb.edu.au/overhere/love-and-loss.html, date accessed 25 August 2015.

27. A. Potts and L. Strauss (1987) *For the Love of a Soldier: Australian War-Brides and their GIs* (Crow's Nest, New South Wales: Australian Broadcasting Corporation); also S. Zeiger (2010) *Entangling Alliances: Foreign War Brides and American Soldiers in the Twentieth Century* (New York: New York University Press).

28. Interview with D. and F. Balester by R. Jenzen, 17 August 1994. Thousands of Australian men in reserved occupations were forbidden from joining the military.

29. D. Balester, *Dawne's Journal*. http://uswarbrides.com/bride_stories/dawne.html, date accessed 25 August 2015.

30. B. Barton, letter to R. Jenzen, 20 April 1994.

31. *Herald Sun*, 14 June 1993.

32. B. Barton, letter to R. Jenzen, 20 April 1994.

33. J. Sharpe, Letter, *Old Breed News*, October 1995, p. 21.

34. McMillan, *The Old Breed*, pp. 155–8.

35. See Darian-Smith, 'World War 2 and Post-war Reconstruction, 1939–49'.

36. T. Malick (1998) *The Thin Red Line*, 20th Century Fox; C. Eastwood (2006) *Flags of Our Fathers*, Warner Bros; C. Eastwood, (2006) *Letters from Iwo Jima*, Warner Bros.; C. Franklin and others (2009) *The Pacific*, HBO, ten-part mini-series.

37. E. Sledge (1981) *With the Old Breed: At Peleliu and Okinawa* (Novatoia: Presidio Press); R. Leckie (1957) *Helmet for My Pillow* (New York: Random House).

38. N. Franklin (2010) 'Hell on Earth: HBO's 'The Pacific', *The New Yorker, vol.* 86, no. 4, 15 March, p. 68.

39. The exhibition *Over-Paid, Over-Sexed and Over Here?: U.S. Marines in Wartime Melbourne 1943*, was held at the City Gallery, Melbourne Town Hall 17 February to 30 April, 2010; with a reworked exhibition, *Over-Paid, Over-Sexed and Over Here?: U.S. Marines in Wartime Victoria 1943*, held at the Gold Museum, Sovereign Hill Historic Park, Ballarat, 5 December 2013 to 30 April 2014. The phrase 'Over-Paid, Over-Sexed and Over Here' was commonly used in Australia during World War II. The exhibition website is at: http://history.unimelb.edu.au/overhere/indexmain.html.

40. Attendance figures were over 15,000 people, a record for the City Gallery. I am grateful to the oversight of E. Butler-Bowdon, Manager, Art and Heritage Collection, City of Melbourne for his support for the exhibition.

41. For part-American children in New Zealand and the Pacific see J. A. Bennett, J. Leckie, and A. Wanhalla (2015) 'Mothers' Darlings: Secrets and Silences in the Wake of the Pacific War', in C. Twomey and E. Koh (eds), *The Pacific War: Aftermaths, Remembrance and Culture* (Abingdon: Routledge), pp. 214–32. See also *US Fathers of Pacific Children* website: http://www.otago.ac.nz/usfathers/, date accessed 25 October 2016.

42. Anonymous, correspondence to K. Darian-Smith, March 2010.

10

Conflicted Memories: Images, Realities, and Politics of Male Homosexuality in France during the Second World War

Florence Tamagne

In France, as in other warring countries, the Second World War resulted in a profound reconfiguration of gender norms and of relations between men and women. France had suffered a swift and traumatic defeat by Germany, characterized by a massive exodus of its population, and 1.6 million soldiers taken prisoner, an ordeal followed by the division of its territory into several zones, the occupation and military administration of the North Zone by Germany and the establishment of a new authoritarian political regime, the French State, headed by Marshal Pétain and based in Vichy, in the South Zone. After the Liberation of France, a period of legal and summary cleansing (*épuration*) took place, aimed at punishing collaborators. A Provisional Government of the French Republic (GPRF), headed by General de Gaulle, leader of the Free French, was established in 1944. It lasted until 1946, when the Fourth Republic was instituted. On 21 April, 1944, French women were granted the right to vote.

Although the Second World War, occupied France, and collaboration and resistance have been matters of heated historiographical debates, the question of gender roles and sexualities during the period has only been addressed very inconsistently.[1] Indeed, a global study of French masculinities during the period is still lacking.[2] Same-sex relations during the Second World War have also never been extensively studied. The subject is problematic in two ways. First, the period has been identified as a turning point for the legislation of same-sex relations in France. Although sodomy laws had been repealed in 1791, in 1942, Pétain's regime introduced a discriminative law that increased the age of consent in the case of same-sex relationships from thirteen to twenty-one, a measure confirmed at the Liberation. Secondly, with the annexation of Alsace-Moselle by Germany in 1940, homosexuals could now fall under Paragraph 175 of the

German Penal Code, which harshly sanctioned same-sex relations between men. A totally taboo topic after the war, the deportation of some Frenchmen for their homosexuality was the subject of increasing controversy from the 1970s, when gay activist movements intent on gaining recognition for 'pink triangles' came up against the hostility of many deportees' associations. It is still unclear today how many Frenchmen were deported for their homosexuality.[3]

This article provides an overview of the research on male homosexuality during the Second World War in France, as well as an assessment of the debates regarding same-sex relationships and memories of the war in the years from the Liberation to today. Despite the lack of thorough study of the daily life of French queer people during the Second World War, some broad tendencies can be identified, which this article explores. One major hypothesis is that the Second World War in France did not so much mark a turning point in terms of homosexual representations as reveal long-term prejudices at work within French society, the expression of which had, however, been relatively contained and circumscribed.

Troubled images of male homosexuality during the war: sadism, effeminacy, and corruption

Although the interwar period had been viewed as a period of greater visibility for the homosexual subculture in France, prejudices remained. From the end of the nineteenth century, France's declining birth rate had been a recurring concern, and homosexuality, as well as gender inversion, was held responsible for this situation, along with feminism, women's place in the workforce, abortion, and birth control movements. The fear of national decline merged with the fear of invasion. Homosexuals had been described for centuries as foreigners; from 1907 and following the Eulenburg affair, a political and sexual scandal that involved the Prussian army as well as favourite counsellors of the Kaiser, German soldiers had been vilified as effeminate sissies in the satirical press, and homosexuality had been dubbed a 'German vice'. During the First World War, homosexuals were represented as a danger to national defence and security. In the 1930s, when fears of communism merged with fears of homosexuality, the naval authorities at the military harbour of Toulon kept records on 'communist homosexual sailors'. [4]

The declaration of war rejuvenated these old clichés. During the phoney war, the popular daily newspaper *Paris-Soir* published a passage of Hermann Rauschning's book, *Hitler Speaks*, stating that the Führer used 'inverts' for missions of intelligence and counter-intelligence, thus reinforcing the image of the homosexual as a spy and traitor.[5] Other articles presented homosexuality as a sign of the moral degeneration of the Nazi regime by exploiting lurid reports of the Night of the Long Knives that saw the killing of the homosexual SA (*Sturmabteilung*) leader, Ernst Röhm.[6] Left-wing newspapers presented homosexuality as a 'fascist perversion', and sometimes made 'inverts' responsible for the 'explosion of cruelty' specific to the Nazi regime.[7] During the Occupation, the clandestine communist newspaper *L'Humanité* described the Nazis as 'robbers, murderers, pederasts, barbarians, depraved, ignoring, heartless and amoral people, capable of all crimes and a disgrace to mankind'.[8] In a similar vein, a Jewish journal quoted the British General Consul in Frankfurt, who wondered whether the tortures perpetrated in concentration camps could be explained by 'a sexual perversion, and more specifically homosexuality, which is very common in Germany'.[9]

This association of homosexuality with criminality and perversion was of course nothing new. It had been cultivated during the nineteenth century in medical and psychiatric literature, and relayed by the popular press, sensational novels, and spectacular scandals. Neither was it unique to French commentators. In various essays and novels, German political emigrants had developed the cliché of the homosexual Nazi, drawing support from the homoerotic aesthetic that pervaded paramilitary institutions such as the SA and the SS (*Schutzstaffeln*) or the *Hitlerjugend*, and the work of artists such as Arno Breker, Josef Thorak, and Leni Riefenstahl, as well as from the psychoanalytical theories of Wilhelm Reich.[10] As Richard Golsan and Melanie Hawthorne note, those 'gyno/homophobic readings' of fascism 'serve as much to condemn femininity and homosexuality as to clarify their role in fascist politics, ideology and psychology'.[11] The French media did not ignore the fact that same-sex relations were severely punished under German law and that homosexual men were deported to concentration camps, and sometimes executed.[12] Nevertheless, 'pink triangles' were clearly distinguished from other deportees, especially Jewish or political prisoners, and were equated with common criminals.[13]

Gender roles were also a subject of debate. As had been the case in 1914, the declaration of war was seen as an opportunity to get rid of any deviancy. In 'The Defeat of Vice', a sensationalist article published in *Détective*, a weekly tabloid dedicated to crime stories and lurid affairs, René-J. Piguet examined the consequences of the war on Parisian criminal nightlife, especially 'pimps, inverts, addicts, prostitutes'. Male prostitutes, such as 'Solange' (a woman's name), who would soon begin his training as a conscript, were forced to 'go straight'. The young man, who regretted the 'ravages of the clippers', which deprived him of his beautiful blond hair, 'could still put on airs for a few hours, act as a star in this mundane milieu; the day draws near when he would have the opportunity to become a man again'.[14] From 1940, following the defeat at German hands, analyses focused on the crisis of masculinity. Cultural representations were at stake. In sharp contrast to the virile heroes of the 1930s, such as Jean Gabin, a new mild and fragile masculine figure emerged in French cinema of the 1940s, with actors such as Charles Trénet and Jean Marais, both notorious homosexuals, enjoying great popular success, but causing outrage in the collaborationist press.[15] The journalist Alfred Fabre-Luce claimed that Pierre Dunoyer de Segonzac, at the time the leader of the School of Uriage (a youth institution created by Vichy to train the nation's future leaders) but who would later join the Resistance, had a sense of foreboding of the pending debacle when seeing soldiers gathered to listen to Tino Rossi's records: 'A eunuch makes the French women dream, and their husbands in uniform revered in him their own mediocrity. Tino Rossi in the trench! Such a scandal called for redemption – a virile worker-song in front of a barren land.'[16]

Youth was also a key issue. For Jacques-Paul Burin, the Chief of Staff to Fernand de Brinon, representative of the Vichy regime in occupied Paris, prisoner of war camps would be a new 'Spartan education system', where young citizens could be 'revilirised'.[17] Robert Brasillach, in the fascist newspaper *Je suis partout*, claimed that 'youth need a leader' instead of being 'entrusted to intellectuals'. Hitler Youth camps should provide the example against 'softening' influences and 'English comfort'.[18] For the Resistance, however, Vichy youth institutions, such as the *Chantiers de jeunesse*, were nothing but hotbeds of corruption. The Resistance newspaper *Libération* claimed that there 'are some youth services where no one is admitted if he's not a passive or active invert' and that there was an urgent need to 'use the big stick on homosexuals' arses'.[19] The accusation was not totally unfounded. Collaborationist François Sentein, himself leader of one *Chantier*, and a self-described 'pederast' recalls in his diary the presence of many homosexuals among the team leaders, one of whom tried to create 'sane relations of sentimental pederasty', a phrase which suggests that although same-sex relationships were not condoned by the institution, homoerotic feelings could have been used by some leaders to reinforce loyalty and solidarity within the group.[20]

Homosexuality and gender inversion were used by all social and political actors as symbols of weakness, inefficiency, corruption, and decline. Among black marketeers, collaborationist Henri Poulain identified a fashion house owner, 'who's of masculine gender only on his birth certificate' and always went about with his 'court of minions'.[21] Prominent figures were outed as homosexual, most of the time a slanderous tactic that had already been used in the 1930s against several left-wing politicians, especially the Jewish Prime Minister Léon Blum.[22] Général Noguès, nominated resident-general in Morocco in 1936 by the Popular Front, was described in *Paris-Soir,* now under German control, as 'self-effacing like a servant and effeminate like an invert whose appearance betrays deceit and conceit'.[23] Allegations of homosexuality were also made against well-known figures of the Vichy regime, either by the Resistance press or by opposition collaborationist newspapers. Fascist journalist Lucien Rebatet dismissed Germanophile writer André Germain, a friend of Proust, as 'a kind of gender-queer larva'; *Paris-Municipal* claimed that the dismissal of Jean Antoine, in charge of the National Radio, would be regretted only by 'the young inverts he liked to surround himself with'; *Libération* made fun of the 'Adonis' of the collaborationist National Popular Rally (RNP) and of their leader, 'homunculus' Déat.[24] The main target remained Abel Bonnard 'peacock writer' and Minister of National Education (1942–1944). 'Characteristic detail: this admirer of Hitler has never been known for having a wife or a mistress. Bonnard, he's Gestapette. Birds of a feather.'[25] The nickname, a portmanteau of Gestapo and *tapette* (poofter), proved very popular. Some high-school students were heard shouting 'Gestapette is an arsehole!' in the Latin Quarter of Paris.[26]

These youngsters were themselves a target of the collaborationist press. Nicknamed 'swing' or 'zazous', jazz fans, conspicuous by their extravagant outfits and British sympathies, could be seen on the Champs-Elysées or the Boulevard Saint-Michel. They came mostly from well-to-do backgrounds and were castigated, depending on the circumstances, as 'spoiled children', dodgers, idle youngsters, or Gaullists. They were also described as 'effeminate'.[27] Although of mixed gender, the homoerotic dimension of the movement did not escape observers, the more so as Jean Marais and Charles Trénet were famous zazous. Some students chose to spank 'three very "swing" little young men' who 'pranced' along the Boulevard Saint-Michel.[28] From 1942, the *Jeunesses Populaires Françaises* (JPF), the youth branch of Doriot's fascist French Popular Party (PPF), organized 'anti-swings' campaigns, in which they captured zazous and shaved their long hair.[29] It is worth noting that these punishments were often used against women – or men – who transgressed gender and sexual norms, such as women 'furies' during the French Revolution, the 'Incroyables and Merveilleuses' of the French Directory, and, later, women accused of collaboration with Germany. The police also raided swing bars. Some youngsters, who wore the yellow star with 'swing' written inside as a protest against discriminations against the Jews, or simply as a provocation, were deported to Drancy and later died in concentration camps.[30] As the Allies bombed France, the collaborationist press wondered: 'Are there still Anglophile snobs and invert patriots to find that "swing"?'[31]

Invisible men: homosexual members of the Resistance

Within the Resistance movement, pleasure-seeking zazous were not held in high esteem either. *Liberation* preferred to celebrate 'rough people in overalls and clogs' and *Combat* 'the men of the Resistance, strengthened by daily trial'.[32] As Mark Meyers argued, 'the well-documented misogyny and homophobia of fascist regimes had a rhetorical counterpart in both liberal and socialist brands of antifascism'.[33] The question of homosexuality within the French Resistance remains a blindspot in historical research. Few homosexual members of the Resistance were out of the closet, or left testimonies. Those who did, such as Roger Stephane or Pascal Copeau, were often criticized for not keeping this information private.[34] Following the Liberation, members of the Resistance wanted to present an image of virtue, courage, and honour. Many of them shared the same prejudices against homosexual people as the rest of French society. Homosexuality was linked to effeminacy and treason, and homosexuals were not deemed fit for armed struggle. Jacques Renouvin, a former Camelot du Roi, the youth organization of far-right Action Française, who later joined the Resistance, was surprised to find among his new comrades a majority of democrats, those same 'fags' he had hated before the war.[35] In his memoirs, Jean Marais, whose relationship with playwright Jean Cocteau was common knowledge and who joined the 2nd Armored Division of General Leclerc at the Liberation, recalled being told by an old member of his company, after eight months of service: 'People in Paris are mean. Why? You remember when you took us to this nightclub? Yes, so what? Well, I was told you were a fag. – So? – Well, now I know very well that it isn't true.'[36] Roger Stephane, imprisoned for acts of resistance in Fort-Barraux, in the Alps, noted in his diary that his fellow inmates had nothing but contempt for 'common-law prisoners' such as pimps, brothel owners, and 'fags'. 'I am surely the only one to show them curiosity, not hostility. Gendarmes go wild.'[37]

In this context, being homosexual *and* in the Resistance was not an easy situation. Pascal Copeau, between the wars, had chosen to hide his homosexuality, boasting of numerous female conquests, although as a young man in Berlin in the 1930s, he had enjoyed the lively gay nightlife and found love with a German boy.[38] As a member of the Resistance, he stated that he had no time for a private life. Roger Stéphane found in T. E. Lawrence's book *Seven Pillars of Wisdom* a guide and a model.[39] Like many who had entered the Resistance under an alias, he saw both queer men and adventurers as transvestites, as well as solitary figures, who shared a similar ethic: 'the transvestite not only flees from himself by putting on peculiar garments, but he escapes the prying eyes of the other [...] Therefore cross-dressing can be seen as a revealer, a facilitator of freedom.'[40] Although Stéphane, as a homosexual man, could feel isolated within the Resistance, the war nevertheless offered him many sexual opportunities. His wartime diaries regularly mention casual encounters, homosexual bars and nightclubs, as well as cruising locations in Nice, Toulon, Paris, and London.[41] 'Soldiers, young cops, aviators, thugs and even an FFI [French Forces of the Interior] chaplain' were among his conquests.[42] The Resistance provided him with a predominantly homosocial milieu, and the Liberation, in which he took part in a series of all-male parties that shocked some of his friends, was for him a time of sexual euphoria. He was not the only one to make the most of the period. Stéphane's lover, Jean-Jacques Rinieri, born in 1925, who joined the maquis, according to him, 'not out of political conviction, but out of love for a man',[43] suggested that the years 1945 and 1946 were the golden age of homosexuality in Paris: the *détente* that follows periods of troubles; the presence of Allied troops, among whom many men had discovered their true sexual orientation in a vacuum by living daily in close contact with their comrades or who had taken advantage of the anonymity of the uniform to give free rein to those penchants that were still repressed because of society's constraints, or who had felt newly freed in a foreign capital city; the return of prisoners or workers from Germany, where they experienced the same situations – all these reasons explain the extension, or rather the exposition in broad daylight of the homosexual world.[44]

Such a life was not without danger, however. In August 1945, Stéphane was arrested for a sexual offence, the victim of a soldier on leave, who acted as an *agent provocateur*, and claimed to be part of a gang of seven police informers, who had already caught seventeen homosexual men.[45] In 1946, Pascal Copeau, then an MP, and still in the closet, was arrested for public indecency while cruising on the banks of the Seine. Although he was released after a night in the cells, his main opponent in the parliamentary elections began to use nasty double-entendres against him in his local newspaper. In the end, Copeau chose not to run for the election and left politics. In 1947, he tried to commit suicide.[46] Despite prejudice, Stéphane did not hesitate, under the influence of Gide and Cocteau, to reveal his homosexuality publicly: 'Socially, the pederast was not better treated than the Jew. As such, with few exceptions, he had not been martyred. But he was condemned, or at least criticised.'[47] Although the presence of self-declared homosexual men among the Resistance may have helped some people in overcoming prejudices, the post-war period saw a surge of homophobic interpretations with regards to collaboration, the most famous example being Sartre's article 'What is a collaborator?', where he argued that there was a strong sexual and gender component to collaboration: 'It seems to me that there is here a curious mixture of masochism and homosexuality. The homosexual Parisian circles did indeed provide many and brilliant recruits.'[48] In his short story 'L'enfance d'un chef' (1939) and in his novel *La mort dans l'âme* (1949), Sartre had already depicted homosexual characters attracted by the far-right or seduced by German troops. For Sentein, 'Sartre reverses the order of abjection: first pederast, then, the absolute end, Camelot du roi'.[49] Sartre was not the only one to link homosexuality and collaboration. In 1945, the writer Jean Queval accused Abel Bonnard, Jean Cocteau, and Maurice Rostand, all well-known homosexuals, of having tried to convince French youth to join the fascist side, while Jean Guéhenno wondered in his diary: 'Why so many pederasts among the collaborators?'[50] Among those, the most famous one was fascist writer and editor of *Je suis Partout* Robert Brasillach, executed on 6 February 1945.[51] His trial, as Alice Kaplan demonstrated well, was tainted by homophobia.[52] In an article published just before the Liberation, his German sympathies had already been interpreted from the standpoint of sexual attraction. Recalling that Brasillach had written that 'the French, from whatever tendencies, have, during [the German occupation], more or less slept with Germany, not without quarrels, but it will remain as a fond memory', *Libération* assumed the writer spoke for himself: 'Mr Brasillach can make love to Germany all he wants, and get voluptuously fucked by our "fair victors", his "effusiveness with the German army", "his 'relations' with the Gestapo" are all but a "monstrous love dream".'[53] The same passages were used during his trial, making him, at least in words, guilty of '*collaboration horizontale*' – of sleeping with the enemy, like the women who were shorn in the same period.[54] Brasillach was not only a fascist, anti-Semite, and collaborationist, he was also 'perverse, sterile and anti-French'. The judge's rhetoric, Alice Kaplan remarks, used 'hatred of homosexuality to reinforce the hatred of Brasillach'.[55] As is quite common, the invasion of the country had been expressed in gendered and sexual terms, with a female France suffering under the assaults of a male Germany. This high point of the prosecution speech 'touched on a crisis of masculinity, targeted a nation of men who had been defeated and powerless for four years, men who were now coming back into their own'.[56]

It is not to be denied, of course, that some homosexual men and women had collaborated. However, others may have been the victims of homophobic prejudices. François Sentein recalls in his diary the case of a hotel valet accused by a woman of having opened fire on the crowd before being arrested by the FFI in September 1944. The hotel manager tried to help him, stating that he was a very gentle and patriotic man, and that he could not see what could be held against him, before adding, suddenly worried: 'Obviously he was homosexual.'[57] Another problem was that the focus on the figures of homosexual collaborators associated homosexuality with treason, while rendering invisible gay and lesbian members of the Resistance, as well as homosexual victims of Nazism and of the Vichy regime.

Dark times and far-reaching shadows: the repression of homosexuality in France during the Second World War

Because of its early decriminalization of sodomy, France had been seen throughout the nineteenth and early twentieth century as a refuge for sexual outcasts. Public space was, however, strictly regulated, with the vice squad organizing unofficial surveillance of the main cruising areas in Paris and other major cities. Indecent exposure (Article 330 of the Penal Code), indecent assault (Article 331), as well as the 'debauching of minors for the purposes of procuring' (Article 334) remained liable to prosecution in the case of homo- or heterosexual relations and could be used to circumscribe same-sex relationships. The most exposed were men who indulged in risky practices such as cruising around urinals, and those whose 'effeminate' looks and behaviour matched the police's criteria for 'inversion'.[58] A male prostitute, condemned in 1940 to fifteen days of prison, was described in *Détective* as a 'beautiful young man ... who did not wear too much makeup for this occasion, and who tried to respond in a masculine voice to the questions of the President [of the *Cour correction-nelle*]'.[59] Homosexual practices, carried out within private or semi-private spaces, such as bars and clubs, fell outside the law, although judges sometimes interpreted the notion of public space quite extensively.

The decriminalization of homosexuality was indeed resented by many. In June 1939, Parisian city councillors used the example of a municipal by-law enacted by the mayor of Nancy against male prostitution to ask for new measures against 'incitement to commit the vice of inversion spread by foreigners freshly naturalized' and 'effective measures against such perversions or propaganda disseminated by the press, theatre and literature'.[60] In Saint-Malo, following a homosexual affair involving a minor, the Deputy Prosecutor regretted that the old 'corporal punishments of the former legislation' (whipping) could no longer be used.[61] A journalist, reporting on an affair involving a man aged sixty, who had filed a complaint against 'two very young and highly made-up men' who had tried to blackmail him, regretted that, although both thieves had been condemned to six months of prison, the plaintiff had been left unpunished.[62]

Two problems were of particular concern. The first was the prostitution of sailors, notably in Toulon, where the prefect organized a close supervision of the homosexual 'milieu'. Convicted sailors suffered disciplinary punishment, civilians convicted of indecent behaviour were fined or imprisoned, and foreigners were expelled from the country, bars, and hotels were closed.[63] The other problem was the so-called 'corruption of minors', at a time when the age of consent was thirteen and the idea that homosexuality was an acquired 'vice' was still quite common. Social anxiety was heightened by detailed reporting of affairs involving underage children, although it remained a taboo subject and only the most dreadful cases, with evidences of rape, violence, and murder, would be discussed publicly.[64] Before and during the war, articles revealed a well-organized subculture of rent boys and self-described 'pederasts'.[65] Their most popular cruising grounds were cinemas, public transport, swimming pools, public parks, and *kermesses* (fairs), which offered revellers pinball machines, table football, and other arcade games. The writer Henry de Montherlant, one of the most famous advocates for virile values at the time and a 'pederast', waited at the entrance of Parisian cinemas and, on the pretext that his nephew had stood him up, offered a spare ticket to an attractive youngster.[66] Such encounters could be dangerous. Apart from the potential tricksters and blackmailers, one risked retaliation from the young victim's friends or family (Montherlant was badly beaten by a group of young men who saw him paw one of their brothers) and reports by the victim to the police. The writer Roger Peyrefitte, who was arrested in Vichy on such charges on 13 October 1940, was told by the police that it was because of 'men like [him] that we have lost the war'.[67]

On 6 August 1942, a new law, modifying Article 334 of the Penal Code, condemned the perpetrators of same-sex sexual acts committed with an underage person to six months' to three years' imprisonment and a fine of 200 to 60,000 francs. The age of consent was raised from thirteen to twenty-one for homosexual relations. Not only same-sex relations committed between an adult and a minor were criminalized, but also between two persons if under twenty-one. Unprecedented was the sanctioning of lesbian acts.[68] The inclusion of the amendment within Article 334, which dealt with prostitution, as well as the vocabulary used ('facilitating the debauchery and corruption of young people of either sex'; 'indecent or unnatural acts') showed that the emphasis was on the repression of immorality. In his diary, pederast and collaborator François Sentein foamed with rage. He felt betrayed; 'fucked in the arse by a majuscule Law' he quoted in its entirety. He thought that this 'foolish idea' would only produce an 'incoherent justice', when men as young as seventeen were executed and he totally refused to consider that a young man could be 'lured' by an older man. 'Fuck you, Pétain!' he concluded. [69]

Recent research by Marc Boninchi has shown that the text had been prepared well before 1942.[70] In 1934, the extent of naval prostitution had led to protests from the Ministry of the Navy, which wanted to be able to bring criminal charges. The debate was relaunched in 1939, following a murder case in Paris involving a rent boy. A project proposing to increase the age of consent to eighteen in the case of same-sex relations was approved by Prime Minister Edouard Daladier, but it arrived too late to be included in the last clutch of measures of 1939.[71] Finally, a report by Charles Dubost, Deputy Public Prosecutor of Toulon, dated 22 December 1941, following an affair that involved a 29-year-old man and several boys aged fourteen to seventeen, proved decisive. Although the boys were of age and there were no grounds to initiate legal action, Dubost considered the situation shameful and worrisome, and he advocated a reform of the law. He would have favoured a condemnation of all 'sexual anomalies' but admitted that such a change would raise much controversy.[72] The report was reviewed by several magistrates and ministers, who supported its conclusion in favour of 'moderate reform'.[73] The main change, compared to the preparatory text of 1939, was that the age of consent had been raised from eighteen to twenty-one, a decision motivated by largely pragmatic reasons, notably the wish to crush any homosexual tendencies in movements such as the *Chantiers de jeunesse*, which welcomed youth in their early twenties.[74]

The law of 6 August 1942 was therefore not a Vichy initiative, or a consequence of the German occupation, as would be assumed in the 1980s.[75] It had its roots in the preparatory works of the Third Republic and received a positive response after the war. When the GPRF reviewed the laws enacted under the Vichy regime, it chose, following a report by Minister of Justice François de Menthon (*Mouvement Républicain Populaire* (MRP), Christian-Democrat), to keep it, since 'this reform, inspired by the necessity to prevent corruption of minors, could not, in principle, be criticised'.[76] It was, however, moved to Article 331, which dealt with indecent assault without violence committed on minors, and the age of consent for heterosexual relations was raised to fifteen, a decision already proposed in 1942 without being followed through.

The scope of this chapter does not permit a full presentation of the statistics but a quick overview shows a rapid and regular rise in the number of persons tried up to 1968, followed by a rapid decline – although one should note that same-sex offences committed under Articles 330 and 331 were not always differentiated.[77] For example, 20 persons were condemned in Metropolitan France in 1945, 78 in 1946, 126 in 1947, 178 in 1948, 227 in 1949, 181 in 1950, and 210 in 1951. Additionally, 85 affairs were tried in Algeria – at that time a French department – in 1945, 9 in 1946, 28 in 1947, 17 in 1948, 32 in 1949 and 1950, and 56 in 1951, which raises questions about the ethnic origins of such offenders, and the ways in which gender, race, and sexuality interacted here.[78] The majority of offenders were condemned to less than one year's imprisonment. Maximum repression was reached in 1961, after the implementation of the Mirguet amendment of 18 July 1960, which defined homosexuality as a 'social plague' and resulted in the aggravation of sentences for 'indecent exposure' in the case of same-sex relations between men or between women (Article 330): 448 persons were condemned, among them women. In 1978, when the age of consent was lowered to eighteen for same-sex relations, 172 people were condemned, among them 10 women. The discrimination law was finally repealed in 1982.

Although the Vichy regime reinforced the repressive apparatus against homosexuality, it did not, as has sometimes been wrongly assumed, organize the deportation of homosexual men or women.[79] This question was raised, however, in Alsace-Moselle, departments annexed to the German Reich, where paragraph 175 of the German Penal Code applied from 1942 onwards. Regis Schlagdenhauffen has recently shown that in Strasbourg, 208 men were arrested for homosexuality between 1940 and 1945. Between 1940 and 1942, these men were sent to the camp of Schirmeck-Vorbrück, before being transferred as 'asocials' to the free zone. Between 1942 and 1944, 41 were tried, 1 was acquitted, and 1 policeman was condemned to death, while the others received a jail sentence from three months to life. Some were sent to a concentration camp.[80] Research is ongoing to discover exactly how many Frenchmen were victims of paragraph 175. In 2007, Arnaud Boulligny counted 62 French men deported for their homosexuality, either in Schirmeck-Vorbrück, Natzweiler-Struhof, or in German camps and prisons: 22 were arrested in Alsace-Moselle, 7 had been deported from occupied France, 32 were in Germany at the time of their arrest, sometimes as *Service du travail obligatoire* (STO) (Compulsory

Work Service) workers.[81] At least 312 men were incarcerated for homosexuality in Natzweiler-Struthof concentration camp, among them 286 Germans and 14 Frenchmen, with a death rate of about 51 to 56 per cent.[82] These figures need to be confirmed, however.

After the war, owing to a lack of direct testimonies, and despite allusions to 'pink triangles' in essays written by deportees and homophile journals such as *Arcadie*, homosexual persecution remained largely ignored.[83] A firm line had been drawn between members of the Resistance and those who were perceived as common criminals. Charles Richet, a doctor who reported in 1945 on the inmates of Buchenwald, regretted that all Frenchmen were considered 'political prisoners', even 'homosexuals, pimps, blackmailers or assassins'. According to him, 'this promiscuity was painful. Nowadays, we are still protesting against this kind of global accreditation of all prisoners.' He argued that such a generalization was all the more damaging given that although 'homosexuality remained rampant throughout the camp', 'it seemed that the French were refractory to it'.[84]

Such an attitude was not exceptional, nor specific to France. In East and West Germany, paragraph 175 remained in force until 1968–69 and 'pink triangles' were not considered victims of Nazism and did not receive reparations. In France, the question of homosexual deportation was not debated publicly until the 1970s, when the new gay and lesbian liberation movements reopened the subject. The publication, in 1972, of Austrian former 'pink triangle' Heinz Heger [Josef Kohout]'s autobiography had a huge impact. It was translated into French in 1981, with a foreword by Guy Hocquenghem, one of the founding members of the Homosexual Revolutionary Action Front (FHAR), who dramatically denounced a homosexual 'genocide' that had voluntarily been hidden by both the Germans and the Allies, who shared a common homophobia.[85] Outrageous and highly controversial, Hocquenghem's essay was, however, reflective of the exasperation of many gay and lesbian activists.[86] Since 1975, homosexual associations had begun to require to be represented at the annual deportation ceremonies, but their demands were generally refused and there were numerous incidents with associations of deportees, who did not recognize the reality of homosexual deportation.[87] The fact that paragraph 175 had applied only to Alsace-Moselle, at that time annexed to Germany, was used as a pretext to deny the existence of any persecution on French territory and avoid official recognition.

A major step forward was taken in 1983, when gay magazine *Gai Pied Hebdo* published the testimonies of two Alsatian gay men. The first, Camille Erremann, aged twenty-eight, had been arrested and expelled to the free zone in December 1940; the second, Pierre Seel, was only eighteen when he was imprisoned and tortured in Schirmeck in May 1941. Both stated that they had been arrested because the French police had held files on them, and their records had later been retrieved by the Gestapo.[88] Published as a book in 1994, Pierre Seel's testimony proved decisive, since he was – and remains – the only French homosexual deportee to have spoken publicly.[89] Recognition has been slow. Since 1995, the Ministry of Veterans has classed homosexuals among the victims of war. In their speeches Prime Minister Lionel Jospin, on 26 April 2001, and President Jacques Chirac, on 24 April 2005, both included homosexuals amongst the victims of Nazism, a choice emulated by their successors. In 2010, a plaque dedicated to homosexual victims of Nazism was unveiled on the site of the former Natzweiler-Struthof camp. Rudolf Brazda, a German 'pink triangle' who had lived in France since 1945, was awarded the Legion of Honour in 2011.

Current research on the subject should in time clarify the nature of the persecution suffered and the numbers of gay and lesbian victims. However, as has been shown, it is important to have a comprehensive and long-term approach. We need further detailed studies on the fates of homosexual men and women in Alsace Moselle (whether French citizens or foreigners), while paying attention to other factors such as age, gender, social, and ethnic backgrounds. However, such research should be put in the more general context of the stigmatization of same-sex relationships before and after the war. Regional studies devoted to other parts of France – and its colonies – could also be useful to assess the continuities of homosexual repression. Most case studies currently deal with Paris and harbours such as Toulon, and most testimonies – apart from judicial affairs – stem from individuals of privileged and intellectual backgrounds. Lesbian lives during the period have remained largely unexplored.

Many scholarly analyses have focused on the gendered rhetoric that shaped both Vichy and Resistance discourses. As Richard J. Golsan and Melanie Hawthorne noted, the Vichy regime 'defines itself from the outset as a "virile" reaction to a Third Republic it considers excessively "feminized"—an "effeminate republic of women or inverts"'.[90] Discussing the post-war period, Tony Judt remarked that the 'association of collaboration with the female gender was a widespread myth of these years. It both symbolized the collective consciousness of national weakness and projected it on others, in this case women.'[91] Because homosexuality was still mostly understood through the theory of gender inversion, male homosexuals were seen as exhibiting female characteristics – they should have been on the side of collaboration. As Andrew Hewitt concluded: 'Fascism is there pathologized sexually, while homosexuality is likewise stigmatized politically. The defeat of fascism feeds the fantasy of returning to a political and sexual normalcy.'[92]

The fact that same-sex relationships during the Second World War have been mostly addressed through the perspective of fantasy, social stigma, and contempt has obscured the realities of queer lifestyles, practices, and destinies. However, as has been shown here, homophobia was not just rhetorical, it shaped realities before, during, and after the war. In the 1950s, 'back to normalcy', in France, as in Germany and the United States, implied the reaffirmation of traditional values and the denunciation of deviancies, notably homosexuality. In France, a country that had early been defeated but which nevertheless stood among the victors in 1945, masculinity was a sensitive and complicated issue. In the 'fight over the meaning of true manliness', Mark Meyers argued, it was essential for the Resistance to distance itself from the hypermasculinity exalted by Fascist regimes, now suspected of being but a 'cover for an ultimately pathological and effeminate nature', and the degraded image of the French soldier or prisoner of war, unable to defend his country – and his women.[93] The less controversial model would therefore be the one of the *père de famille* (husband and father), a familiar feature of French masculinities and the ideal citizen of the French republic, praised on all sides of the political spectrum.[94] Usually presented as a rather authoritarian but benevolent figure, he was now reinvented as a domesticated, hard-working, and gently virile man, whose sexual desires were happily channeled through marriage. Such a transformation implied, however, a strict redefinition of gender roles along patriarchal norms, with stay-at-home mothers who would not challenge a deeply damaged sense of self, and the stigmatization of threatening virilities, notably those of rebellious colonized men and single North African migrants. In this context, the construction of homosexuality, by both Vichy and the Resistance, as a symbol of corruption, treason, and decadence at least partly explains the difficulties experienced after the war by queer people, who often found themselves unable to speak on their own terms, although some of them would soon regroup and form the first and long-lasting French homophile movement 'Arcadie'.[95]

Recommended reading

Boninchi, M. (2005) *Vichy et l'ordre moral* (Paris: Presses universitaires de France).

Kelly, M. (1995) 'The Reconstruction of Masculinity at the Liberation', in H. R. Kedward and N. Wood (ed.), *The Liberation of France. Image and Event* (Oxford and Washington, DC: Berg Publishers), pp. 117–28.

Koos, C. and D. Sarnoff (2003) 'France', in K. Passmore (ed.), *Women, Gender and Fascism in Europe 1919–1945* (Manchester: Manchester University Press), pp. 168–88.

Meyers, M. (2012) 'Gender, Sexuality, and Crowd Psychology. French Antifascism, 1929–1945', in A. M Moore (ed.), *Sexing Political Culture in the History of France* (Amherst, NY: Cambria Press), pp. 241–65.

Pollard, M. (1998) *The Reign of Virtue: Mobilizing Gender in Vichy France* (Chicago: University of Chicago Press).

Schlagdenhauffen, R. (2014) 'Désirs condamnés. Punir les "homosexuels" en Alsace annexée (1940–1945)?", *Clio*, vol. 1, no. 39, pp. 83–104.

Tamagne, F. (2004) *A History of Homosexuality in Europe. Berlin, London, Paris, 1919–1939*, 2 vols (New York: Algora).

Notes

1. See for example M. Hawthorne and R. J. Golsan (ed.) (1997) *Gender and Fascism in Modern France* (Hanover, NH and London: University Press of New England); M. Pollard (1998) *The Reign of Virtue: Mobilizing Gender in Vichy France* (Chicago: University of Chicago Press); L. Capdevila, F. Rouquet, F. Virgili, and D. Voldman (2003) *Hommes et femmes dans la France en guerre (1914–1945)* (Paris : Payot); C. Koos and D. Sarnoff (2003) 'France', in K. Passmore (ed.), *Women, Gender and Fascism in Europe 1919–1945* (Manchester: Manchester University Press), pp. 168–88; M. Meyers (2012), 'Gender, Sexuality, and Crowd Psychology: French Antifascism, 1929–1945', in A. M Moore (ed.), *Sexing Political Culture in the History of France* (Amherst, NY: Cambria Press), pp. 241–65. Patrick Buisson has published a well-documented synthesis on sexualities in Vichy France, but it is weakened by biased analysis and sketchy references. P. Buisson (2008) *1940–1945: Années érotiques*, 2 vols (Paris: Le Livre de Poche).

2. See, for example, M. Kelly (1995) 'The Reconstruction of Masculinity at the Liberation', in H. R. Kedward and N. Wood (ed.), *The Liberation of France: Image and Event* (Oxford, and Washington, DC: Berg Publishers), pp. 117–28; R. Revenin (2007) *Hommes et masculinités de 1789 à nos jours* (Paris: Autrement); L. Capdevila (2010) 'La quête du masculin dans la France de la défaite (1940–1945)', *Annales de Bretagne et des Pays de l'Ouest*, vol. 117, no. 2, pp. 101–22.

3. M. Bertrand (ed.) (2011) *La déportation pour motif d'homosexualité en France* (Lyon: Mémoire Active).

4. See F. Tamagne (2004) *A History of Homosexuality in Europe: Berlin, London, Paris, 1919–1939*, 2 vols (New York: Algora).

5. *Paris Soir*, 11 December 1939.

6. *Le Petit Parisien*, 24 September 1939; *Le Matin*, 8 October 1939.

7. *Le Populaire*, 12 September and 1 November 1939. The phrase had been used for the first time by Gorki in the *Pravda* on 23 May 1934.

8. *L'Humanité*, 5 March 1943.

9. *Paix et Droit. Organe de l'alliance israélite universelle*, October–December 1939.

10. See, for example, K. Theweleit (1979) *Männerphantasien* (Frankfurt-on-Main: Roter Stern Verlag); A. Hewitt (1996) *Political Inversions: Homosexuality, Fascism, and the Modernist Imaginary* (Stanford: Stanford University Press); D. Herzog (ed.) (2005) *Sexuality and German Fascism* (New York and Oxford: Berghahn Books).

11. Hawthorne, Golsan (ed.) (1997), p. 4.

12. *Le Petit Parisien*, 14 August 1939; *Le Temps*, 1 February 1939; *Le Journal*, 4 April 1939, 5 April 1939, 11 April 1939; *L'écho d'Alger*, 31 January 1940.

13. *Le Journal*, 7 April 1939; *L'avenir du Canton de Vanves* [a resistant newspaper], May 1943.

14. *Détective*, 12 October 1939.

15. N. Burch and G. Sellier (1996) *La drôle de guerre des sexes du cinéma français, 1930–1956* (Paris: Nathan).

16. F. Sentein (2000) *Nouvelles minutes d'un libertin 1942–1943* (Paris: Gallimard), pp. 196–7. Tino Rossi was straight.

17. *Libération*, 5 October 1941.

18. *Je suis partout*, 23 May 1942, 5 March 1943.

19. *Libération*, 11 January 1944. *Trique* (stick) also means erection in French slang.

20. Entry of 13 June 1942, Sentein, *Nouvelles minutes*, p. 88.

21. *Je suis partout*, 26 March 1943.

22. F. Tamagne (2003) 'Caricatures homophobes et stéréotypes de genre en France et en Allemagne : la presse satirique de 1900 au milieu au milieu des années 30', *Le temps des médias*, vol. 1 (Autumn), pp. 1, 42–53.

23. *Paris-Soir*, 7 December 1942.

24. *Je suis partout*, 18 April 1941; *Paris-Municipal*, 9 August 1942; *Libération*, 21 December 1943.

25. See *Paris-Municipal*, 6 February 1944, 17 May 1942 and *Combat*, June 1942.

26. See *Libération*, 26 October 1943, 21 April 1944 and J.-C. Loiseau (1977) *Les zazous* (Paris : Le Sagittaire), p. 90.

27. See *Ouest-Éclair*, 4 August 1944, *Je suis partout*, 24 January 1942, 7 February 1942.

28. *Le Cri de Paris*, 12 June 1942.

29. Loiseau (1977), pp. 156–62.

30. Archives de la Préfecture de Police de Paris, BA2436.

31. *Paris-Soir*, 6 March 1942.

32. *Libération*, 18 April 1942; *Combat*, February 1943.
33. Meyers, 'Gender, Sexuality, and Crowd Psychology', pp. 264–5, 244.
34. Born in a Jewish family in 1919, Roger Worms took the alias Stéphane when he joined resistance movement Combat in September 1941. He took an active part in the liberation of the Hotel de Ville of Paris in August 1944. See O. Philipponnat and P. Leenhardt (2004) *Roger Stéphane : Enquête sur l'aventurier* (Paris: Grasset). Pascal Copeau, born in 1908, joined resistance movement Libération in 1942 and became the leader of Libération Sud from summer 1943 onwards. He was elected MP at the end of the war but later returned to journalism. See P. Leenhardt (1994) *Pascal Copeau (1908–1982) : L'histoire préfère les vainqueurs* (Paris: L'Harmattan).
35. Philipponnat and Leenhardt, *Roger Stéphane*, p. 195.
36. J. Marais (1975) *Histoires de ma vie* (Paris: Albin Michel), p. 170.
37. R. Stéphane (2004a) *Chaque homme est lié au monde*, 1st ed. 1946 (Paris: Grasset), p. 205.
38. Leenhardt, *Pascal Copeau*, pp. 60–80.
39. T. E. Lawrence (1935) *Seven Pillars of Wisdom* (London: J. Cape).
40. R. Stéphane (1965) *Portrait de l'aventurier* (Paris: Grasset), pp. 83–4.
41. Stéphane (2004a) and Stéphane (2004b) *Fin d'une jeunesse. Carnets 1944–1947* (Paris: La Table Ronde).
42. Philipponnat and Leenhardt, *Roger Stéphane*, p. 374.
43. Stéphane (2004b), *Fin d'une jeunesse*, p. 175.
44. J.-J. Rinieri (1950), 'Amour et homosexualité', *La Nef*, October–November, 85. This situation was not peculiar to France: see A. Berube (1990) *Coming Out Under Fire* (New York: The Free Press) and M. Houlbrook (2005) *Queer London: Perils and Pleasures in the Sexual Metropolis, 1918–1957* (Chicago: Chicago University Press).
45. Diary entry of 13 May 1946, Stéphane (2004b), *Fin d'une jeunesse,* and Philipponnat and Leenhardt (2004), p. 373.
46. Leenhardt, *Pascal Copeau*, pp. 175–81.
47. R. Stéphane (2005) *Parce que c'était lui* (Paris: H&O), 1st edn, 1953, p. 23.
48. J.-P. Sartre (1949) *Situations III* (Paris: Gallimard), p. 58.
49. Entry of 31 January 1942, Sentein, *Nouvelles minutes*, p. 29.
50. M. Studnicki (2010) *Extrême-droite, genre et homosexualités dans les années trente en France* (University of Lille 3: unpublished Master's dissertation), p. 5.
51. Writer Maurice Sachs and sportswoman Violette Morris were other famous homosexual collaborators, as well as Marcel Bucard, founder of the fascist Mouvement Franciste, executed for treason in 1946. Jean Genet's fascination for Nazism and German soldiers has been discussed at length, notably by J.-P. Sartre (1952) *Saint Genet, comédien et martyr* (Paris: Gallimard); A. Hewitt (1997) 'Sleeping with the Enemy: Genet and the Fantasy of Homo-Fascism', in Hawthorne and Golsan (ed.), *Gender and Fascism*, pp. 119–40; I. Jablonka (2004) *Les vérités inavouables de Jean Genet* (Paris: Seuil), pp. 155–227.
52. A. Kaplan (2000) *The Collaborator: the Trial and Execution of Robert Brasillach* (Chicago: Chicago University Press).
53. *Libération*, 29 February 1944.
54. See F. Virgili (2002) *Shorn Women: Gender and Punishment in Liberation France* (Oxford: Berg).
55. Kaplan, *The Collaborator*, p. 164.
56. Kaplan, pp. 162–4.
57. Entry of 12 September 1944, F. Sentein (2002) *Minutes d'un libéré (1944)* (Paris: Gallimard), pp. 134–5.

58. Tamagne, *A History of Homosexuality.*

59. *Détective*, 4 January 1940.

60. *Bulletin Municipal de la Ville de Paris*, 16 June 1939, p. 1615.

61. *L'Ouest-Eclair*, 11 March 1939.

62. *Détective*, 16 May 1940.

63. Tamagne, *A History of Homosexuality.*

64. A.-C. Ambroise-Rendu (2014) *Histoire de la pédophilie XIXe-XXIe siècles* (Paris: Fayard).

65. See, for example, *Le Populaire*, 9 May 1939; *Ce Soir*, 8 May 1939, 10 May 1939, 13 June 1939; *L'écho d'Alger*, 11 July 1940.

66. R. Peyrefitte (1977) *Propos secrets* (Paris: Albin Michel), pp. 50–60. Montherlant was arrested in Marseille in July 1940 and Peyrefitte was once again questioned by the police in March 1941: H. de Montherlant and R. Peyrefitte (1983) *Correspondance* (Paris: Robert Laffont), pp. 83–90, 231–53.

67. Peyrefitte, *Propos secrets*, p. 70.

68. For examples of lesbian victims of this law, see C. Olivier (2005) *Le vice ou la vertu : Vichy et les politiques de la sexualité* (Toulouse: Presses Universitaires du Mirail), pp. 259–70.

69. Entry of 12 September 1942, Sentein, *Nouvelles minutes*, pp. 201–3. Sentein added some further comments in the 1970s, blaming 'Christians and communists' for the 'persecution of pederasts' and castigating these 'petainist-communist-gaullist laws'.

70. M. Boninchi (2005) *Vichy et l'ordre moral* (Paris: Presses universitaires de France), pp. 143–93.

71. Olivier, *Le vice*, p. 259.

72. Boninchi, *Vichy et l'ordre moral*, pp. 143–8.

73. For more details, see Boninchi, pp. 147–60. One magistrate advocated castration in the case of repeat offenders, but the measure was ruled out in the name of Christian principles. Most experts considered that the penalization of same-sex relations would not only prove ineffective but would give unnecessary visibility to 'sexual perversion'.

74. Boninchi, pp. 156–7.

75. Boninchi, pp. 144–5 and M. D. Sibalis (2002) 'Homophobia, Vichy France, and the "Crime of Homosexuality": The Origins of the Ordinance of 6 August 1942', *GLQ*, vol. 8, no. 3, pp. 301–18.

76. *Journal Officiel de la République Française. Ordonnances et décrets*, 9 February 1945.

77. See for each year *Compte général de la justice criminelle* published by the Ministry of Justice under different names. Judiciary statistics do not provide the number of persons condemned for same-sex relations with minors before 1945. Men and women are not differentiated until 1953. Between one and twelve women were judged for same-sex relations with minors per year between 1953 and 1978.

78. Some studies have been devoted to (homo)sexual tourism in the French colonies, but there is currently no research available on the repression of homosexuality in Algeria. See R. Aldrich (2003) *Colonialism and Homosexuality* (London: Routledge). The very high number of arrests in 1945 should be investigated.

79. Recent research by Arnaud Boulligny suggests, however, that more than thirty men were arrested in occupied France by German authorities on homosexual charges, notably because they had sex or tried to have sex with German soldiers or officers. Some were imprisoned, others deported to concentration camps. A. Boulligny (2016) 'La repression des homosexuels français sous domination allemande (1940–1945)', paper delivered at the conference 'Etat et homosexualités au XXe siècle,

ruptures et continuités dans les pays francophones et germanophones' (Centre Marc Bloch, Berlin, 27–28 May 2016), unpublished.

80. R. Schlagdenhauffen (2014) 'Désirs condamnés. Punir les "homosexuels" en Alsace annexée (1940-1945)?', *Clio*, vol. 1, no. 39, pp. 83–104. Paragraph 175 had been extended in 1935, so that any homosexual act could be prosecuted. Repeat offenders, prostitutes, and 'corrupters of youth' were liable to ten years in the penitentiary. Between 5,000 and 10,000 men were sent to concentration camps as 'pink triangles', where the majority died. Although lesbianism was not criminalized, some lesbians were arrested and deported as 'asocials'.

81. A. Boulligny, "La déportation de France pour motif d'homosexualité", in Bertrand *La déportation*, pp. 51–72.

82. Arnaud Boulligny and Jean-Luc Schwab propose the number of about 150 Alsatian or Alsatian residents imprisoned for their homosexuality, about 15 of whom were sent to a concentration camp. http://yagg.com/2015/04/27/natzweiler-struthof-et-la-deportation-pour-homosexualite-en-france-eclairage-chiffre-dune-realite-complexe-par-jean-luc-schwab/, date accessed 24 July 2015.

83. For a full discussion of the memory of homosexual deportation, see F. Tamagne in Bertrand, *La déportation*, pp. 29–50 and R. Schlagdenhauffen (2011) *Triangle rose: La persecution nazie des homosexuels et sa mémoire* (Paris: Autrement).

84. *Bulletin de l'Académie nationale de Médecine*, 12 June 1945, pp. 384, 396.

85. H. Heger (1981) *Les hommes au triangle rose: Journal d'un déporté homosexuel 1939–1945* (Paris: Persona).

86. See A. Finkielkraut (1982) *L'avenir d'une négation* (Paris, Seuil), pp. 319–49.

87. See, for example, *Gai Pied Hebdo*, 28 April 1985 and 11–15 May 1985.

88. *Gai Pied Hebdo*, 26 March–1 April 1983, pp. 20–4.

89. Pierre Seel (1994) *Moi, Pierre Seel, déporté homosexuel. Récit écrit en collaboration avec Jean Le Bitoux* (Paris: Calmann-Lévy). Seel came from a Catholic and well-to-do family. In Schirmeck, he never wore the pink triangle but a blue bar for 'asocial'. Set free in February 1941, he was later conscripted into the Wehrmacht as a *malgré-nous*. It was only after his divorce in 1978 and the reading of Heger's book that he chose to speak publicly about his ordeal. A speech by the Archbishop of Strasbourg, Elchinger, in which he called homosexuality a sickness was the trigger. Seel died in 2005. The municipality of Toulouse, where he lived, renamed a street in his honour.

90. Hawthorne, Golsan (ed.) (1997), p. 7.

91. T. Judt (1992) *Past Imperfect: French Intellectuals, 1944–1956* (Berkeley: University of California Press), p. 49.

92. Hewitt, 'Sleeping with the Enemy', p. 119.

93. Meyers, 'Gender, Sexuality, and Crowd Psychology', pp. 264–5, 244.

94. See J. Surkis (2006) *Sexing the Citizen: Morality and Masculinity in France, 1870–1920* (Ithaca, NY and London: Cornell University Press).

95. J. Jackson (2009) *Living in Arcadia: Homosexuality, Politics, and Morality in France from the Liberation to Aids* (Chicago and London: University of Chicago Press).

Part 4
Representing Gender Identities

11

Peculiar Poster Girls: Images of Pacifist Women in American World War II Propaganda

Katherine Jellison

During American participation in World War II, the nation's propaganda machine produced numerous images of scantily clad models and actresses designed to appeal to the heterosexual male gaze and inspire young men to vanquish the enemy so they could soon return to the pleasures of home.[1] Not all propaganda that focused on the female body, however, did so in order to appeal to young men's sexual desires. A lesser known category of images appealed to the patriotism of wartime servicemen and home front civilians alike by focusing on the female body enacting the Four Freedoms that President Roosevelt told Congress in January 1941 the nation must protect and extend around the globe: Freedom of Speech, Freedom of Religion, Freedom from Want, and Freedom from Fear.[2] Photographers working for the federal government scoured the nation's cities, towns, and countryside looking for women who seemed to embody these ideals in their daily lives. In the process, photographers frequently ignored the young adult men who lived and worked beside these women, perpetuating the notion that able-bodied men should be on the war front rather than the home front. The Anabaptist farmwomen of Lancaster County, Pennsylvania – a location widely represented in popular and scholarly literature as the nation's archetypal agricultural district – were among the women government photographers selected as subjects. But these war propaganda photos were steeped in irony: the Amish and Mennonite women who appeared in them were members of religious sects who strongly opposed armed conflict.[3]

Ideal images

The Amish and Mennonite residents of Lancaster County, who made up 9 per cent of the county's population by the time of World War II, were the descendants of Swiss and South German Anabaptists – or 're-baptizers' – whose insistence

171

on adult rather than infant baptism and rejection of armed resistance placed them at odds with other Reformation sects and caused them to seek refuge in colonial Pennsylvania.[4] Now, over 200 years later, these former outcasts became favourite subjects of government propaganda. Even before Germany's September 1939 invasion of Poland launched the war in Europe, the administration employed visual images of Pennsylvania Anabaptists to promote Roosevelt's Depression-era domestic agenda, known as the New Deal. Attention centred especially on the most conservative Anabaptist sect, the Old Order Amish, and on the location of their largest Pennsylvania settlement, Lancaster County. Several reasons existed for this fascination with the Amish. In segregated America, the Amish and other white farm families were safer subjects for New Deal celebrations of the nation's 'common man' than were members of the racially diverse urban working class. The Amish division of labour between male farmers and female homemakers appealed to New Dealers eager to glorify traditional gender roles at a time of high male unemployment. And with their theologically based commitment to nonconformity and agricultural self-sufficiency, the Old Order Amish neatly reflected the national creation myth. Like the Puritan founders, these thrifty, hard-working, Christian agrarians were admirable role models for Depression-weary and war-wary Americans of the late 1930s and early 1940s. With their rejection of electricity and automobiles, their use of horse-drawn transportation and farm equipment, and their wearing of plain, unfashionable clothing, the physical circumstances of the Old Order Amish even resembled those of the nation's Puritan forebears. Their race and agrarian way of life thus made the Lancaster County Anabaptists ideal photographic subjects, even as the beliefs that sustained their culture were at odds with their nation's commitment to total war.[5]

Although they were pacifists who frequently assisted male relatives and neighbours in avoiding conscription and military service, the Amish and Mennonite women in government propaganda photos nevertheless communicated ideas central to America's wartime mission. As portrayed by government photographers, these women were archetypal freedom-loving Americans whose activities mirrored those of the figures Norman Rockwell portrayed in his famous 1943 *Saturday Evening Post* portraits of the Four Freedoms.[6] Whereas Rockwell represented Freedom of Speech as a young man rising to speak at a town hall meeting, a government photographer pictured a Mennonite school-girl rising to speak in class. While the artist's representation of Freedom from Fear featured parents standing protectively over their sleeping children, a photographer's portrait pictured a watchful Mennonite teacher hovering over her pupils. Rockwell painted Americans of diverse faiths at prayer in his representation of Freedom of Religion, while photographers pictured the bowed heads of Anabaptist women and girls practising the faith that had caused their ancestors' banishment from Europe. And just as Rockwell portrayed Freedom from Want as a family enjoying their abundant Thanksgiving feast, photographers frequently portrayed well-fed Anabaptist women presiding over tables laden with agricultural bounty (see Figure 11.1).[7]

Contemporary viewers of wartime Lancaster County photos may assume that government photographers deliberately imitated Rockwell's paintings, but they actually created their images prior to the public debut of Rockwell's

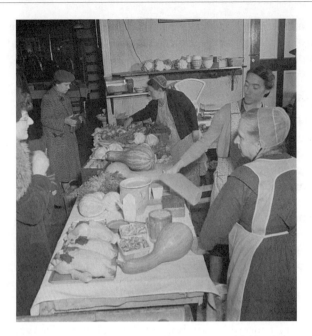

Figure 11.1 Photographer Marjory Collins's November 1942 picture of Anabaptist women selling farm produce at the Lititz, Pennsylvania, farmers' market depicted Freedom from Want in wartime America.
Photograph LC-USW3-011233-E, FSA/OWI Collection, Library of Congress.

portraits in February and March 1943. Although Rockwell's portraits became – and remain – the most widely reproduced and celebrated images of the Four Freedoms, they were far from unique. Speakers earnestly stating their case, heads bowed and hands folded in prayer, tables laden with food, and innocent little children appeared throughout wartime America in numerous forms – from a city hall mural in southern California to a billboard-sized photo montage in New York's Grand Central Palace, sculptures in New York's Rockefeller Plaza, and even patriotic fabric designs. After all, only a limited number of ways existed to create visual representations of Freedom of Speech, Freedom of Religion, Freedom from Want, and Freedom from Fear. But while Rockwell and other creators of Four Freedoms imagery necessarily coaxed models into position or conjured figures from their own imaginations, photographers in Lancaster County seemingly found ready-made representations all around them.[8]

A close examination of the work of two government photographers who visited Lancaster County in 1942 – John Collier, Jr., and Marjory Collins – demonstrates how American war propaganda used female bodies – even those of modestly clothed pacifists – to promote the Four Freedoms, inspire its fighting men, boost home front morale, and showcase the wonders of American life to friends and enemies overseas. Their portrayal of Amish and Mennonite women demonstrates in dramatic fashion the extent to which women who posed for wartime image makers – whether pin-up girls or pacifists – typically lacked control over the ways in which their bodies were used and displayed in wartime propaganda.

Collier's photographs

In March 1942, when 28-year-old John Collier, Jr., arrived in Lancaster County, he was on the payroll of the New Deal's Farm Security Administration (FSA), an agency that provided loans and other services to the nation's poorest farm families and employed photographers to document rural life and gather information about the historical, sociological, and economic aspects of federal relief programmes. At the time of Collier's arrival, FSA photographers and other New Deal representatives had been focusing on rural Pennsylvania and its noticeable Anabaptist population for several years. Following established precedent, the photographs Collier took in 1942 portray the Amish, and particularly Amish women, as representatives of an idealized agrarian past. The reasons for employing the Amish in this way, however, were changing. Arriving in Pennsylvania three months after the Japanese attack on the US naval base in Pearl Harbor, Hawaii, Collier sought images of what President Roosevelt later described as America shifting care of its national health from 'Dr New Deal' to 'Dr Win-the-War'.[9]

The FSA's photography unit, under the direction of economist Roy Stryker, did not officially transfer to the Roosevelt administration's war publicity organization, the Office of War Information (OWI), until September 1942, but its photographers were already beginning to produce what were essentially war propaganda pictures. As early as autumn 1940, Stryker began sending new shooting scripts to his team, urging them to downplay images of poverty, struggle, dust storms, and soil erosion in favour of rural 'abundance'. Prefiguring the January 1941 Congressional address in which President Roosevelt called on Americans to cherish, protect, and export the Four Freedoms, Stryker urged FSA photographers to create more 'horn of plenty' pictures. At the end of a long memo issued only a month before Collier's arrival in Lancaster County, Stryker described for his employees the ideal subject matter for war-era photos: 'People—*we must have at once* [Stryker's emphasis]: Pictures of men, women and children who appear as if they really believed in the U.S. Get people with a little spirit.'[10]

As they had been in the New Deal era, children were popular subjects for photographers who visited Lancaster County after Pearl Harbor. In part, this was because children were not yet baptized members of the faith and therefore not subject to Old Order Amish proscriptions against posing for photographs, a belief centred in the importance of face-to-face communication and biblical injunctions against graven images and personal pride. Collier's photograph of children at a farm auction's well-stocked confectionery stand, for example, shows 'people with a little spirit' and also fulfilled Stryker's request for 'horn of plenty' pictures illustrating Freedom from Want. Collier's frequent focus on children also yielded Lancaster County photos that reflect other of the Four Freedoms. His image of children praying in an Old Order Mennonite church, for instance, shows descendants of European religious protesters now enjoying Freedom of Religion in America.[11]

As Collier's photograph of the confectionery stand demonstrates, public auctions were an especially rich location for creating the type of pictures that Roy Stryker requested, and these events were easy for Collier to find during his stay in Lancaster County because March was the month when renters and buyers took possession of new farmsteads and acquired new equipment. As one Old Order Amish woman described a typical Lancaster County March, 'Work among the men folks is attending sales while some are getting ready to move. Work among the women folks is sewing and cleaning house.'[12] Collier's pictures of Old Order Amish attending an auction at Lancaster County's New Holland Sales Barn include posed images of children as well as candid 'action shots' of adults whose faces are in profile or partially obscured. Collier also met Stryker's request for pictures of wholesome rural residents by focusing on adult Anabaptists who resembled the Old Order Amish but faced fewer restrictions on worldly behaviour. Collier's New Holland photos include full-faced portraits of people who belonged to various Mennonite denominations, including Old Order Mennonites known as 'Team' Mennonites because – like the Old Order Amish – they continued to travel and perform farm work in conveyances pulled by horse teams after other Mennonites had adopted the automobile and tractor. Among Collier's auction photos are several full-faced portraits of subjects that the captions describe as 'Amish and Mennonite women'. In reality, however, the women pictured are predominantly Team Mennonites. Like other Lancaster County women, they had been busy sewing spring garments and sweeping and scrubbing for moving day but now took time to socialize at the auction while their husbands inspected farm equipment (see Figure 11.2).[13]

Figure 11.2 The caption for John Collier, Jr.'s picture of attendees at a March 1942 farm auction identified them as Amish women, but they were probably Old Order Mennonites. *Photograph LC-USF34-082262-E, FSA/OWI Collection, Library of Congress.*

As Collier's photos indicate, the wholesome, corn-fed – and all-white – Old Order Amish, Old Order Mennonites, and other Lancaster County Anabaptists were seemingly perfect subjects for the type of morale-boosting photos that Roy Stryker believed would appeal to Middle Americans of the 1940s. And Collier's attention to women, like his focus on children, had precedent among the other photographers who documented America's home front for the Stryker unit. In most locations, photographers gravitated to women and children because they – along with older men – were the home front population the government most wanted to praise and publicize. When government photographers turned their lenses on young men, they preferred those men to be in uniform and ideally headed to the war front. In Lancaster County – with its relatively large population of draft-age men receiving farm and ministerial deferments or claiming conscientious objector status on religious grounds – Collier had ample opportunity to include young men in his home front photographs, but he rarely did so. Even though one of the goals of Stryker's photographers was to show that the home front still possessed a sufficient civilian workforce, images of military-age men who stayed out of uniform did not make the best propaganda.[14] Collier was on safer ground photographing their sisters, wives, and sweethearts, whose sex disqualified them from consideration for combat service. The American public would not automatically interpret the women in Collier's photos as war opponents, even though, as the historian Rachel Goossen's scholarship demonstrates, Anabaptist women often provided significant assistance to male neighbours and relatives who sought or obtained conscientious objector status. Most of the people who would have viewed Collier's pictures in public exhibits or government publications, however, were probably unaware of Anabaptist women's controversial wartime activities. Deluged with other propaganda images that gendered the home front female and ignored young men unwilling to serve in uniform, the audience for Collier's photos likely accepted his portrayal of auction attendees as wholesome farmwomen whose well-dressed and well-nourished bodies provided yet another example of America's Freedom from Want.[15]

Collins's photographs

Eight months after Collier's Pennsylvania sojourn, with Roy Stryker's photographic unit now fully ensconced in the OWI, another of Stryker's employees travelled to Lancaster County in search of photos that served the war propaganda mission. Like Collier, 30-year-old Marjory Collins met Stryker's demand for morale-boosting pictures of men, women, and children by photographing people in public gathering places. Women figured prominently in the 'horn of plenty' photos that Collins created for Stryker both at the farmers' market in the town of Lititz and at the Central Market in the city of Lancaster. Stryker wanted pictures that proved the Roosevelt administration correct in its assertion that America would out-produce the Axis and supply servicemen, civilians, and overseas allies with enough food to 'win the war and write the peace'. Collins complied with her boss's demands, capturing images of women's market stalls overflowing with poultry, baked goods, fruits, and vegetables. But the corpulence of the women's bodies in most of these pictures also communicates the theme of rural prosperity and Freedom from Want.[16]

In some ways, the full-bodied Mennonite farmwomen in these photos presaged yet another of Norman Rockwell's well-known propaganda images – the solidly built female war worker he portrayed on the cover of the *Saturday Evening Post* in May 1943. But Rockwell's famous Rosie the Riveter character is a quintessentially urban, industrial character. With her well-muscled body and riveting machine and her penny-loafers propped defiantly on top of a copy of Hitler's *Mein Kampf*, Rockwell's war worker represents an active, combative, modern, self-sufficient, masculine America. Portrayed with her sleeves rolled up and ready for action, Rockwell's Rosie echoes the pose of countless male subjects in wartime propaganda photos, posters, and films. In fact, although Rockwell used his slender teenage neighbour Mary Doyle as the model for Rosie's face, he modelled Rosie's body on a male figure – Michelangelo's representation of the prophet Isaiah on the ceiling of the Sistine Chapel.[17]

In contrast to Rockwell's masculinized Rosie, the soft, round bodies of the women in Marjory Collins's photographs are conventionally feminine, invoking a theme popular a few years earlier among regional artists who equated the supposedly passive, voluptuous female body with the fertile countryside that receives – and perhaps is exploited by – the plough and farmer. For example, in a 1936 painting entitled *Erosion No. 2 – Mother Earth Laid Bare*, the artist Alexandre Hogue portrayed a dust bowl scene in which an abandoned plough lies at the base of eroded soil mounded in the shape of a naked, curvaceous female torso. Similarly, Missouri artist Thomas Hart Benton's 1938 portrait of *Persephone* imagines her as a nude and shapely pin-up girl lying near a stream, oblivious to the leering Farmer Hades who peers from around the lush vegetation emanating from her body. Unlike these New Deal-era artists who denounced the rape of the land – and perhaps implicitly promoted Roosevelt administration conservation projects as a solution – wartime photographer Collins now celebrated successful cooperation between the land and its stewards. Anabaptist women, whose religion taught that farming was a sacred way of life to be passed on to the next generation, were the ideal representatives of successful care for and use of the land.[18]

Collins's marketplace photos – with their focus on full-figured women displaying (literally) the fruits of their labour – emphasize both the fertility of Lancaster County farms and Lancaster County farmwomen. While a few years earlier Stryker's FSA employee Dorothea Lange had famously demonstrated the poverty of California's migrant farm workers by focusing on the undernourished body of a ragged *Migrant Mother* and her dust-streaked children, Collins now centred on the successful productive and reproductive capabilities of Lancaster County women to illustrate their community's agrarian abundance. The differences in Lange's and Collins's presentation of the female body reflect the altered mission of Stryker's photographic unit. In the New Deal period, Stryker directed his photographers to document rural suffering in a way that would arouse middle-class sympathies and elicit support for Roosevelt's agricultural reforms. But in the 'we're all in this together' spirit of wartime, he wanted pictures of people the viewer could relate to rather than pity.[19] Collins

Figure 11.3 Marjory Collins's picture of a smiling, well-fed Mennonite woman selling celery at Lancaster city's Central Market was an effective visual representation of America's wartime abundance.
Photograph LC-USW3-011003-E, FSA/OWI Collection, Library of Congress.

frequently achieved this goal by having her well-fed farmwomen face the camera head on, addressing the viewer directly and returning the observer's gaze as an equal (see Figure 11.3).[20] And unlike Lange's women, those in Collins's photos had something more to show for their life on the land than tattered clothing and hungry children. Collins's subjects proudly display the results of women's labour in the henhouse, garden, orchard, and farm kitchen, demonstrating that most farm homemakers were also farm producers. This aspect of Collins's work distinguishes it from that of her male colleague John Collier, Jr. The women in Collier's pictures of public space chat while their husbands purchase farm equipment, but the women in Collins's photos participate actively in the business of farming. Collins's photographs acknowledge that women's widespread participation in production and marketing–along with their role in reproducing the large farm family work force–contributed significantly to Lancaster County's reputation as the 'garden spot of the country'.[21]

By focusing on well-nourished female bodies, Collins also avoided more controversial subject matter – such as the strong, able bodies of young men who remained in Lancaster County while the war raged overseas. Like Collier, Collins rarely acknowledged the problematic presence on the Lancaster County home front of draft-age Anabaptist men. On the infrequent occasions that she produced images of young men out of uniform, the captions for her photos always carefully note that the men were soon entering the military or were deferred to perform vital home front service. The one time that Collins dealt with a young man's crisis of conscience, she focused not on a man struggling with the question of military service but on one weighing the propriety of war industry employment. Like other OWI photographers, Collins photographed a wide variety of activities when on assignment, and her photos of the Lancaster County countryside include images of mechanized farming and manufacturing as well as pastoral depictions of traditional Anabaptist life. On her visit to the town of Lititz, Collins not only took pictures of residents attending a public auction and buying and selling produce at the local farmers' market but also captured images of workers at a former animal trap factory that now made 'armor-piercing bullet cores and other war essentials'. Among those she photographed at their work stations was lathe-operator Raymond Newswanger, a pleasant-looking, clean-cut young man in work shirt and overalls, whose rolled-up sleeves and well-muscled forearms resemble those of numerous other men portrayed in the era's military recruitment posters, propaganda films, and commercial advertising. The photo's poignant caption describes Newswanger as 'a Mennonite, about thirty, ... [who] hopes his church won't find out he's doing defense work. Most Mennonites are farmers, and Newswanger used to be'.[22]

The caption for Collins's photo seemingly ignores the idea – so prevalent in much of the rest of her work for the OWI – that as a farmer Newswanger had already been 'doing defense work' long before he took a job in a munitions factory. According to the OWI, farmers were home front warriors who produced essential war materials and helped America achieve Freedom from Want. As Secretary of Agriculture Claude Wickard had told Congress in September 1942, 'Food is just as much a weapon in this war as guns.' But the caption for Collins's portrait of Raymond Newswanger reflects the man's own opinion – and that of his church – that farm work was not necessarily war work. It was simply the traditional way of life for Lancaster County Amish and Mennonites.[23]

Pacifist 'warriors'

When Marjory Collins and John Collier, Jr., portrayed the men, women, and children of Lancaster County working on their farms, praying, attending and teaching school, and meeting at auctions and farmers' markets, they simply recorded the usual round of tasks that rural Anabaptists performed whether or not the nation was at war. The subjects of these pictures likely never thought of these activities as serving the war effort and had no control over how the OWI employed and interpreted their images. Most Lancaster County Anabaptists did not place their activities within a pro-war context, but the OWI personnel who captured and distributed their images did. There were some exceptions. When, for instance, middle-aged Mennonite farmer Moses Zimmerman, his wife, and family participated in the making of a 1943 OWI motion picture entitled *Farmer at War*, they had to know that their Lancaster County farm was the setting for a war propaganda film. And the words and actions of Zimmerman and his family clearly reference the Four Freedoms. Zimmerman attends a local farmers' meeting where participants rise to speak their minds. The family prays for the safety of American servicemen. The stout

Mrs Zimmerman brings a plump roast turkey to the Thanksgiving dinner table. And, like the patriarch in Norman Rockwell's *Freedom from Fear* portrait, Zimmerman – newspaper in hand and wife by his side – ascends the stairs to the attic bedrooms where the couple's young nephew is already peacefully asleep. But Zimmerman was a special case. His age exempted him from the suspicion he should be in uniform and thus made him an acceptable male subject for the propagandists' lens. And his paternal, life-affirming statements about feeding the hungry and protecting those in harm's way – expressed both in the film and behind the scenes to family members and neighbours – allowed him to remain a member in good standing at his local Mennonite church.[21]

The Zimmermans, Raymond Newswanger, and a minority of other Lancaster County Anabaptists actively cooperated with the American war effort. At a time when military service represented the highest expression of American masculinity, some of the community's young men even served in uniform. Urban Anabaptists and those belonging to less restrictive sects were those most likely to register for regular military service, but even 2.9 per cent of the nation's draft-eligible Old Order Amish were classified as regular military rather than as conscientious objectors or military noncombatants. For the cooperators, World War II was such a popular national cause and a crisis of such magnitude that the usual code of conduct did not apply. Most of Lancaster County's Anabaptists, however, maintained their commitment to what their religion termed 'nonresistance' and continued to avoid participating in or supporting armed conflict in any way.[25]

In describing the types of pictures he wanted from his photographers in 1942, Roy Stryker emphasized the need for photos of Americans at their everyday activities – 'woman sewing, man reading … [people] coming from church'. Marjory Collins and John Collier, Jr., fulfilled Stryker's requests with their pictures of Pennsylvania Anabaptists. Collins photographed a Mennonite woman making a dress at her sewing machine and took several pictures of middle-aged men reading local newspapers and national magazines. Collier photographed worshippers leaving a modest Mennonite meeting house, and Collins captured a similar scene outside a more elaborately appointed Moravian church. For a government eager to tell its citizens why their nation was at war, the version of Lancaster County life portrayed in Stryker unit photos represented an America worth fighting for and an image of the nation as it ostensibly wanted to be.[26]

Conclusion: 'Peculiar' legacy

After facing increasing interference from his superiors at the OWI and losing several of his male photographers to the military draft, Stryker disbanded his photographic unit and resigned from government service less than a year after Collins completed her Lancaster County assignment. Prior to his September 1943 resignation, Stryker arranged that control of his employees' photographs be transferred from the OWI to the Library of Congress. With Stryker and the OWI no longer managing the vast photo collection and promoting its use in publications and exhibits specifically designed to tout the American war cause, the Lancaster County images had a more limited wartime audience than Stryker had originally intended. Records, in fact, are unclear about the number of viewers who saw the photos during the war and how they reacted to these images. Thirty years after his resignation from the OWI, however, Stryker finally published a collection of the photos he felt best represented the purpose and goals of his government photographic unit. From over 70,000 FSA/OWI pictures printed in the 1930s and 1940s, the 80-year-old Stryker chose nearly 200 for inclusion in his 1973 volume. Among them were two Lancaster County pictures – Marjory Collins's photo of a dishevelled man selling newspapers full of war news on the streets of Lancaster city and her picture of an elderly Mennonite couple attending a public auction in Lititz. With the pleasant-looking, bonneted wife standing in front of her bearded husband, the pair in Collins's photograph securely inhabits the OWI's idealized home front of wholesome women, children, and senior citizens. Their portrait is the perfect fulfilment of Stryker's 1942 request for photographers to produce more pictures of 'contented-looking old couples'.[27]

When Marjory Collins and John Collier, Jr., portrayed the women, girls, and other Anabaptist residents of Lancaster County, they simply recorded the daily activities their subjects engaged in in times of peace as well as war. These women and girls, regardless of their compliance with friendly government photographers, did not think of their activities as innately serving the war effort and ultimately had little or no control over how the OWI employed and interpreted their images in photo exhibits and other wartime venues. For the pacifist Old Order Amish, Old Order Mennonites, and other Anabaptists whose separation from the mainstream world and distinctive habits and dress prompted themselves and others to label them a 'peculiar people', the use of their images in pro-war publicity was peculiar indeed and starkly highlights the extent to which women lacked control over construction of the messages their bodies were intended to convey in wartime propaganda.[28]

Recommended reading

Casey, J. G. (2009) *A New Heartland: Women, Modernity, and the Agrarian Ideal in America* (New York: Oxford University Press).

Goossen, R. W. (1997) *Women Against the Good War: Conscientious Objection and Gender on the American Home Front, 1941–1947* (Chapel Hill: University of North Carolina Press).

Guimond, J. (1991) *American Photography and the American Dream* (Chapel Hill: University of North Carolina Press).

Kollmorgen, W. M. (1942) *Culture of a Contemporary Rural Community: The Old Order Amish of Lancaster County, Pennsylvania* Rural Studies Series. vol. 4 (Washington, DC: Government Printing Office).

McEuen, M. A. (2011) *Making War, Making Women: Femininity and Duty on the American Home Front, 1941–1945* (Athens, GA: University of Georgia Press).

Murray, S. and J. McCabe. (1998) *Norman Rockwell's Four Freedoms* (New York: Gramercy Books).

Reschly, S. D. and K. Jellison (1993) 'Production Patterns, Consumption Strategies, and Gender Relations in Amish and Non-Amish Farm Households in Lancaster County, Pennsylvania, 1935–1936', *Agricultural History*, vol. 67, no. 2, pp. 134–62.

Stryker, R. E. and N. Wood (1973) *In This Proud Land: America 1935–1943 as Seen in the FSA Photographs* (Greenwich, CT: New York Graphic Society).

Walbert, D. (2002) *Garden Spot: Lancaster County, the Old Order Amish, and the Selling of Rural America* (New York: Oxford University Press).

Weaver-Zercher, D. (2001) *The Amish in the American Imagination* (Baltimore: Johns Hopkins University Press).

Notes

1. For discussion of the problematic effects of using highly sexualized images of the female body to motivate America's military servicemen, see R. B. Westbrook (1990) '"I Want a Girl, Just Like the Girl That Married Harry James". American Women and the Problem of Political Obligation in World War II', *American Quarterly*, vol. 42, no. 4, pp. 587–614; M. E. Hegarty (2008) *Victory Girls, Khaki-Wackies, and Patriotutes: The Regulation of Female Sexuality During World War II* (New York: New York University Press); and M. A. McEuen (2011) *Making War, Making Women: Femininity and Duty on the American Home Front, 1941–1945* (Athens, GA: University of Georgia Press).

2. Roosevelt first enunciated his Four Freedoms in an address delivered to Congress a full eleven months prior to America's December 1941 entry in the war. See J. M. Burns (1970) *Roosevelt: The Soldier of Freedom* (New York: Harcourt Brace Jovanovich), pp. 34–5.

3. Several publications promoting Lancaster County Amish and Mennonite agriculturalists as the nation's best farmers and touting the county as America's 'garden spot' appeared just as the country was mobilizing for and entering the war in 1941–1942. See E. C. Stauffer (1941) 'In the Pennsylvania Dutch Country', *National Geographic Magazine*, vol. 80, no. 1, pp. 37–74; C. G. Bachman (1942) *The Old Order Amish of Lancaster County* (Norristown, PA: Pennsylvania German Society); W. M. Kollmorgen (1942) *Culture of a Contemporary Rural Community: The Old Order Amish of Lancaster County, Pennsylvania*, Rural Life Studies, vol. 4 (Washington, DC: Government Printing Office). For a thoughtful analysis of these and other works that have portrayed Lancaster County as America's ideal agrarian location, see D. Walbert (2002) *Garden Spot: Lancaster County, the Old Order Amish, and the Selling of Rural America* (New York: Oxford University Press).

4. Population calculation derives from information in T. F. Murphy (1941) *Religious Bodies: 1936*, vol. 1 (Washington, DC: Government Printing Office), p. 812; Kollmorgen, *Culture of a Contemporary Rural Community*, pp. 1, 85; and R. L. Forstall (1995) *Population of Counties by Decennial Census: 1900 to 1990*, available at www.census.gov/population/cencounts/pa190090.txt, date accessed 5 September 2016.

5. D. Weaver-Zercher (2001) *The Amish in the American Imagination* (Baltimore: Johns Hopkins University Press), pp. 11–12, 22, 49; J. G. Casey (2009) *A New Heartland: Women, Modernity, and the Agrarian Ideal in America* (New York: Oxford University Press), pp. 28–9, 37.

6. These can be viewed at the Norman Rockwell museum and website 'The Four Freedoms': http://www.nrm.org/four-freedoms/, date accessed 15 July 2016.

7. See material throughout S. Murray and J. McCabe (1998) *Norman Rockwell's Four Freedoms* (New York: Gramercy Books). All government-sponsored photographs reproduced or discussed in this chapter are from the Farm Security Administration/Office of War Information Collection, Library of Congress, Washington, DC. Available online at www.loc.gov/pictures/collection/fsa/sampler.html, date accessed 5 September 2016. Hereafter cited as FSA/OWI Collection.

8. Murray and McCabe, *Norman Rockwell's Four Freedoms*, pp. 40–3, and photos and captions for photographs LC-USE6-D-004863, LC-USW3-018411-E, and LC-USW3-021102-C, FSA/OWI Collection.

9. Roosevelt declared an end to the New Deal at a 1943 press conference in which he said 'Dr New Deal' had cured the nation of its internal economic malady and was now turning the patient over to his partner, 'an orthopedic surgeon, Dr Win-the-War', to tend the external injuries the nation sustained in its 'pretty bad smashup' of 7 December 1941. See Burns, *Roosevelt*, p. 423.

10. J. Guimond (1991) *American Photography and the American Dream* (Chapel Hill: University of North Carolina Press), pp. 137–9.

11. For discussion of Amish school children as popular subjects for New Deal poster artists and photographers, as well as other visual artists, see Weaver-Zercher, *The Amish in the American Imagination*, pp. 51, 67, 70–2, and D. Eitzen (2008) 'Reel Amish: The Amish in Documentaries' in D. Z. Umble and D. L. Weaver-Zercher (eds) *The Amish and the Media* (Baltimore: Johns Hopkins University Press), pp. 48–51.

12. R. S. Glick (19 March 1936) 'Lancaster, PA', *The Budget*. For discussion of the weekly newspaper *The Budget* and its frequent reliance on Old Order Amish and other Anabaptist women as reporters or 'scribes', see S. M. Nolt (2008) 'Inscribing Community: *The Budget* and *Die Botschaft* in Amish Life', in Umble and Weaver-Zercher (eds), *The Amish and the Media*, pp. 181–98.

13. For discussion of Amish adults pushing religious boundaries by allowing photographers to take pictures of their faces in profile or obscured, see D. B. Kraybill (2008) 'Amish Informants: Mediating Humility and Publicity', in Umble and Weaver-Zercher (eds), *The Amish and the Media*, p. 176. In an interview with Katherine Jellison and Steven D. Reschly, in Lancaster, PA, on 18 December 2008, Amish women 'Rebecca' and 'Ada' identified the location of Collier's auction photos as the New Holland Sales Barn and identified the women in this set of photos as Team Mennonites. Rebecca, born in 1930, and Ada, born in 1926, were both raised in Lancaster County as members of the Old Order Amish, although Ada later joined the Beachy Amish. In contrast to the Old Order Amish, the Beachy Amish own automobiles and hold their worship services in church buildings rather than in members' homes. Amish proscriptions against prideful behaviour prevent the use of Rebecca's and Ada's real names in interview citations.

14. Guimond, *American Photography*, p. 139.

15. See R. W. Goossen (1997) *Women Against the Good War: Conscientious Objection and Gender on the American Home Front, 1941–1947* (Chapel Hill: University of North Carolina Press).

16. Guimond, *American Photography*, p. 138; M. C. Wilson (1941) *How and to What Extent is the Extension Service Reaching Low-Income Farm Families* (Washington, DC: Government Printing Office), p. 18.

17. E. Izadi (2015) 'Model for Norman Rockwell's "Rosie the Riveter" Dies at 92', *The Washington Post*, 22 April, available at www.washingtonpost.com/blogs/style-blog/wp/2015/04/22/rosie-the-riveter-model-dies-at-92/, date accessed 23 April 2015; K. A. Marling (1997) *Norman Rockwell* (New York: Harry N. Abrams), p. 101. For discussion of portrayals of the male body in World War II America, see C. S. Jarvis (2004) *The Male Body at War: American Masculinity during World War II* (DeKalb: Northern Illinois University Press).

18. This interpretation is based on arguments in Casey, *A New Heartland*, p. 4.

19. An excellent discussion of Lange's use of the human body in her photos for the Stryker unit is L. Gordon (2006) 'Dorothea Lange: The Photographer as Agricultural Sociologist', *Journal of American History*, vol. 93, no. 3, pp. 698–727. For discussion of the changing nature of Stryker unit photos of Lancaster County

as the Roosevelt administration shifted from New Deal to wartime concerns, see S. D. Reschly and K. Jellison (2008) 'Research Note: Shifting Images of Lancaster County Amish in the 1930s and 1940s', *Mennonite Quarterly Review*, vol. 82, no. 3, pp. 469–83.

20. L. Aleci (2008) 'The Rural Feminine in Place: Marjory Collins' and David Scherman's Photographs of Lancaster, Pennsylvania', unpublished paper presented at the Berkshire Conference on Women's History, 13 June, Minneapolis, MN.

21. For detailed discussion of Anabaptist women's farm and home production activities in Lancaster County – as well as their significant reproductive rate – see S. D. Reschly and K. Jellison (1993) 'Production Patterns, Consumption Strategies, and Gender Relations in Amish and Non-Amish Farm Households in Lancaster County, Pennsylvania, 1935–1936', *Agricultural History*, vol. 67, no. 2, pp. 134–62. In the same year that Collier and Collins made their photographs of Lancaster County, the federal Bureau of Agricultural Economics released cultural geographer Walter M. Kollmorgen's report designating the county's Old Order Amish the most stable and successful farming community in the nation. For discussion of this report and Amish women's role in their community's success, see K. Jellison (2001) 'An "Enviable Tradition" of Patriarchy: New Deal Investigations of Women's Work in the Amish Farm Family' in C. M. Stock and R. D. Johnston (eds) *The Countryside in the Age of the Modern State: Political Histories of Rural America* (Ithaca, NY: Cornell University Press), pp. 240–57, and Jellison (2002) 'The Chosen Women: The Amish and the New Deal', in K. D. Schmidt, D. Z. Umble, and S. D. Reschly (eds), *Strangers at Home: Amish and Mennonite Women in History* (Baltimore: Johns Hopkins University Press), pp. 102–18.

22. Captions for photographs LC-USE6-D-004655 and LC-USW3-011777-D, FSA/OWI Collection.

23. Wickard is quoted in Goossen, *Women Against the Good War*, p. 87.

24. *Farmer at War* (1943), Record Group 208: Records of the Office of War Information, 1926–1951, National Archives II, College Park, MD; R. Z. Hershey (5 December 2010) interview with K. Jellison and S. D. Reschly, Lititz, PA; D. Hershey (7 December 2010) conversation with K. Jellison and S. D. Reschly, Elizabethtown, PA. For further discussion of the film and the Zimmerman family, see Jellison and Reschly (2014) 'Picturing World War II on the "Garden Spot" Home Front: Images and Memories of Mennonite Farm Families in Lancaster County', *Pennsylvania Mennonite Heritage*, vol. 37, no. 4, pp. 114–18.

25. G. F. Hershberger (1950, reprint 2000) *The Mennonite Church in the Second World War* (Eugene, OR: Wipf and Stock Publishers), pp. 34–48; P. Toews (1996) *Mennonites in American Society, 1930–1970: Modernity and the Persistence of Religious Community* (Scottdale, PA: Herald Press), pp. 173–4; K. L. Sprunger and J. D. Thiesen (1992) 'Mennonite Military Service in World War II: An Oral History Approach', *Mennonite Quarterly Review*, vol. 66, no. 4, p. 483. The entire vol. 66, no. 4 issue of *Mennonite Quarterly Review* is devoted to the topic of Mennonites and alternative service in World War II.

26. Guimond, *American Photography*, p. 138.

27. Guimond, *American Photography*, pp. 139–40; R. E. Stryker and N. Wood (1973) *In This Proud Land: America 1935–1943 as Seen in the FSA Photographs* (Greenwich, CT: New York Graphic Society), pp. 19, 59, 63, 188.

28. In their examination of the Old Order Amish in Iowa, sociologist Elmer Schwieder and historian Dorothy Schwieder even use the word 'peculiar' in their book title. See E. Schwieder and D. Schwieder (2009) *A Peculiar People: Iowa's Old Order Amish*, expanded edn (Iowa City: University of Iowa Press).

12

Beyond the Dichotomy of Prostitutes versus Sex Slaves: Transnational Feminist Activism of 'Comfort Women' in South Korea and Japan

Sachiyo Tsukamoto

The 2015 Japan–South Korea agreement on the issue of 'comfort women' struck the world like a bolt from the blue. Tokyo and Seoul agreed to settle the thorny issue 'finally and irreversibly' by establishing a foundation to support the survivors.[1] However, the unilateral deal was 'outrageous' to both Korean survivors and activists because it 'never reflected the victims' demand' that Japan offer an official apology and compensation to the individual victims.[2] Neither did it reflect the silence-breaker Kim Hak-sun's desire to convey the history of Japan's war crimes to younger generations of the two countries.

Kim Hak-sun was the first silence-breaker, whose testimony in 1991 led to a paradigmatic change, transforming 'comfort women' from prostitutes to sex slaves.[3] In the aftermath of Hak-sun's courageous testimony, the emergence of Japanese historical revisionism placed binary concepts of prostitution or sexual slavery at the forefront of the debate. Since 1991, Japanese historical revisionists have mobilized the sex-work feminist proposition as justification to evade the state's responsibility by depicting 'comfort women' as voluntary prostitutes.[4] Their constant attack against the transnational 'comfort women' justice movement has contributed to the exclusion of the first victims from such activism. The initial victims were Japanese women, many of whom were construed as state-sanctioned prostitutes at the time of recruitment.[5] As a feminist activist scholar, I argue that the fundamental problem of the Japanese and South Korean feminist engagement with the transnational activism lies in their binary representation of 'comfort women'.

Representations of 'comfort women'

The euphemistic term 'comfort women' refers to women and girls forced into prostitution for the Japanese Army during the Asia-Pacific War (1931–1945). [6] During the war, the Japanese government and army collaborated with police and agents of occupied countries in organizing a large-scale trafficking system designed to recruit women and girls from poor families either through deception or by force.[7] As a consequence of the vast spatial expanse of the Empire of Japan a diverse range of nationalities were forced to work in the 'comfort stations', including Japanese, Chinese, Taiwanese, Koreans, Filipinas, Indonesians, Vietnamese, Malays, Thais, Burmese, Indians, Timorese, Chamorros, Dutch, and Eurasian women.[8] When the war ended in 1945, the Japanese army abandoned the 'comfort women' or burned/bombed 'comfort stations' with them confined within. Surviving 'comfort women' remained silent out of fear of social stigmatization.[9]

In Japan, the story of Korean 'comfort women' was first told in 1947 through the novel written by the Japanese veteran, Tamura Yasujirō, entitled *Shunpūden* (A Prostitute's Story). In 1973, a Japanese journalist, Senda Kakō, expressed sympathy with their intolerable lives in his *Jūgun Ianfu* (Military Comfort Women). The 'comfort women' binary was reinforced by the Korean writer, Kim Il-myon. He represented Korean and Japanese 'comfort women' as 'younger and older, amateur and professional, deceived and voluntary, sincere and jaded' in his *Tennō no Guntai to Chōsenjin Ianfu* (The Emperor's Army and the Korean Comfort Women: 1976).[10] None of the three male writers could reach a wider readership beyond Japanese males, most of whom were veterans. More importantly, they lacked the perspective of gender in which the feminine–masculine dynamic was investigated in the context of societal norms.[11] The three authors' gender-blind thinking valued and legitimized the patriarchal system of 'comfort women'.

Gender-sensitive scholarship on 'comfort women' which challenged the naturalization of masculinity emerged after the wake of Hak-sun's testimony of 1991. In 1995, the first comprehensive English book was written by George Hicks. His careless use of the contentious binary without any evaluation is nonetheless evident in his use of Il-myon's stereotypical comparison between Korean and Japanese 'comfort women' cited above.[12] David A. Schmidt (2000) similarly failed to examine the binaries when he concluded that the military brothel system 'was one of the largest systems of state-sponsored rape and sexual enslavement in history'.[13] In contrast, the Japanese historian, Yoshimi Yoshiaki (1996) uncovered the comprehensive mechanism of the 'comfort women' system based on extensive archival research, drawing the radical feminist conclusion that Japan's pre-war state-sanctioned prostitution system and the 'comfort women' system were both systems of sexual slavery.[14] In 2002, a Japanese historian studying in Australia, Tanaka Yuki, expanded Yoshimi's historical analysis into a comparative study of military prostitution, seeking to examine the complex interaction between militarism and masculinity.

In 2000, debate was sparked when feminist scholars, Margaret D. Stez and Bonnie B. C. Oh applied a radical feminist orientation to their examination of the binaries to 'overturn hierarchies of gender'.[15] Writing in 2008, feminist anthropologist, Chunghee Sarah Soh demonstrated the plight of Korean victims 'as a prominent instance of gendered structural violence'.[16] However, she evaluates victimization of Japanese 'comfort women' differently, pointing out that, 'Some Japanese comfort women apparently led relatively secure lives.'[17] In her analysis, 'the degree of sexual violence and abuse the comfort women suffered varies with geographical and chronological factors as well as with the ethnicity of individual women'.[18] Conversely, in a critique of Soh's examination of prostitution, Caroline Norma, an abolitionist feminist, notes that all 'comfort women' were sex slaves regardless of their prior experiences.[19] This chapter draws on Norma's analysis and will explain how and why survivors' voices were ignored in Japan, before considering the consequences of that disregard.

Ignored silence-breaking in Japan

Suzuko Shirota (pseudonym, 1921–1993) was the first Japanese survivor who broke her silence in her 1971 autobiography, *Maria no Sanka* (*Maria's Song of Praise*). Her life story was published by a Christian group that helped to run a shelter for women in Tateyama, where she would spend more than two decades until her death. In 1986, her radio interview under her real name (Yoshie) was broadcast.[20] However, her testimonies attracted very little attention within Japanese society. The life stories of other Japanese survivors, Kikumaru (professional name, 1925–1972) and Aya Suzumoto (pseudonym, 1924–) interviewed by a female journalist, Hirota Kazuko, (1975) did not draw much public attention either. The following statement by Sister Amaha, who cared for Shirota on her deathbed, explains the predicament faced by Japanese survivors: 'There is an unspoken pressure not to come forward and bring shame on the nation. I think that is why none have spoken out.'[21] Thus 'comfort women' also fell victim to the masculine sexism within their own country where female virginity is highly valued. Their ability to become active agents in coming to terms with their past plight had been effectively denied by their own patriarchal government and society.

Nonetheless, in 1977 a new opportunity arose for Japanese feminists to reshape the male-dominant his-story into an alternative her-story. A Korean survivor and Japanese resident, Pae Pong Gi, personally came forward under interrogation by immigration officials when she sought special permission to stay in Japan.[22] She consulted with Japanese lawyers about a possible compensatory lawsuit against the Japanese government. However, the lawyers predicted a slim chance of victory owing to conditions contained within the Treaty on Basic Relations between Japan and the Republic of Korea (1965).[23] Without gaining any support from the Japanese community, she abandoned her court appeal.[24] In 1979, her documentary film was released, while her biography, *Akarenga no Ie* (*The Redbrick House*) edited by Fumiko Kawata, was published in 1987.[25] Neither attracted the attention of feminists.

A feminist historian, Yuki Fujime criticizes the marginality of the 'comfort women' justice movement in Japan. She regrets the failure of Japanese feminists to respond to Shirota's courage in revealing the harsh reality of 'comfort women'.[26] The following section of this chapter will consider the position of Japanese feminism within a broader historical context. Special attention will be given to the post-war period and particularly the effects of the US occupation upon Japanese social forces.

Feminist movements in Japan: 1945–1990

Even though the term feminism (*feminizumu*) did not exist until the 1970s, the first wave of the Japanese feminist movement emerged in the 1920s.[27] It was not a direct import from the West, but was based on Japanese women's experiences of gender segregation.[28] As Ueno Chizuko, a Japanese feminist sociologist, emphasizes, Japanese feminism traditionally valued motherhood while distancing itself from the Western values of individual equality.[29] In the post-war US occupation period (1945–1952), some female activist groups vigorously lobbied Douglas MacArthur, Supreme Command for the Allied Powers (SCAP) and the Japanese government for women's rights, including the right to vote.[30] The SCAP identified the promotion of women's political and economic status as a significant component in the democratization of Japan, and regarded feminist activists as 'potential allies' in pursuit of the common goal: Japan's democratization.[31] Eventually, Japan's new peace constitution initiated by the United States dramatically improved the legal status of females and fulfilled the demands of the pre-war suffrage movement.[32]

The immediate needs of women soon after the end of the war were directed at the shortages and the increases in the price of food. To voice their demands, the League of Regional Women's Organisations (*Chifu-ren*) and the Housewives' Association (*Sufu-ren*) were established.[33] Both of them emerged as 'the prominence of housewives' (*shufu*), connecting them beyond their social and political differences. Ever since, housewives have become 'the backbone' of Japanese feminist activism.[34]

During the period of the US occupation, Japanese feminists who comprised the peace movement and shared strong anti-war sentiments were restricted from expressing 'any antinuclear rhetoric' as it was regarded 'as potentially anti-U.S.' by SCAP.[35] In the wake of the official ending of the US occupation, Japanese feminists raised their voices as part of the anti-nuclear and anti-war movements, demanding the demilitarization of Japan, the removal of all US bases from Japan, and the return of Okinawa.[36] For example, an early 1950s Japanese Women's Association (*Nihon Fujin Kai*) appealed for the eradication of nuclear bombs whereas *Shufu-ren* launched a pacifist campaign.[37] This led to fierce criticism against the 'reverse course' of the US occupation policy, which transformed the nascent process of Japan's democratization into a process of remilitarization in the contest against global communism. As part of this process, the SCAP released a large number of Japanese war criminals including wartime leaders such as Kishi Nobusuke, the grandfather of Japanese Prime Minister Shinzo Abe. Kishi was released by the United States and was appointed prime minister between 1957 and 1958. Within this context, the Japanese feminist movement began to engage more in political issues. The 1960 nationwide protest against the ratification of the Japan–US Security Treaty under the Kishi cabinet attracted more than forty female organizations.[38] After signing the pact, Kishi resigned in 1960.

The birth of the Japanese women's liberation movement (*wōman ribu*) took place on 21 October 1970, organized by the Fighting Women Group (*Tatakau Onna*). Launching a female-only demonstration, Tanaka Mitsu, the head of the feminist group, issued a radical manifesto: 'Liberation from the Toilet.'[39] In the script, she critiqued Japanese masculine sexism symbolized by the patriarchal dichotomy between mothers (*shufu*) and prostitutes (*shōfu*). Whores are implied by 'the toilet' where men sate their sexual drive. During the Second World War, the term 'public toilets' was used as a common metaphor for 'comfort women' by Japanese soldiers. The placards held in the demonstration stated that virgins and 'comfort women' supported invasion.[40] In November 1970, Tanaka inserted the following paragraph into a flyer against the retrogressive revision of the Abortion Law and the Labour Standards Act:

> The duty of virgins to their country and family was to defend the home front as mothers of their nation, thereby revealing themselves as women who were characterized by both mothers' affection and female sexuality as their expression of love. On the front line, comfort women fulfilled their husbands' lust by serving as public toilets for soldiers, thus raising men as the emperor's babies who would become competent killers totally obedient to the military rules. Japanese virgins were complicit in violating Korean women with Japanese men's semen [author's translation].[41]

As Ueno points out, Tanaka argued that Japanese women became perpetrators by viewing themselves as victims. Tanaka posed a fundamental question to all Japanese women in addressing the 'comfort women' issue as women of the aggressor state. However, the first reference to the 'comfort women' issue raised by the Japanese feminist movement was ignored under patriarchal media bashing which labelled *wōman ribu* as female hysteria.

Spurred by Japan's miracle economic growth, in the 1970s there was a Japanese male sexual invasion of Asian women in sex tourism. Some Japanese women urged that attention should therefore shift from the West to Asia. They realized that Japan's patriarchal social structure perpetuated the binary, but interchangeable female roles such as wife and prostitute to ease the stressful lives of male corporate warriors.[42] Despite the fact that the system of legal prostitution was abolished at the end of the Second World War, Japanese public attitudes which regard prostitution as a necessary evil are deeply embedded within Japanese society.[43] As Ueno argues, 'The patriarchal paradigm denies women's agency, and reduces the infringement of women's sexual human rights to a dispute over property rights between fellow men within the patriarchal system.'[44]

Matsui Yayori (1934–2002), at the time the only female member of the editorial staff of a major newspaper *Asahi Shimbun*, was one of the concerned feminists. In her memoir, she mentioned a small newspaper article about the demonstrations by Korean women at Seoul Airport in 1973 against Japanese male sex tours to Korea (*Keysen Tourism*) and emphasized how the news shocked Japanese women.[45] Matsui sought to raise public awareness of the issue of prostitution tours by producing a comprehensive report about *Keysen Tourism*. After a long wait, only the introduction of her article was included in the evening paper, a lesser publication than the morning edition. Realizing she would have enormous difficulties breaking through the male-dominated media industry, she founded the Women's Group Against *Keysen Tourism* and answered Korean feminist critiques by passing a flyer to Japanese tourists at Seoul Airport, calling for the abolition of sex tourism. Matsui recalled that it was 'the first time that Korean and Japanese women had taken joint action against a common enemy'.[46] In exchanging information with Korean feminists, Matsui became aware of the 'comfort women' issue and Japanese women's responsibility for Japan's war crimes. In pursuit of addressing those issues, Matsui established the Asian Women's Association in 1977, the Asian Women Resource Centre in 1995, and Violence Against Women in War Network, Japan (VAWW-NET) in 1997. Later in 2000, VAWW-NET Japan organized the International Women's War Tribunal in Tokyo, culminating in the movement of transnational feminist activism with featured 600 Japanese participants and 500 additional non-Japanese participants including 64 surviving 'comfort women', lawyers, historians, and researchers. Through the efforts of the women's solidarity movement which crossed national boundaries, the tribunal's final judgement opined that Emperor Hirohito was guilty.[47]

The feminist movement in South Korea: 1945–1990

As in Japan, the patriarchal values of Korean society, with its great emphasis upon female virginity, forced the survivors to remain silent for fear of stigmatization and social exclusion. Nevertheless, the post-war Korean feminist movements did not emerge until the 1970s, when protests against the successive military governments gained national momentum. The growing concern of Korean women was about female sexual exploitation by Japan in sex tourism and the United States in military prostitution. When the then president Park Chung Hee facilitated the economic policy to gain foreign currencies through tourism in 1972, the South Korean Church Women's Alliance launched the 1973 airport demonstrations despite the prohibition on political activism. The feminist group was led by Yun Chung Ok, a professor at Ehwa Women's University. She discovered that the common theme between the issue of 'comfort women', prostitution located on the perimeter of US bases, and sex tourism was the 'sexual exploitation and abuse of Korean women by foreign men'.[48] She then became a central figure in the raising of public awareness of the 'comfort women' issue in South Korea in the 1980s.[49] She presented her 'ground-breaking' analysis of the *chongsindae* women (Korean 'comfort women') for the first time in 1988.[50]

Thus, in the 1970s, Korean feminists were engaged in protests against the Korean sex tourism industry conducted on behalf of the Japanese.[51] Then, in the mid-1980s, Korean feminists waged a public campaign to protect prostitutes working around US military installations (*kijich'on*) from sexual exploitation owing to their dire financial circumstances.[52] Soon after the *chongsindae* movement (CM) was organized in the late 1980s, it pursued an alliance with the *kijich'on* movement (KM) 'as part of a larger Asian women's human rights movement against the sexual exploitation of women'.[53] Although both movements seemed to have 'shared values and concerns' about the violation of women's rights, they ultimately fragmented and ceased cooperation until recently.[54] This schism is attributable to the emphasis upon the virginity of the victims. The *chongsindae* survivors and activists denied any association in terms of 'cause' or 'identity' with the *kijich'on* women, who were regarded as 'willing whores'.[55]

Prostitutes or sex slaves

The crucial difference between the *chongsindae* and the *kijich'on* women lies in the fact that the former was a gang-raped victim while the latter was a professional prostitute. A feminist scholar of international relations, Katharine Moon, explains that despite many parallels between the two groups, the particular similarities entailing 'the lasting effects of such sexual labour in terms of bodily damage, social alienation, loss of dignity, shame, and loneliness', have been ignored.[56] Moon describes further similarities between *chongsindae* and *kijich'on* women such as the poverty of their families and their poor education.[57] She suggests that there are some cases in which the same woman might be both.[58] For instance, Kim Hak-sun, the first silence-breaker, was a *Keysen* trainee before she was forced to work as a *chongsindae*. She never worked as a *Keysen* because she was too young to become one after her graduation.[59]

For the CM, the essential issue concerns the methods and practices employed in recruiting the women. The majority of its leading figures, including the survivors, have emphasized the virginity of the *chongsindae* victims. Of particular relevance to this chapter is the politicization of this debate by Japanese nationalists, particularly those in the government, who insist that 'comfort women' were prostitutes. As mentioned earlier, Korean women were mobilized as labourers under the colonial Korean system. Furthermore, Japanese colonial policy permitted the recruitment of young women as prostitutes on the basis of 'voluntary' participation. This perspective frames the public debate in Japan in terms of whether women were 'forced-or-not-forced'.[60]

This 'forced-or-not-forced' argument as it relates to the recruitment of 'comfort women' corresponds to a major split within Western feminist debates regarding prostitution. The polarization among feminists is based on the dichotomy between voluntary prostitution versus forced prostitution. Sex-work feminists including Kempadoo and Doezema insist that prostitution is a woman's occupational choice.[61] In contrast, abolitionist feminists such as Barry and Mackinnon argue that prostitutes are sexually exploited victims within a patriarchal capitalist society.[62]

This dichotomy is all the more significant as feminist movements place great emphasis on the construction of the norms surrounding prostitution within both the domestic and international communities. In reality, this agency-versus-slavery debate has divided women into binary categories – 'Good Women or Whores' – paralleling the division between good wives and prostitutes in

Japanese society or between the *chongsindae* victims and the *keysen* victims in Korean society. [63] As a result, the debate has effectively encouraged the condemnation and suppression of prostitutes because of the absence of a universal moral judgement against prostitution.[64] In effect, the patriarchal domination of women's sexuality and state-led capitalism represented by the commercialization of women's bodies as in sex tourism have been played down. In return, 'the patriarchal assumption that prostitution is a problem about women' has been internalized and enhanced.[65]

1991 silence-breaking

The global wave of reparation movements for social justice propelled by the emergence of human rights activism in the 1980s finally reached Japan. Emperor Hirohito's death in 1989 contributed to breaking down the chrysanthemum taboo (which forbids discussion or criticism of the Emperor of Japan and his family), which shielded him from debates within Japan about his role in the war during his lifetime. However, hundreds of documents, diaries, and scholarly studies were published in the wake of his death, including Hirohito's 'Monologue' which gave an account of his role in the war years. These provided a platform for sparking debates about his war responsibility both inside and outside Japan. This global backdrop encouraged war victims of Japan to call for compensation for their suffering caused by wartime slave labour.[66]

In South Korea during the early part of 1988, Yun and her church women's group started their research on 'comfort women' by travelling to Japan to see Pae Pong Gi and to Thailand to meet Yuyuta, who was identified by the South Korean Embassy.[67] However, Yun's 1989 article did not cover survivors' testimonies, which motivated her to discover surviving 'comfort women'.[68] In 1990, Yun published her investigative report on 'comfort women', raising awareness among both the South Korean government and the public towards the forgotten issue. In response to the women's advocate groups' request, then South Korean president Roh Tae Wu raised the issue of labour draftees during his official visit to Tokyo in 1990. This spotlighted the 'comfort women' issue since many female draftees were believed to have been mobilized by force or deception to 'comfort stations'. As a result, a watershed moment in the history of the Korean women's movement occurred in June 1990 with the establishment of the Korean Council for the Women Drafted for Military Sexual Slavery by Japan (cited as the Korean Council).[69] This organization was formed in response to an explicit denial of the historical fact of 'comfort women' issued by Japanese lawmakers.[70] Accordingly, the Korean Council initiated research by collecting survivors' testimonies, retrieving public records, and facilitating the availability of information amongst academics.[71] It was hoped that the issue might be resolved by disseminating the historical truth.[72] The success within the South Korean 'comfort women' movement can also be attributed to a significant reshuffle in the global and local political landscapes including the end of the Cold War and the 1980s democracy movement in South Korea.[73]

South Korean feminists' dedication to resolving the 'comfort women' issue culminated on 14 August 1991, when Kim Hak-sun, a 68-year-old Korean survivor, broke the silence of nearly half a century and provided personal testimony at a South Korean press conference.[74] Her unprecedented courage was driven by indignation at Japan's denial of accountability for the 'comfort women' system and for her wartime and post-war plights. She stated in the interview with NHK (the Japan Broadcasting Corporation), 'I wanted to sue for the fact that I was trampled upon by the Japanese military and have spent my life in misery. I want the young people of South Korea and Japan to know what Japan did in the past.'[75] The following December, Kim and two other Korean survivors, claiming as Plaintiff A and B, filed a lawsuit against the Japanese government. Even though the lawsuit was carried out as part of a class action which included the cases of eleven former soldiers, the first legal challenge by former 'comfort women' galvanized Japanese society.[76] For the Japanese public, it was a pivotal moment in which Hak-sun exposed the contested terrain of war-memory in Japanese society. Japanese historical consciousness as war victims has been challenged ever since.

After 1991, the Korean Council and other women's groups launched a Volunteer Service Corps Report Line in Seoul, followed by one in Pusan, which sought more survivors who were willing to go public as former 'comfort women'. As a result, six other survivors including Mu Ok Ju participated in the Hak-sun lawsuit.[77] Thus, the 1991 silence-breaking was also a moment when a voiceless victim transformed herself into a courageous activist.[78] However, it provoked a fierce battle between Japanese conservatives and progressives over the validity of survivors' testimonies. The new terminology known as 'military sexual slaves' adopted in the 1996 report of the United Nations Special Rapporteur Radhika Coomaraswany became the subject of a concentrated attack from Japanese conservatives who criticized the former 'comfort women' as ex-prostitutes who had volunteered to be military prostitutes. This debate has developed into a political argument focusing on the way 'comfort women' were recruited: forced or not forced. As mentioned earlier, the emphasis on female virginity is so deeply embedded in both Korean and Japanese society that Japanese historical revisionists, including Prime Minister Abe, have taken advantage of this view of female sexuality in their argument that 'comfort women' were prostitutes.[79]

The current 'comfort women' debate in Japan has followed the prostitute-versus-sex slavery argument in the West. Fujioka Nobukatsu and other Japanese revisionists mobilize the sex-work feminist proposition in pursuit of justification of the military brothel system, relegating the issue to an individual's freedom to choose a profession. Their negative campaign against 'comfort women' has encouraged the pro-'comfort women' activists to clearly differentiate rape victims from prostitutes as shown by the dichotomy between the *chongsindae* and the *kijich'on* in the South Korean feminist movement. The Japanese feminist argument also lacks the broader human rights perspectives developed by Western feminist abolitionists who equate both prostitutes and rape victims as victims of sexual violence against women. Prostitutes cannot exercise any freedom to determine their role in the power relationship of domination and subordination that characterizes prostitution.[80] Prostitution involves 'male self-centred, one-way acts on female bodies'.[81] Inevitably, as a survival mechanism, a prostitute protects herself by separating her personal identity and emotional presence from her body during sexual intercourse. This situation effectively deprives her of human qualities thereby contributing to her dehumanization.[82] In this understanding, 'comfort women', whether prostitutes or not at the time of recruitment, were victims of gendered structural violence.

Conclusion

This chapter has explored the development of post-war feminist activism surrounding 'comfort women' in both Japan and South Korea, and the controversial binaries of prostitutes versus sex slaves which have perplexed the transnational 'comfort women' justice movement. The common dominator between Japan and Korea is the commodification of female sexuality embedded within the patriarchal masculinity of both countries which has been perpetuated on a daily basis, whether in times of war or peace. This masculine exploitation of female bodies has created sex tourism, US military prostitution, and 'comfort women' for the Imperial Japanese Army. Thus, all 'comfort women' for the Japanese military, Japanese 'comfort women' for the Allied occupation forces, and sex workers in US military camp towns in Korea constitute instances of sexual slavery.

The 'comfort women' feminist activists, in both Japan and South Korea, have, however, avoided the fundamental debate surrounding the nature of sexual slavery associated with the diverse forms of female sexual exploitation by males. This situation has caused feminist activists in both countries to become trapped by the gender dilemma. The emphasis by feminist activists on 'not-forced' recruitment of 'comfort women' has greatly stigmatized Japanese survivors who have in turn remained silent. However, the recent cooperation between the Korean CM and the KM provides some hope for the future resolution of the issue.

Korean survivors have illustrated their transformation from forgotten victims to resilient activists in pursuing their autonomy, dignity, and justice. Their aspirations have been empowered by feminists from both victim countries and a victimizing country. This signifies 'comfort women' transnational feminist activism as a new chapter of women's history in Asia in which victims overcame their brutal past and created their alternative history. The 'comfort women' issue is a multilayered controversy. The transnational feminist activism surrounding 'comfort women' in Japan and South Korea has encountered the complex interplay between gender and other elements such as racism, classism, militarism, colonialism/imperialism, and nationalism embedded in the psyche of both nations. The category gender has been impacted by a variety of influences from place to place and from time to time. However, by peeling back those layers, the core issue comes into focus. This is the question of women's human rights. If the transnational feminist activism supporting 'comfort women' in Asia can transcend the dichotomy of the prostitution-versus-sexual slavery argument, it will open the door for creating a new official narrative. This new gender history will represent an accomplishment that Western feminists have not yet achieved.

Recommended reading

Hicks, G. (1995) *The Comfort Women: Sex Slaves of the Japanese Imperial Forces* (St Leonards, New South Wales: Allen & Unwin).

Kimura, M. (2016) *Unfolding the 'Comfort Women' Debates: Modernity, Violence, Women's Voices* (Basingstoke: Palgrave Macmillan).

Moon, K. H. S. (1999) 'South Korean Movements against Militarized Sexual Labor,' *Asian Survey*, vol. 39, no. 2, pp. 310–27.

Norma, C. (2016) *The Japanese Comfort Women and Sexual Slavery during the China and Pacific Wars* (London: Bloomsbury Publishing).

Schmidt, A. D. (2000) *Ianfu-The Comfort Women of the Japanese Imperial Army of the Pacific War: Broken Silence* (New York: Edwin Mellen Press).

Soh, S. C. (2008) *The Comfort Women: Sexual Violence and Postcolonial Memory in Korea and Japan* (Chicago: University of Chicago Press).

Stez, M. and B. B. C. Oh (2001) *Legacies of the Comfort Women of World War II* (New York: East Gate Books).

Tanaka, Y. (2002) *Japan's Comfort Women: Sexual Slavery and Prostitution during World War II and the US Occupation* (London: Routledge).

Ueno, C. (2004) *Nationalism and Gender* (Melbourne: Trans Pacific Press).

Yoshimi, Y. (2000) *Comfort Women: Sexual Slavery in the Japanese Military during World War II*, trans. by S. O'Brien (Ithaca, NY: Columbia University Press).

Notes

1. Ministry of Foreign Affairs of Japan (28 December 2015) 'Announcement by Foreign Ministers of Japan and the Republic of Korea at the Joint Press Occasion', http://www.mofa.go.jp/a_o/na/kr/page4e_000364.html, date accessed 5 September 2016.

2. Y. Mee-hyang (2016) 'Toward Righteous Resolution Over the Dec 28 Jap-Kor Outrageous Agreement on the Japanese Military Sexual Slavery Issue', paper at the 14th Asian Solidarity Conference for Resolution of the Issue of Military Sexual Slavery by Japan (Seoul: the Korean Council for the Women Drafted for Military Sexual Slavery by Japan), pp. 103–14, here p. 103. She is the representative of the Korean Council.

3. See G. Hicks (1995) *The Comfort Women: Sex Slaves of the Japanese Imperial Forces* (St Leonards, New South Wales: Allen & Unwin); Yoshimi, Y. (2000) *Comfort Women: Sexual Slavery in the Japanese Military during World War II*, trans. by S. O'Brien (Ithaca, NY: Columbia University Press); ; A. D. Schmidt (2000) *Ianfu-The Comfort Women of the Japanese Imperial Army of the Pacific War: Broken Silence* (New York: Edwin Mellen Press); Y. Tanaka (2002) *Japan's Comfort Women: Sexual slavery and Prostitution during World War II and the US Occupation* (London: Routledge); M. Stez,and B. B. C. Oh (2001) *Legacies of the Comfort Women of World War II* (New York: East Gate Books); C. Ueno (2004) *Nationalism and Gender* (Melbourne: Trans Pacific Press); S. C. Soh (2008) *The Comfort Women: Sexual Violence and Postcolonial Memory in Korea and Japan* (Chicago: University of Chicago Press); Kimura, M. (2016) *Unfolding the 'Comfort Women' Debates: Modernity, Violence, Women's Voices* (Basingstoke: Palgrave Macmillan).

4. Among scholars of historical revisionism are Hata Ikuhiko and Fujioka Nobukatsu See, for example, Hata, Ikuhiko (2007) 'No Organized or Forced Recruitment: Misconceptions about Comfort Women and the Japanese Military.' Society for the

Dissemination of Historical Fact Available at: http://www.sdh-fact.com/CL02_1/31_S4.pdf, date accessed 5 September 2016; and (1998) 'The Flawed U.N. Report on Comfort Women' in E. R. Beauchamp (ed.), *Women and Women's Issues in post World War II Japan* (New York: Garland). For Nobukatsu, see, for example, (1996–7) *History Not Taught in School Textbooks* (Tokyo: Sankei Publishing).

5. On the subject of Japanese 'comfort women', see C. Norma (2016) *The Japanese Comfort Women and Sexual Slavery during the China and Pacific Wars* (London: Bloomsbury Publishing) and VAWW RAC (2015) *Nihonjin 'Ianfu': Aikokushin to Jinshinbaibai to [Japanese 'Comfort Women': Patriotism and Human Trafficking]* (Tokyo: Gendai Shokan).

6. From the Asian perspective, the Second World War is part of the Asia-Pacific War, which overlaps with Japan's fifteen-year war beginning with the Manchurian Incident (1931) and ending in Japan's surrender (1945).

7. Y. Yoshimi, *Comfort Women.*

8. See Yoshimi (2015) 'Why Do the Comfort Women Matter?', paper at the Conference on 'The Challenge of Overcoming the Past and its Significance', 17 August, Edinburgh.

9. See Yoshimi, *Comfort Women*, Hicks, *The Comfort Women* (1995), and Tanaka, *Japan's Comfort Women.*

10. Hicks, *The Comfort Women*, p. 39.

11. A. S. Runyan and V. S. Peterson (2014) *Global Gender Issues in the New Millennium: Fourth Edition* (Boulder, CO: Westview Press), pp. 7–8.

12. Hicks, *The Comfort Women*, p. 39.

13. Schmidt, *Ianfu*, pp. 12, 21.

14. Yoshimi, *Comfort Women*, pp. 29, 203. His English translation was published in 2000.

15. Stez & Oh, *Legacies*, p. xiii.

16. Soh, *The Comfort Women*, p. xv.

17. Soh, p. 30.

18. Soh, p. 30.

19. Norma, *Japanese Comfort Women*, pp. 40–4.

20. See G. Hicks (1994) *The Comfort Women: Japan's Brutal Regime of Enforced Prostitution in the Second World War* (New York: W.W Norton), pp. 119–20.

21. 'Memoir of Japanese "comfort woman" recounts "this hell"', *The Japan Times*, 9 July 2007.

22. F. Kawata (1993) *Kōgun ianjo no onnatachi [Women in the Comfort Stations for the Imperial Japanese Army]* (Tokyo: Chikuma Shobo), p. 20.

23. Until today, the Japanese government has consistently refused to pay compensation to individual Koreans including former 'comfort women' for their wartime suffering on the grounds of the Japanese–South Korean Basic Treaty.

24. Kawata, *Kōgun ianjo no onnatachi*, pp. 12–13.

25. Soh, *The Comfort Women*, p. 147.

26. Y. Fujime (2015) *'Ianfu'mondai no Honshitu: Kōshōseido to Nihonjin'ianfu' no Fukashika [Fundamental Problems of the 'Comfort Women' Issue: State-Licensed Prostitution System and Invisibilizing Japanese 'Comfort Women']* (Tokyo: Hakutakusha), p. 65. Fujime testified at the 2000 Women's International War Tribunal, arguing that Japanese 'comfort women' were victims of Japan's military sexual slavery system.

27. W. T. D. Bary, C. Gluck, and A. E. Tiedemann (2006) *Sources of Japanese Tradition 1600 to 2000: Part Two: 1968 to 2000,* (Ithaca, NY: Columbia University Press), p. 473.

28. D. Khor (1999) 'Organizing for Change: Women's Grassroots Activism in Japan', *Feminist Studies*, vol. 25, no. 3, p. 643.
29. C. Ueno (2012) *Nationalism to Gender*, new edition (Tokyo: Iwanami Shoten), p. 36.
30. S. Buckley (1994) 'A Short History of the Feminist Movement in Japan', in J. Gelb and M. Lief Palley (eds), *Women of Japan and Korea: Continuity and Change* (Philadelphia: Temple University Press), p. 151. Some examples of Japan's post-war women's groups were the Women's Committee for Post-war Policies (1945), the League of Democratic Women (1946), Women's Bureau within the Ministry of Labor (1947), and the Housewives Association (1948).
31. See Buckley, 'A Short History', pp. 152–7. The real concern for most Japanese women was the day-to-day survival of them and their families given the food shortage caused by the defeat of the war. This split in female concerns created two binary women's movements after the end of the US occupation: 'pro-motherhood' versus pro-working-mothers.
32. V. Mackie (1996) 'Feminism critiques of modern Japanese politics', in M. Threlfall (ed.), *Mapping the Women's Movement* (London: Verso), p. 266.
33. Mackie, 'Feminism critiques', p. 267.
34. Khor, 'Organizing for Change', pp. 648–9.
35. Buckley, 'A Short History', p. 167.
36. Buckley, pp. 160–7.
37. Mackie, 'Feminism critiques', p. 268.
38. Mackie, p. 268
39. M. Tanaka (2004) *Inochi no Onnatachi he [For Women of Life]* (Tokyo: Gendai Shokan).
40. C. Ueno (2013) *Onna no Shisō [Women's Thought]* (Tokyo: Shūeisha international), p. 72.
41. Ueno, *Onna no Shisō*, p. 72.
42. H. Yamazaki (1995) 'Military Sexual Slavery and the Women's Movement', *AMPO Japan-Asia Quarterly Review*, vol. 25, no. 4, pp. 49–54, here p. 52.
43. On 13 May 2013, former Osaka Mayor Toru Hashimoto said that the Japanese military's 'comfort women' were necessary to maintain discipline in the ranks and provide respite for soldiers who risked their lives in battle and came under fierce attack from around the world. See BBC News (2013) 'Japan WWII "comfort women" were "necessary" – Hashimoto', 14 May, available at http://www.bbc.co.uk/news/world-asia-22519384#TWEET754330, date accessed 14 May 2013.
44. Ueno, *Nationalism*, p. 73.
45. Y. Matsui (2001) 'Women's International War Crimes Tribunal on Japan's Military Sexual Slavery: Memory, Identity, and Society', *East Asia*, vol. 19, no. 4 (Winter), pp. 119–42. Yayori Matsui (2003) *Ai to Ikari to Tatakau Yūki [Love, Anger and Courage to Fight]* (Tokyo: Iwanami Shoten).
46. Matsui, 'Women's International War Crimes', p. 139.
47. VAWW-NET Japan (2001) *The Women's International War Crimes Tribunal: Judgement* (Tokyo, VAWW-NET Japan).
48. Moon, 'South Korean Movements', p. 311 (see Recommended reading).
49. Hicks, *The Comfort Women*, pp. 133–6.
50. Moon, 'South Korean Movements', p. 311.
51. C. S. Soh (1996) 'The Korean "Comfort Women": Movement for Redress', *Asian Survey*, vol. 36, no. 12, pp. 1226–40, 1931. Protest to the Korean Tourism Association was launched in 1973.
52. Moon, 'South Korean Movements', p. 311.

53. Moon, p. 311.

54. Moon, pp. 311–12. On 25 June 2014, 123 *kijich'on* women sued their own government for compensation. According to Reuters' report entitled 'Former Korean "comfort women" for U.S. troops sue own government' (11 July 2014), this collective legal action has marked 'a culmination of work by a handful of small and regional NGOs that came together in 2008 to gather their testimonies and seek legal advice': http://www.reuters.com/article/2014/07/11/us-southkorea-usa-military-idUSKBN0FG0VV20140711, date accessed 12 July 2014.

55. Moon, 'South Korean Movements', p. 319.

56. Moon, p. 312.

57. Moon, pp. 312–14.

58. Moon, p. 314.

59. Soh, *The Comfort Women*, p. 127; p. 128; Hicks, *The Comfort Women*, pp. 148–9.

60. Soh, 'The Korean "Comfort Women"', pp. 1227–8.

61. K. Kempadoo and J. Doezema (eds) (1998) *Global Sex Workers: Rights, Resistance, and Redefinition* (New York: Routledge).

62. K. Barry (1995) *The Prostitution of Sexuality* (New York: New York University Press); C. A. MacKinnon (1993) 'Prostitution and Civil Rights', *Michigan Journal of Law and Gender,* vol. 1, no. 13, pp. 13–31.

63. Barry, *The Prostitution of Sexuality*, p. 705.

64. C. Pateman (1992) *The Sexual Contract* (Cambridge: Polity Press), p. 191.

65. Pateman, p. 192.

66. P. A. Seaton (2007) *Japan's Contested War Memories: The 'Memory Rifts' in Historical Consciousness of World War II* (London: Routledge), p. 68.

67. Hicks, *The Comfort Women*, pp. 138. About Pong Gi and Yuyuta, see Hicks, pp. 136–40.

68. According to Hicks (pp. 136–9), Pae declined Yun's interview while Yuyuta forgot the Korean language.

69. Soh, 'The Korean "Comfort Women"', p. 1234. The Korean Council was co-chaired by Yun Chung-ok and Lee Hyo-chae. Lee and Yun were professors at Ewha Womans University, teaching 'sociology and English literature until their retirement in 1990 and 1991, respectively. Both are from a Christian family and their fathers were pastors. Neither has ever married.' According to Hicks, a variety of groups joined the Korean Council such as the Voluntary Service Corps Study Association (the affiliation of the Church Women's Alliance and Alliance of South Korean Women's Organisations), the YMCA, and student groups, p. 143. Their official website can be found at https://www.womenandwar.net/contents/general/general.nx?page_str_menu=2101, date accessed 5 September 2016.

70. Before the Korean Council was established in June 1990, the Korean feminists took advantage of the May official visit of President Roh Tae Woo to Japan to compile their demands to the Japanese government. One demand was that the 'comfort women' cases be investigated. However, the Japanese government refused to do so and insisted that the military 'comfort stations' were operated by private enterprise. See Soh, 'The Korean "Comfort Women"', p. 1232.

71. In 'South Korean Movements' (pp. 310–27), Moon explains that 'one of the first organizational actions that the CM (Comfort Women) leaders took was to establish a research committee in Seoul, initially under the auspices of the Church and Society Committee of Korea Church Women United (July 1988) and then independently as the Research Committee on the Chongsindae (July 1990).'

72. C. Chou (2002) 'An Emerging Transnational Movement in Women's Human Rights: Campaign of Nongovernmental Organizations on "Comfort Women" Issue in East Asia', *Journal of Economic and Social Research*, vol. 4, no. 2, pp. 153–81, here pp. 159–60, p. 231.

73. One of the most famous movements was the 1980 Kwangju uprising. After the uprising, one of the main slogans in the democracy movement in South Korea was 'Remember Kwangju'.

74. In Japan, 15 August marks the end of the Second World War and on this day the Japanese government commemorates the war dead at an annual commemoration ceremony in presence of the Emperor and the Empress. Every year, this attracts considerable attention from China and Korea, specifically whether the current prime minister pays a visit to the Yasukuni Shrine, which has enshrined the war dead including the A-class war criminals.

75. Yoshimi, *Comfort Women*, p. 33. Yoshimi confessed that this statement moved him to focus on the research of the 'comfort women' issue.

76. About the life stories of Plaintiff A and B, see Hicks, *The Comfort Women*, pp. 150–2.

77. Hicks, pp. 152, 158. Mun Ok Jun's story is described in pp. xiii–xv.

78. Yoshimi, *Comfort Women*, pp. 57–65. Kim's interview with NHK (the Japan Broadcasting Corporation, the Japanese counterpart of the BBC) was conducted on 28 November 1991.

79. The revisionist school is called the 'Liberal School of History' and was founded by Fujioka Nobukatsu, a professor at Tokyo University, in 1995. What Fujioka means by the *Jiyū-shugi shikan*, or 'Liberal School of History', is the association for the 'unbiased' view of Japanese history. His logic is underpinned by the *Jiyū-shugi shikan*, which is regarded as 'neo-nationalism'. On Fujioka and his Liberal School of History, see Rikki Kersten (1999) 'Neo-liberalism and the "Liberal School of History"', *Japan Forum*, vol. 11, no. 2, 1pp. 91–203.

80. C. Overall (1992) 'What's Wrong with Prostitution? Evaluating Sex Work', *Signs*, vol. 17, no. 4, pp. 705–24, 721.

81. Pateman, *The Sexual Contract*, p. 198.

82. Pateman, p. 207. S. Pollock Sturdevant and B. Stoltzfus (1992) *Let the Good Times Roll: Prostitution and the U.S. Military in Asia* (New York: The New Press, New York), p. 505. Barry categorizes the 'dehumanization' process in prostitution into four stages: 'Distancing', 'Disengagement', 'Dissociation', and 'Disembodiment and Dissembling' (*The Prostitution of Sexuality*, pp. 30–5).

13

The Visual as Memory: Gender, Memory, and Chinese Political Cartoons in the Second Sino-Japanese War

Danke Li

Women, especially ordinary women, rarely left any written records about their experiences during the Second Sino-Japanese War, fought between China and Japan from 1937 to 1945. This conflict resulted from Japanese imperialist expansion and eventually became part of World War II. The study of ordinary Chinese women's wartime experiences has therefore relied heavily on oral histories. Might other sources help us better to understand gender, war, and memory? This study examines political cartoons and wood-block prints produced during the war.[1] I employ the perspective of the visual image as memory to investigate the history of the war from a gendered perspective.

The topics of gender and visual war memory are not new to academic discourse. These themes have been discussed in scholarship on wars of other places and times, from Sarah Barber's study of a seventeenth-century English Civil War wood-cut image to Craig Larkin's work on Lebanon in the 1990s.[2] John Dower pioneered the study of visual images in the Pacific War, using American and Japanese wartime cartoons to examine the racialized aspect of the war.[3] However, Dower's study did not examine the gendered aspects of visual images and war memory. Yet visual images offer powerful resources for examining more deeply the gendered aspects of wartime experiences in particular. Visual images, especially the visual images of the Holocaust during World War II, have left deep and profound visual memories of Nazi atrocities against the Jewish people and humanity. In particular, though, these images, especially the images of naked and terrified Jewish women at the moment of being murdered by Nazi soldiers, helped fuel intensive debate on the Holocaust as a *gendered* experience.[4]

The Vietnam War offers yet another powerful case. We all know that hundreds and thousands of Vietnam women sacrificed their lives for their country's independence and unification during the war, yet their contributions went largely unrecorded in post-war official Vietnamese history. However, Vietnamese popular culture produced during and after the war, such as the paintings and statues created by ordinary Vietnamese artists and exhibited in museums, included vivid images of Vietnamese women. These images provide us with a gendered war memory in which women played active and important roles.[5]

Visual images also play an important role in the history of Japan's memories of the Pacific War. Some Western scholars believe that while establishing a democratic political system in the image of the West, post-war Japan either deliberately tried to forget the tragic end of the Pacific War or only selectively remembered Japan's role as victim, not victimizer. Visual images, however, tell a different story. In his study on Japanese popular culture of the 1950s and 1960s, the Japanese scholar Nakar relates that a large number of comic books, especially children's comic books, portrayed Kamikaze pilots as war heroes and victors. This not only created a masculine memory of the Pacific War for Japan, but also planted this memory into the hearts and minds of many Japanese children who were born after the war's end.[6]

The aforementioned cases reveal that visual images have played an important role in the study of war, gender, and memory. Yet the study of gendered visual memory of World War II in the China theatre has not attracted sufficient scholarly attention. In the following pages I show how gender, war, and memory were constructed in political cartoons and wood-cut pictures during China's War of Resistance against Japan. Some of the images were created by a feminist woman artist and others by left-wing male artists or even government-sponsored art groups. Sarah Barber points out that, over time, visual images can be interpreted by different people for various purposes with varying value judgements attached.[7] With the images I examine, I suggest that their significance does not depend upon what their creators' initial intentions were. Whether the images were created as government propaganda or merely for popular consumption, these visual representations have preserved the imagery of public memories of war and gender. As historical artefacts, they also provide us with rich information about how and why the memories were constructed and the messages the creators of the images wanted their viewers to see, remember, or forget.

Visual images, war, gender, and memory in the Second Sino-Japanese War

On 7 July 1937, Japan launched an all-out war against China. The rapid advance of Japanese military forces through north and central China forced the Nationalist government to call for an 'all-people's' war against the Japanese invasion and for the development of war-related national resistance policies. Many Chinese artists answered this call by using their paintbrushes as weapons in support of the war effort. As Chen Erkang, a wartime cartoonist, declared: 'The cartoon is an effective propaganda weapon … Ever since the beginning of the anti-Japanese war, it has been transformed from being leisurely after-tea entertainment for the bourgeoisie to becoming a part of the War of Resistance ... Cartoons promoted a national anti-invasion sentiment and fighting spirit and courage, and were widely welcomed by ordinary people.'[8] During China's War of Resistance against Japan, political cartoons and wood-block prints were the second-most popular wartime objects of popular cultural consumption, second only to anti-Japanese war-themed drama.[9] These wartime cartoons and wood-block prints therefore served as powerful public platforms of communication and representation of public discourse at the time. Looking back on them now as a visual record of this discourse, they offer us a valuable window into the nature of gendered public memories of the war.

The changing content of these visual images over time illustrates the evolution of the war's gendered discourse, and it captures a complex relationship between women's participation in the war effort and their representation in war propaganda. As we know from sources such as the memoirs of the female soldier Xie Bingyin, and as documented in Danke Li's *Echoes of Chongqing*, women contributed to the War of the Resistance against Japan both on and off the battlefield from the early days of the war.[10] However, they were not so well represented in mainstream public images until later in the war, when women's participation became recognized as vital to the survival of the nation. A shift in the representation of women in wartime visual images then gave increasing recognition and impetus to women's participation in the war efforts at the time while etching them into public memories of the war for posterity.

In the early phases of the war, many Chinese politicians and artists simply did not realize that the war would be a long one that would require the active participation of Chinese women. Therefore most of the wartime cartoons and wood-block prints propagandized the theme of men going to the front line to fight against Japanese invaders in order to protect women and children at home. The typical resistance fighters portrayed in some of the wartime cartoons were men in uniform; in contrast, women and children were treated as the mere victims of the war, as seen in a cartoon titled 'Protecting Our Wives and Children' (Figure 13.1). This kind of chauvinist image conveyed a wartime mainstream ideology of family and social order – such polarized representations promoted images of strong men and weak women as well as the gendered division of men in the public domain and women in the private sphere. These types of image not only portrayed women as weak beings and accessories to men, but also assigned men the role of symbolizing the country and the nation. Their purpose was to arouse in Chinese men a sense of responsibility to take up arms, to go to the front line to fight against the Japanese invaders to protect the country and their families. During the early years of the war, most male artists' cartoons, including some by the left-wing and progressive artists Ding Cong and Ye Qianyu, belonged to this masculinized-war school.[11] However, if we turn to feminist wartime images, we see a different portrayal of women in the war from its early days onward. This can be seen in the work of female artist Liang Baibo.

Figure 13.1 'Protecting our Wives and Children' by Wang Zimei (1940), in *Kangzhan Huaxuan*, p. 15.

Liang Baibo and the feminist memory of the War of Resistance against Japan

In 1937, some Chinese artists organized the National Association of Cartoonists for National Salvation (NACNS) and used their paintbrushes to mobilize ordinary people to participate in the War of Resistance. Liang Baibo was the one and only active female member of the organization.

Liang was born in Shanghai and in the late 1920s attended the New China School of Arts in Shanghai. There she was influenced by the then young Chinese communist movement and joined the Youth League of the Chinese Communist Party (CCP). Later, she also became a member of the left-wing writers' and artists' organization. She illustrated a book for Yin Fu, a renowned leftist poet who was executed by the Nationalist government in 1931. In the early 1930s, Liang participated in some of the activities organized by the underground CCP in Shanghai. When anti-communist and anti-left-wing political activities intensified, Liang went to the Philippines to teach art at a school for overseas Chinese. In the mid-1930s, she returned to Shanghai and became a contributor to the Shanghai-based art magazine, *Modern Sketch*. Her professional relationship with *Modern Sketch* brought her into contact with Ye Qianyu, an editor of the magazine and one of the best known Chinese cartoon artists. Subsequently Liang had a three-year affair with Ye who was a married man. This relationship stirred up a sensation in Shanghai's media world.[12]

Liang belonged to the generation of the May Fourth era, the period of intellectual revolution and the movement for sociopolitical reform between 1917 and 1921; her idol was none other than the free spirit American dancer Isadora Duncan. Liang was one of what Tani Barlow called the 'New Women' of the 1920s whose personal lives intertwined with the political currents as well as with the growing pains and contradictions of the modern Chinese nation.[13]

When Japan launched total war against China in 1937, Liang joined the Cartoonist Association for National Salvation. During the early war years, Liang published numerous war-themed political cartoons in various journals and magazines and left us with unique memories of the war from a feminist perspective.[14] Like the famous male cartoonist Ding Cong, Liang also produced a cartoon called 'the New Great Wall' to showcase the Chinese people's determination against the Japanese invasion. Unlike Ding, whose images portrayed male figures only, Liang's images of China's War of Resistance against Japan depicted Chinese men but also both genders standing together.[15]

Her signature piece was the 'The Giant Who Stood in Front of the Enemy' (Figure 13.2) in which a strong, armed Chinese man towered over a dwarfed

Figure 13.2 Baibo's "Giant": 'The Giant Who Stood in Front of the Enemy' by Liang Baibo (1938), *Kangzhan Manhua*, no. 3, p. 1.

and a buck-toothed Japanese soldier.[16] What distinguishes Liang's cartoon from the images created by her male contemporaries is that, in Liang's depiction, this Chinese Giant was neither a Nationalist government soldier nor a representative of a social elite. Instead, this giant was an ordinary Manchurian peasant resistance fighter.[17] Liang's leftist and populist interpretation of the war was also expressed in another picture titled 'Military and Civilians Work together Fighting against Ferocious Enemies'.[18] This cartoon depicts uniformed government soldiers and peasant militants fighting together on the front line. More importantly, men and women are pictured working together in the War of Resistance, representing the true meaning of the 'all people's War of Resistance against Japan'. Liang Baibo's wartime cartoons vividly showcased and projected visual memories of women's participation in the mobilization of the war efforts. Even after seventy-five years, viewers of Liang's cartoons still receive the clear message that Chinese women made significant contributions to the War of Resistance.

As the only female artist who joined the NACNS, Liang created various images of women in the War of Resistance. In contrast to her male counterparts, women in Liang's cartoons were positive, active, strong, and powerful. In one of her cartoons entitled 'Organizing Rural Women to Participate in the Mobilization of the Second Stage of the War of Resistance', she portrays a group of rural Chinese women wearing typical peasant-style aprons and headscarves and holding babies, hoes, and guns.[19] The women appeared as strong and determined as the male soldiers' images portrayed by male artists in wartime cartoons. Viewers of this image would be wary of suggesting that these women needed the protection of men. Liang presented peasant women as mother-warriors who demonstrated a spontaneous anti-Japanese nationalism. In her cartoons, Liang thoroughly established the strong determination of Chinese women to prevent the Japanese invaders from taking over their country. In so doing, she was able to showcase ordinary women as the symbols of Chinese anti-Japanese nationalism.

Moreover, Liang made use of her wartime cartoons boldly to propagandize ideas of gender equality and to promote women's rights. In her pictures, she portrayed women as citizens who took on equal responsibilities in the war-torn country. Liang cast women's wartime engagement as conscious decisions made as citizens of the Republic of China, not as solely private actions in their roles as wives and mothers of male citizens. In a cartoon called 'the Total Mobilization of Women', Liang presented various images of women, from soldiers, nurses, girl-scouts, students, and nursery-school pupils to urban and peasant women, all contributing to the salvation of their country.[20]

In another cartoon, Liang portrayed women as the decision makers. In the caption, a peasant wife says to her husband 'Give me the hoe and you pick up the gun!', and a worker's wife says to her husband 'Give me the machine and you pick up the gun!' (Figure 13.3).[21] Both cartoons challenged the stereotypical image of the conventional Chinese gender order in which the husband makes the decisions for his wife to follow. Liang also used the images to remind people that after men were drafted women took over and carried on work and life on the home front. In Sichuan Province alone, a total of 3 million Chinese

Figure 13.3 Liang Baibo depicts women taking over men's roles, from *Kangzhan Manhua*, 1. 'Give me the hoe and you pick up the gun'. 2. 'Give me the machine and you pick up the gun' by Liang Baibo (1938) *Kangzhan Manhua*, no. 10, p. 1.

males, mostly peasants, were conscripted, leaving the female members of their families to continue life at home.[22] Liang's cartoons remind people of the wartime gendered reality.

Liang's portrayals of women's citizenry and contributions to the war efforts were best conveyed through her cartoon titled 'Explanation of Evenly Distributed Responsibilities'.[23] Under a fluttering republican flag, five young Chinese women represent every aspect of life in the Chinese Republic. They were the resistance war heroines and the soul of the wartime Chinese nation. Most importantly, Liang's cartoon images articulated a feminist version of wartime nationhood as an 'imagined community'.[24] In Liang's imagined wartime Chinese nation, women citizens played important roles in every aspect of life in the War of Resistance, asserting their rights and carrying out their responsibilities. It was women's participation that made wartime China a modern nation.

Liang's cartoons gave ordinary Chinese women both subjectivities and representation. However, as a left-wing feminist artist, her portrayal of women in the war at the time was exceptional. It was only later on in the war, when women's war participation became obviously vital to the total war effort, that their representation in popular wartime images became more common.

Further images of women's participation in the war

With the intensification of the War of Resistance after 1940, some government institutions and male artists began to publish more and more positive, women-themed wartime political cartoons and wood-block prints to reflect and mobilize ordinary women's participation in the war effort. Some of the publications combined political propaganda cartoons with folk songs clearly intended for popular consumption.

One such collection was published by the Chengdu Mass Educational Hall in 1941. In this publication, China's War of Resistance was linked to the construction of a modern state and women were included as an important part of the mobilization and the construction of the imagined modern nation.[25] In one of the pictures in the collection entitled 'A Picture of the Pledge of the Citizens', a group of ordinary people, including two women, sit on the floor listening intently to the explanation of the' 'Three People's Principles' by a young student (Figure 13.4). In this cartoon, women were not only publicly recognized as citizens but were also seen to enjoy learning the 'Three People's Principles' on

Figure 13.4 'A Picture of the Pledge of the Citizens' in Chengdu Mass Educational Hall (1941).

equal terms with men. In the accompanying rhymed caption, women were included as members of the imagined wartime national community.[26]

This collection of wartime cartoons and folk songs included cartoons and captions aimed at mobilizing ordinary Chinese women to send their husbands, fiancés, and sons to the front to fight against the Japanese. One of the cartoons in this collection featured a family of three, a peasant husband, a wife, and a small child. The caption printed beneath the picture reads: 'I put down the hoe and pick up the rifle to go to the front line this morning. It does not matter how many Japanese devils are out there, I guarantee that they will all soon go to the King of Hell!' The picture depicted the wartime reality that while peasant men were drafted to join the army, rural women replaced their male family members to carry on the muck-spreading in the fields. A second cartoon from the collection portrays a young rural woman working in a paddy field. In the background, a young man with a rifle is waving goodbye to her. The accompanying rhymed caption (intended to be sung) runs: 'Taking off my embroidered shoes to transplant rice seedlings in a square paddy field. My love, please leave quickly. While you defend the country, I take care of the work in the fields' (Figure 13.5). Both cartoons depict the same theme of women playing a decisive role of sending their beloved ones to the front, and assuming the male role in agricultural production at home. There is also a cartoon illustrating a pair of elderly parents sending their young son off to the front and telling him: '... Do not come home until the enemies are all defeated.' The collection also includes a cartoon of a

图 11 成都民教馆:《抗战漫画歌谣集》,
成都:成都民教馆,1941 年,第 15 页

Figure 13.5 'I will take over the field work and you go to the front to fight the enemy' in Chengdu Mass Education Hall (1941), p. 15.

Figure 13.6   Nursing depicted in Chengdu Mass Education Hall (1941), p. 16.

female nurse who is taking care of several wounded soldiers. The caption under-neath the picture runs: '... Brothers, you are the soldiers and I am the nurse. If you are wounded when fighting against the Japanese, I feel so much better that it will be me who will take care of you' (Figure 13.6).[27]

The Chinese have a traditional saying that 'good iron is not made into nails; good men do not become soldiers'. However, during the Second Sino-Japanese War, China needed a large number of men to join the army to fight against the Japanese invaders. To change ordinary people's attitudes toward soldiers, the Chengdu Mass Educational Hall publication deliberately used cartoons to educate people that good men should become soldiers. One of the cartoons in the collection shows a young male soldier aiming at a target. The caption runs: '... A good man aims at the enemies and is determined to kill all Japanese devil invaders.'[28] The cartoon aimed to convey that desirable men were those willing to bear arms and go to the front line to kill the enemy. Although during the early war years many political cartoons and war-themed wood-block prints featured male soldiers and used them as the symbol of Chinese anti-Japanese nationalism, those cartoons were mostly published in magazines that circulated among educated elites and did not try to remake Chinese mascu-linity and propagandize it to the ordinary people. In contrast, the aforemen-tioned cartoon in the Chengdu Mass Educational Hall collection was a deliberate attempt to reconstruct Chinese masculinity for mass consump-tion with the message that soldiers were good men.

To drive home further this revised idea of military masculinity, another interesting cartoon in the same collection featured a woman dressed in a floral jacket leaning against a fence under a Chinese scholar-tree. The caption reads:

> With a long sigh and two lines of tears, thousands of regret rushed to my heart! Why I was so blind to marry a man with no aspirations? Instead of joining the army to fight the Japanese invaders, he preferred to stay at home and be close to his wife. How blessed is Zhang my sister-in-law whose husband joined the army. She smiles before speaking, holding her head high in front of people! It kills me when I compare my situation with hers; it is even more dreadful when people look down upon me. I feel that a fresh flower has been placed on dung, how can I live and go through the rest of my life?[29]

This cartoon and caption drove home the same message that good men should become soldiers and that it was the role of women actively to encourage men to do so, not only by sending them to war, but also by taking up the men's civilian roles so that they did not need to worry about leaving their responsibilities at home. It not only labelled men who refused to join the army as men without aspirations, but also as men who thus brought shame on their wives in the local community.

An examination of the wartime political cartoons of the Chengdu Mass Educational Hall through the lens of gender reveals many similarities with the cartoons and wood-block prints produced by the masculinized school artists. For example, in the abovementioned Women and Scholar Tree cartoon, the initial intention of the artist was probably to use social pressure to encourage women to send their male family members to join the army. However, as the captions demonstrated, women's social status and acceptance were still dependent on their husbands' positions. Men's behaviour determined their wives' happiness and status in the local community. This kind of presentation clearly undermined women's self-worth and agency. Moreover, most of the cartoons in the Chengdu Mass Educational Hall collection still promoted the gendered social division of labour: men went out to the public sphere and to the front line to fight against the invaders; women remained in the domestic sphere, tilling the land and taking care of children and families. Despite the similar chauvinist tone in the Chengdu collection, we can still distinguish the differences between this group of wartime cartoons from the masculinized images produced during the earlier years of the war. One great difference was that during the early stage of the war, male-authored political cartoons mostly portrayed women as weak, helpless, and passive beings who needed the protection of armed men. The Chengdu collection clearly showed that as the war continued, women's participation in the war had become necessary to ensure the nation's survival. Despite the fact that in the mainstream ideology upheld by the Nationalist government in Sichuan, China's War of Resistance was conceived of as a male-centred masculine war, in practice, women's participation in the war effort came to exceed their domestic roles. Therefore, from 1940 onwards, wartime cartoons and wood-block images had to go beyond the dominant masculine ideology to reflect the reality that women were part of the war effort in order to ensure women's continued support for the war. As previously discussed, the images in the Chengdu collection began to acknowledge women as citizens of the nation with rights and responsibilities. In addition, the images also began to show women as engaged in wartime production and national construction. The cartoon that portrayed a woman as a nurse even reversed the power roles. It labelled wounded male soldiers as the weaker and needy ones that required the female nurse's help and care. The role reversal was in sharp contrast to the image of women in the cartoon entitled 'Protect Our Wives'.

Another collection of wartime cartoon and wood-cut prints edited by Zhao Yunwan, a well-known progressive male artist, also included women-centred images.[30] In this collection there is a picture entitled 'Women's Voluntary Team' (Figure 13.7), which portrays a group of young and energetic women soldiers in military formation. The leading female soldier has a dynamic youthful personality, displaying the determination of those women soldiers to defeat the invading enemies. A wood-cut print in the same collection called 'A Nation-wide Good Harvest', features a smiling full-figured rural woman holding a sickle and a bundle of freshly harvested wheat. The peasant woman featured is very

Figure 13.7 'Women's voluntary team' by Hou Zibu (1940), *Kangzhan Huaxuan*, p. 23.

confident and full of life and energy. Those pictures followed in Liang Baibo's footsteps and suggest a growing recognition of women's vital role in the war.[31]

If we consider all of the wartime propaganda images together – both the masculinized and feminist cartoons and the wood-cut prints – we can see that these images reveal a complex and sometimes even contradictory gendered interpretation of the war. During the early phase of the war, Liang Baibo was the main force behind the feminist school. As the war dragged on and women's participation was needed and became a reality, some male artists and even government agencies also began to use cartoons and woodblock pictures to mobilize women's support for the war effort. This complexity and contradiction was actually the wartime social reality in the Nationalist government-held areas. This contradictory reality left us with a complex set of gendered war representations. From the multifaceted images I have discussed, we can see the coexistence of both the chauvinistic depiction of women as weak and passive prevalent in early war images and the more enthusiastic recognition and acceptance of women's participation in the war efforts increasingly seen later in the war. The complexity and contradictions remind us that there were multiple images of the war and there were also multiple memories of Chinese women's participation in the War of Resistance.

The visual memory of Japanese soldiers' sexual violence against Chinese women

In recent years, sexual violence against women in military conflicts, especially those of the late twentieth century, has captured much scholarly attention in the West.[32] Yet relatively little scholarship is available on the subject regarding China's War of Resistance against Japan. Existing English works on sexual violence against Chinese women during this war mostly focus on the Rape of Nanjing and the 'comfort women'. Despite the fact that during the war years Japanese soldiers committed sexual violence against ordinary non-comfort Chinese women in many localities, it is difficult to find English-language scholarly works on the subject. In 2004 a group of Japanese scholars published on this topic. In a review of the book by a mainland Chinese scholar, the author pointed out that among the historical archives and documents 'there are many statistics on the massacres, arsons, and looting of the Japanese military in China, but records on rape are scarce, even non-existent…Regarding the subject of the Japanese military's sexual violence against Chinese women, there is a gap in both official and non-official Chinese historical documents.'[33] Both the Japanese authors and the Chinese reviewer pointed out that several reasons contributed to the lack of recorded documents on the Japanese military's sexual violence against Chinese women who were not 'comfort women'. One of the major reasons was that the victims were 'the enemies' women' who were 'used and abused by the Japanese soldiers'. These women's very existence created a scarred memory that damaged the collective reputation and masculine honour of the local community because being raped was regarded as a shameful thing in rural Chinese societies and the blame was placed on the victims, not the rapists. Therefore, in the invaded rural local communities, for the sake of preserving national and local collective self-esteem and honour, after the war there was no active effort to record or investigate Japanese military's sexual violence against Chinese non-comfort women. There was no effort to inter-view the victims of such sexual crimes. Moreover, China also did not attempt to hold the Japanese military accountable for such crimes. For these reasons, insufficient attention was paid to the subject of the Japanese military's sexual violence against non-comfort Chinese women during the Second Sino-Japanese War in post-war scholarly publications.[34]

However, these crimes were clearly recorded in Chinese wartime cartoons and wood-cut prints. Regardless of what the intentions of their male authors were, these visual images have kept the Japanese military's sexual violence against Chinese women alive in both the private and the public Chinese gaze for seventy-five years.

The work of these Japanese scholars revealed that in rural villages of the Yu County, Shanxi Province, the Japanese military employed multiple methods of sexual violence towards non-comfort Chinese women in the area. One was to kidnap and force rural women into Japanese military pillboxes and the cellars of blockhouses to be raped.[35] In a wood-block print entitled 'Naked Women in Detention Room' by Zhao Yunwang, the artist clearly captured a scene in which Japanese soldiers imprisoned and sexually violated Chinese women in military pillboxes.[36] In the same collection, a paper-cut picture by Zhang Leping named 'Horrific Death of a Pregnant Chinese Woman' vividly depicted Japanese mili-tary's sexual violence against ordinary Chinese women. In this picture, a preg-nant Chinese woman is stripped naked with her hands tied to tree branches. Her stomach is cut open and a dead unborn child and the woman's intestines fall out of her stomach. The picture is so gruesome to behold that it creates a powerful and unforgettable image of Japanese sexual violence against Chinese women (Figure 13.8).

Another cartoon in the collection portrayed a similarly horrible scene of Japanese sexual violence against ordinary Chinese women. In this picture, a Japanese soldier holding a smoking pistol stands in front of the dead bodies of multiple Chinese women.[37] In a cartoon titled 'Bestial Behaviour of the Enemies', a Chinese woman is depicted being raped and killed by a drunk Japanese soldier. In the window we can see that the entire village is on fire. The dagger in the Japanese soldier's hand drips with the Chinese woman's blood (Figure 13.9).[38]

It is often said that a picture is more powerful than a thousand words. Those wartime political visual images vividly portrayed and broke the silence about the sexual violence against ordinary Chinese women by the Japanese military. It is true that some wartime newspapers and literature also exposed the crimes committed by the Japanese military. However, information conveyed by newspaper reports and literary narratives was not as direct and not as easily understood by ordinary Chinese. Feng Zikai, a

Figure 13.8 Horrific death of a pregnant Chinese woman depicted by Zhang Leping (1940), *Kangzhan Huaxuan*, p. 53.

renowned Chinese cartoonist explained in 1938 that cartoons became one of the most effective wartime propaganda tools for two reasons. First, looking at a cartoon was much faster than reading any written document. Even the shortest article will take people a few minutes to finish. But people could comprehend the message of a cartoon in seconds. Second, cartoons offered a universal language which could be understood by people all over the world, including the illiterate.[39] As Sarah Barber suggests, images of sexual assault against women by foreign invaders also function as metaphors designed to arouse an invaded people's condemnation of such crime.[40] Sexual violence against ordinary women represents the violation of Chinese civilians, the Chinese community and the Chinese nation. Thus, political cartoons and wood-cut prints were able to attract Chinese public and private gazes and instilled in them collective memories of Japanese sexual violence against ordinary Chinese women and the Chinese nation. These wartime political cartoons also informed viewers that China's War of Resistance against Japan was indeed a gendered war. In the study of the war, gender, and memory, we must pay attention to the visual images and memories.

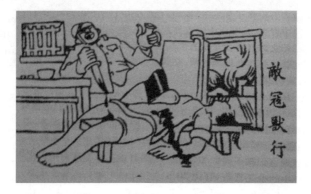

Figure 13.9   Images of Japanese sexual violence by Chen Erkang (1940), *Kangzhan Manhuaji*, p. 9.

Gender and the memory of the forgotten war

During the Second Sino-Japanese War in the Nationalist-held areas, some poor Chinese women experienced another kind of sexual victimhood through selling their bodies to make a living. Some wartime Chinese writers recorded this phenomenon. Li Luzi believed that during the war, there were roughly over one thousand Chinese women who made a living by selling their bodies in the wartime capital city of Chongqing.[41] Lu Sihong echoed Li's account and reported: 'Since there were too many prostitutes in Chongqing, it was difficult to have accurate statistics. The licensed prostitutes who registered with and paid taxes to the Police Bureau were at least over a thousand, and this number did not include the unlicensed ones.'[42] Despite the exposure, during the war years information about prostitutes in Chongqing was, in most cases, reported as tabloid gossip with negative comments. Most of the reports blamed the victims, casting prostitutes as the cause of wartime Chongqing's social problems and moral decay. In reality, many of these women were driven into the profession by poverty and the displacement caused by the war, like their counterparts in early twentieth-century Shanghai.[43]

To date, literature on the Second Sino-Japanese War has hardly discussed the subject of wartime prostitution. Because prostitutes belonged to a marginalized social group, they were collectively silenced in the studies of the history of the war. Their wartime experiences were never even included or considered in the scholarly research agenda; they were the forgotten people and memories in the history of the war. Apart from writers' brief descriptions and scattered oral histories, official historical documents do not provide us with much information about their experiences. [44]

Wartime political cartoons, however, drew attention to these marginalized women even though these cartoon images did not attract much scholarly attention. Ding Cong, a renowned left-wing artist, created a few prostitute-themed cartoons during the war years. Some of them mocked the prostitutes and others were used as social critiques of wartime Chongqing politics and society. One of them depicted a 'Cheap exchange'. The artist drew a rickshaw puller and a prostitute in conversation. Prostitute: 'Don't act like you are somebody! I toss you a few coins, you have to pull me and run.' Rickshaw puller: 'Don't kid yourself! If I stop, you will for sure go after me'.[45] This cartoon was mocking the prostitute, portraying her as chasing after all the men she encountered. In another cartoon named 'Flower Street', Ding depicted wartime Chongqing's well-known red light district (see Figure 13.10). Beneath a dim street light, a fat brothel madam is depicted dragging customers into the brothel by force, shameless men come to the street to seek pleasure, a pale-faced young prostitute faints on the street, while the bystanders watch all the ongoing drama without emotion. The artist adopted a sharp and sarcastic tone in his portrayal of a group of ugly human characters in a dark corner of society in Chongqing in the midst of the national crisis of war. Two mainland scholars have praised the fact that Ding's 'Flower Street' uses an energetic lay out and offers a vigorous depiction of human characters. It combines the approaches of realism and exaggeration to achieve an extraordinary artistic effect. The picture not only reflected the artist's careful observation, profound understanding, and bold exposure of the social reality

Figure 13.10 'Flower Street' by Ding Cong (1946) *Qingming,* Inauguration issue, p. 1.

in the Nationalist government-held wartime capital Chongqing.[46] Ding himself later also frankly admitted that to create 'Flower Street', he had visited Chongqing's red-light district several times to observe various people who lived, worked, and visited the area. Ding stated that the picture was aimed at exposing the corruption and moral decay of the Nationalist Government-held Chongqing during the war period.[47]

Although Ding Cong's 'Flower Street' aimed to expose the corruption and decay of the society in wartime Chongqing, he fell short of offering a gendered critique of Chongqing society nor did he defend the marginalized street prostitutes. Nevertheless, his wartime cartoons at least preserved rare and valuable historical images of these otherwise voiceless and powerless women, allowing us the opportunity to include their wartime experiences in future scholarship on the war.

Conclusion

China's War of Resistance against Japan has left us a large number of visual images, yet few existing scholarly works on visual images and the war are women-centred or use a perspective of gender analysis. Even fewer have analysed visual images as gendered memories of the war. This study argues that wartime images should be viewed as visual public war memories that inform us about the gendered nature of World War II and its public representations. While during the early years, China's resistance against the Japanese invasion had been portrayed in the visual world as male-dominated, feminist artists such as Liang Baibo were able to use gendered wartime visual images to challenge the conventional masculine story of the war and articulate ordinary women as equal and strong citizens who made vital contributions to the mobilization for war. With the escalation of the war and when women's participation in the war effort became essential, even government-sponsored male artist groups started to feature women's images in propaganda political cartoons. Regardless of the intent with which these images were authored, either for promoting feminist views of the war or for governmental propaganda, the prominent presence of women's images in wartime political cartoons and wood-cut prints sends an unambiguous message that ordinary women were a significant part of China's War of Resistance and they demand a public image and voice in the history of the war. Women's images in wartime political cartoons also reveal that the propaganda war of World War II contains gendered discourse as well. At stake is the redefinition of the meaning of modern resistance. When women play an important role in the war effort, the meaning of resistance is no longer just masculine but feminine as well.

Wartime political cartoons are especially powerful in exposing Chinese people to the Japanese military's sexual violence against Chinese non-comfort women. When official history is largely silent on Japanese soldiers' sexual assault of ordinary Chinese women, wartime visual images on the subject expose the issue to the public gaze and keep it alive in collective Chinese memory. The relatively few images of women who had to sell their bodies to make a living during the war remind us also of the need to pay more attention to the forgotten gendered social groups. Visual images created during the war not only offer resources for studying the gendered discourse of World War II, but also point toward a new research method for discovering new research directions and reimagining old narratives.

Recommended reading

Barber, S. (2010) 'Curiosity and Reality: the Context and Interpretation of a Seventeenth-Century Image', *History Workshop Journal*, no. 70, (Autumn), pp. 21–46.

Dower, J. (1986) *War without Mercy: Race and Power in the Pacific War* (New York: Pantheon Books).

Chavez, L. (2007) 'Vietnamese Women's Museums: A Form of Resistance', *Asian Women*, vol. 23, no. 4, pp. 107–27.

Gottschang Turner, K. with P. Thanh Hao (1998) *Even Women Must Fight: Memories of War from North Vietnam* (New York: John Wiley & Sons).

Larkin, C. (2012) *Memory and Conflict in Lebanon: Remembering and Forgetting the Past* (New York: Routledge).

Li, D. (2010) *Echoes of Chongqing: Women in Wartime China* (Urbana and Chicago: University of Illinois Press).

Nakar, E. (2003) 'Memories of Pilots and Planes: World War II in Japanese Manga, 1957–1967', *Social Science Japan Journal*, vol. 6, no. 1, pp. 57–76.

Young, J. E. (2009) 'Regarding the Pain of Women: Questions of Gender and the Arts of Holocaust Memory', *PMLA*, vol. 124, no. 5, pp. 1778–86.

Xie, B. (2001) *A Woman Soldier's Own Story* (Ithaca, NY: Columbia University Press).

Notes

1. For more background on the war, see R. Mitter (2013) *Forgotten Ally: China's World War II, 1937–1945* (New York: Houghton Mifflin Harcourt).

2. S. Barber (2010) 'Curiosity and Reality: the Context and Interpretation of a Seventeenth-Century Image', *History Workshop Journal*, no. 70, (Autumn) 21–46. C. Larkin (2012) *Memory and Conflict in Lebanon: Remembering and Forgetting the Past* (New York: Routledge).

3. J. Dower (1986) *War without Mercy: Race and Power in the Pacific War* (New York: Pantheon Books).

4. B. Zelizer (2001) 'Gender and Atrocity; Women in Holocaust photographs', in B. Zelizer (ed.), *Visual Culture and the Holocaust* (New Brunswick: Rutgers University Press). J. E. Young (2009) 'Regarding the Pain of Women: Questions of Gender and the Arts of Holocaust Memory', *PMLA*, vol. 124, no. 5, pp. 1778–86.

5. K. Gottschang Turner with P. Thanh Hao (1998) *Even Women Must Fight: Memories of War from North Vietnam* (New York: John Wiley & Sons); L. Chavez (2007) 'Vietnamese Women's Museums: A Form of Resistance', *Asian Women*, vol. 23, vo. 4, pp. 107–27.

6. E. Nakar (2003) 'Memories of Pilots and Planes: World War II in Japanese Manga, 1957–1967', *Social Science Japan Journal*, vol. 6, no. 1, pp. 57–76.

7. Barber, 'Curiosity and Reality'.

8. E. Chen (1941) *Kangzhan manhuaji* (Collection of anti-Japanese wartime cartoons), Preface. (Chengdu: Chengdu Mass Education Hall).

9. Z. He (1997) 'Kangzhan shiqi Chongqing meishu huodong lueying' (A fleeting view of the art activities in Chongqing during the War of Resistance), *Journal of Literature and History*, vol. 4, pp. 37–8.

10. X. Bingying (2001) *A Woman Soldier's Own Story* (Ithaca, NY: Columbia University Press); D. Li (2010) *Echoes of Chongqing: Women in Wartime China* (Urbana and Chicago: University of Illinois Press).

11. For example, Ding Cong's cartoon (1937) 'All People's War of Resistance against Japan', *Kanzhan huakan*, no. 7, p. 1. Ye Qianyu's cartoon, "Change into Our New Outfit," *Ziyoutan*, 1938, Inaugural Issue, p. 28.

12. For example, "Liang Baibo yu Ye Qianyu: yishuhua de qinglu" (Liang Baibo and Ye Qianyu: An artistic couple), Shidai Shenghuo, 1937, vol. 5, no. 4–5, p. 6. "Ye Qianyu xiatang zhiqi, Liang Baibo yeying fei jiaji' (Ye qianyu's current woman Liang Baibo is not the legal wife), *Kuaihuolin*, 1947, no. 51, p. 2.

13. Tani Barlow (2004) *The Question of Women in Chinese Feminism* (Durham, NC: Duke University Press).

14. For sources for the brief biography of Liang Baibo, please see: P. Hu (2011) 'duomian numanhuajia – Liang baibo de huihua shijie' (Various faces of female cartoonist – the painting world of Liang Baibo), *Aesthetics and Time*, vol. 4, pp. 72–4. Q. Ye. (2006) Ye Qianyu zizhuan (Autobiography of Ye Qianyu) (Beijing: China Social Science Press), pp. 78–379.

15. J. Shen (ed.) (2005) *Kangzhan Manhua* (Resistance War cartoons) (Shanghai: Shanghai Social Science Academia Press) p. 133.

16. Shen, p. 151.

17. X. Cao (2005) 'Lun kangzhan manhua' (On the political cartoons of China's War of Resistance against Japan), *The Journal of Studies of China's War of Resistance against Japan*, no. 4, p. 68.

18. Shen, *Kangzhan Manhua*, p. 190.

19. Shen, p. 233.

20. Shen, p. 233.

21. Shen, p. 245.

22. Chongqing Kangzhan congshu bianzhuan weiyuanhui (The compilers of the book series of War of Resistance against Japan in Chongqing (1995), *Chongqing renmin dui kangzhan de gongxian* (The Chongqing people's contributions to the War of Resistance against Japan), (Chongqing: Chongqing Press), p. 84.

23. The compilers of the book series of War of Resistance against Japan in Chongqing (1995), p. 136.

24. B. Anderson (2006) *Imagined Communities* (London: Verso), p. 6.

25. Chengdu Mass Education Hall (1941) *Kangzhan manhua geyaoji* (Collection of China's War of Resistance against Japan cartoons and folk songs). Also in Y. Zhou (ed.) (2011) *Kangzhan dahoufang geayo huibian* (Selected folk songs from the Great Rare) (Chongqing: Chongqing Publishing House), pp. 470–92.

26. Chengdu Mass Education Hall, *Kangzhan manhua geyaoji*, p. 4.

27. Chengdu Mass Education Hall, pp. 10, 15, 18, 16.

28. Chengdu Mass Education Hall, p. 28.

29. Chengdu Mass Education Hall, pp. 22–3, 28.

30. Y. Zhao (ed.) (1941), *Collection of pictures of China's War of Resistance against Japan* (Chongqing: Zhonghua Books).

31. Zhao, p. 23.

32. For example, J. Leatherman (2011) *Sexual Violence and Armed Conflict* (Cambridge: Polity Press) and (2007): 'Sexual Violence and Armed Conflict: Complex Dynamics of Re-Victimization', *International Journal of Peace studies*, vol. 12, no. 1, pp. 53–71.

33. P. Liu (2010) 'Japanese military's sexual violence in the eyes of Japanese scholars' (Book review of *Japanese military soldiers' sexual violence in the yellow earth plateau – the old ladies' war is not yet over*), *The Journal of Studies of China's Resistance War against Japan*, no. 2, pp. 153–60.

34. Liu, p. 160.
35. I. Yoneko (2008) *Kodo no mura no seiboryoku-danyantachi no senso ha owaranai* (Japanese military's sexual violence in the yellow earth plateau – the old ladies' war is not yet over), trans. by J. Zhao (Beijing: Social Science Press), pp. 61–62.
36. Zhao, *Collection of pictures*, p. 56.
37. Zhao, pp. 53, 80.
38. E. Chen (1941), p. 9.
39. Z. Feng (2005) 'Manhua shi bigan kangzhan de xianfeng' (Cartoons are the vanguard of fighting against the Japanese invaders with pen), in J. Shen (ed.), *Kangzhan manhua*, (Shanghai: Shanghai Social Science Press), p. 220.
40. Barber, 'Curiosity and Reality', p. 29.
41. L. Li (1944) *Chongqing neimu* (Inside stories of Chongqing) (Chongqing: publisher unknown). This information is from the 1986 reprint by Chongqing Publishing House, p. 206.
42. S. Lu (1939) *Xin Chongqing* (New Chongqing) (Chongqing: Zhonghua Press), p. 185.
43. G. Hershatter (1997) *Dangerous Pleasures: Prostitution and Modernity in Twentieth Century Shanghai* (Berkeley: University of California Press).
44. D. Li (2010) *Echoes of Chongqing: Women in Wartime China* (Urbana and Chicago: University of Illinois Press), pp. 133–4.
45. Q. Xie (2006) *Manhua manhua: 1910–1950 shijianxiang* (Cartoon chatting: images in the world, 1910–1950) (Beijing: Xinxing chubanshe), p. 89.
46. C. Lin and H. Zhang (2010) 'Duanjianzhili: dahoufang kanzhan manhua yundong' ('The power of the short sword: cartoon movement in the Great Rear during the War of Resistance'), *Hongyan Chunqiu*, vol. 6. p. 67.
47. Unknown (2010) 'Ding Cong: Bidi caiqing diwangfu'(The talent shown by his pen is better than ten thousand people), *Arts China*, available at http://art.china. cn/tslz/2010-09/07/content_3703588_2.htm, date accessed 16 July 2016.

Index